Feelings

Series in Affective Science

Series Editors
Richard J. Davidson
Klaus Scherer

The Nature of Emotion
Fundamental Questions
Edited by Paul Ekman and
Richard J. Davidson

Boo!
Culture, Experience, and the Startle Reflex
by Ronald Simons

Emotions in Psychopathology
Theory and Research
Edited by William F. Flack Jr.
and James D. Laird

Shame
Interpersonal Behavior, Psychopathology,
and Culture
Edited by Paul Gilbert and
Bernice Andrews

Affective Neuroscience
The Foundations of Human and
Animal Emotions
By Jaak Panksepp

Extreme Fear, Shyness, and Social Phobia
Origins, Biological Mechanisms,
and Clinical Outcomes
Edited by Louis A. Schmidt
and Jay Schulkin

Cognitive Neuroscience of Emotion
Edited by Richard D. Lane
and Lynn Nadel

The Neuropsychology of Emotion
Edited by Joan C. Borod

Anxiety, Depression, and Emotion
Edited by Richard J. Davidson

Persons, Situations, and Emotions
An Ecological Approach
Edited by Hermann Brandstätter
and Andrzej Eliasz

Emotion, Social Relationships, and Health
Edited by Carol D. Ryff and Burton Singer

Appraisal Processes in Emotion
Theory, Methods, Research
Edited by Klaus R. Scherer, Angela
Schorr, and Tom Johnstone

Music and Emotion
Theory and Research
Edited by Patrik N. Juslin
and John A. Sloboda

Handbook of Affective Sciences
Edited by Richard J. Davidson, Klaus R.
Scherer, and H. Hill Goldsmith

Nonverbal Behavior in Clinical Settings
Edited by Pierre Philippot, Robert S.
Feldman, and Erik J. Coats

Memory and Emotion
Edited by Daniel Reisberg and
Paula Hertel

Psychology of Gratitude
Edited by Robert A. Emmons and
Michael E. McCullough

Thinking about Feeling
Contemporary Philosophers on Emotions
Edited by Robert C. Solomon

Bodily Sensibility
Intelligent Action
By Jay Schulkin

Who Needs Emotions?
The Brain Meets the Robot
Edited by Jean-Marc Fellous
and Michael A. Arbib

What the Face Reveals
Basic and Applied Studies of Spontaneous
Expression Using the Facial Action Coding
System (FACS) (second edition)
Edited by Paul Ekman
and Erika L. Rosenberg

The Development of Social Engagement
Neurobiological Perspectives
Edited by Peter J. Marshall
and Nathan A. Fox

Feelings
The Perception of Self
By James D. Laird

FEELINGS

The Perception of Self

JAMES D. LAIRD

OXFORD
UNIVERSITY PRESS

2007

OXFORD
UNIVERSITY PRESS

Oxford University Press, Inc., publishes works that further
Oxford University's objective of excellence
in research, scholarship, and education.

Oxford   New York
Auckland   Cape Town   Dar es Salaam   Hong Kong   Karachi
Kuala Lumpur   Madrid   Melbourne   Mexico City   Nairobi
New Delhi   Shanghai   Taipei   Toronto

With offices in
Argentina   Austria   Brazil   Chile   Czech Republic   France   Greece
Guatemala   Hungary   Italy   Japan   Poland   Portugal   Singapore
South Korea   Switzerland   Thailand   Turkey   Ukraine   Vietnam

Library of Congress Cataloguing-in-Publication Data
Laird, James D.
Feelings : perception of self / by James D. Laird.
   p. cm.
ISBN 978-0-19-509889-1
1. Emotions.   2. Self-perception.   3. Psychophysiology.   I. Title.
BF531.L29 2006
152.4—dc22   2005025705

9 8 7 6 5 4 3 2
Printed in the United States of America
on acid-free paper

For Nan, who worked harder on this project than I did.

Preface

Over 100 years ago, William James proposed a view of emotions that most of us would know immediately was incorrect, if not downright silly, because it directly contradicts our common sense. Common sense says that the feelings of emotion are the first part of an emotional response, and the rest of the response—facial expressions, physical responses of the body and actions—are caused by the feelings. Common sense says we see a loved one, feel happy, and the happiness makes us smile and approach them. James argued that this was exactly backwards—that first we react and our perception of these reactions as they are occurring is the feeling. We first attack and then feel angry, flee and then feel afraid, approach and then feel love.

Although James' view is counter-intuitive, in fact the evidence is strong that James was correct, and his "silly" hypothesis true. Indeed, James' claims seem to have been too modest. The purpose of this book is to review the evidence supporting the Jamesian view of emotion, and to extend his hypothesis to include all kinds of feelings, not just those of emotion. This latter, more general view is usually called Self-Perception Theory. The basic test of the Self-Perception Theory sequence is to manipulate the behaviors that are related to feelings, and then to observe whether the appropriate feelings occur. In literally hundreds of experiments, manipulations of behaviors have led to corresponding changes in feelings. The emotional behaviors have included facial expressions, postures, patterns of gaze, autonomic arousal, and instrumental actions. These behaviors have been used to induce happiness, anger, fear, sadness, disgust, pride, surprise, and romantic love. In addition to these emotional behaviors and feelings, other bodies of research have manipulated actions and speech, and found changes in attitudes and beliefs. Even such cognitive feelings as familiarity and the tip-of-the-tongue feeling fit this model. In fact, wherever people have explored the origins of feelings, the result has been to confirm the Self-Perception view. However, the volume and breadth of this evidence seems not to be widely known, and the first task of this book is to persuade the reader that Self-Perception Theory is probably true.

One unexpected observation emerged from some of the Self-Perception research, that not all people fit the simple version of the theory. While some people feel happy if they are induced to smile, and love if they share mutual gaze with an appropriate partner, others do not. These differences in response to bodily and behavioral cues are stable and emerge with many kinds of feelings. This apparent limitation of the theory has actually been extremely useful in extending its application to new phenomena, such as anxiety, panic, placebo response, and premenstrual tension.

We might expect that a theory that directly contradicts common sense would have substantial reverberations in broader theoretical realms, and the second purpose of this book is to explore those ideas. The most direct implication of Self-Perception Theory is that feelings cannot be causes of behavior. A simple reversal, that feelings are results rather than causes, is also too simple. Instead, feelings seem to be different kinds of things from behaviors and bodily responses. Feelings are information, or knowledge, about just those behaviors and responses.

The later chapters of this book are directed at developing a way of thinking about feelings, knowledge and action that is not simply mechanistic, that lacks simple mechanistic causes, and instead sees feelings as components of control systems. These control systems are stacked to operate at increasing levels of organization. These levels of organization of our behavior are in turn matched by levels of organization in the world as well. I would not claim that any of these more abstract theoretical insights are original with me, but I hope that taken together, and organized as I have presented them, they will provide a useful perspective on psychological processes.

Acknowledgments

Academics lead really excellent lives. We get to choose the problems and questions that interest us most, and then we get paid (granted, not like investment bankers) to try to answer these questions. It is not much different from doing crossword puzzles, except that sometimes the solutions have practical significance too. I hope this book conveys some sense of how much fun it was to write it and to do the thinking and research that led me to write it.

One of the major reasons this kind of project is so much fun is the people that you get to work with. I have been very lucky to have had many colleagues, and even more students, who helped along the way, and who made the work even more enjoyable by their participation. All of my own research has involved collaboration with a series of extremely bright, creative people who really did make it all possible. Rather than listing them here, in a long and boring list that would only be read by those who wanted to make sure I hadn't forgotten them, I have preferred to try to make their various contributions explicit in the book itself. However a few important people and institutions do not get explicit mention in the main body of the text and deserve specific thanks.

Among my research collaborators whose contributions are mentioned in the text, some also read parts or all of the book in its earlier forms, and made many useful suggestions. Bill Flack, Simone Schnall, Alex Genov, Sarah Strout, Boyd Timothy, and Nick Thompson were especially helpful at various stages of the project.

Two institutions were extremely accommodating in helping me work on the book while on sabbatical: Oxford University and the Maison des Sciences de l'Homme. Maison Suger in Paris, which is maintained by MSH to provide accommodations for visiting social scientists, provided the perfect kind of apartment, in an ideal location, in a wonderful city. Friend and colleague Monique deBonis was especially helpful, in too many ways to list.

Jodie Zdrok Boduch was a remarkably able and accommodating editor and helper at all the final stages, including those that arrived long after we thought the final stage had been passed.

Contents

Feelings

1

The Problem of Feelings

As part of my clinical training in graduate school, one of my supervisors watched my therapy sessions through a one-way mirror. One day my client smiled in a peculiar way, which I was sure was significant. I was even more certain that my supervisor would have thought the smile important, too, and that he was sure to ask about it in my supervision session the next day. As I drove home that night, I tried furiously to figure out the significance of that smile, without much success. At one point I tried smiling the way my client had done. That did not help much, so I tried smiling the way I normally do, and I noticed something interesting: When I deliberately smiled, it made me feel happier. So I tried an angry frown, and that made me feel angry; a sad, slumped posture made me feel sad, and so forth. This seemed remarkable, since I knew as well as anyone else that the relationship between expressions and feelings was supposed to be the reverse: Feelings were the causes of facial expressions. But by the time I reached home, I was convinced that at least sometimes feelings were the results, rather than the causes, of expressions. (I have often wondered what the other drivers thought of me as I drove away from a mental health facility making dramatic emotional faces for no apparent reason.)

Over the next few weeks I spent as much time as I could reading the emotion literature, trying to find out if others had experienced the same thing. Eventually I discovered William James's theory of emotion. James expressed his point of view elegantly in talking about emotional feelings:

> Common sense says, we lose our fortune, are sorry and weep; we meet a bear, are frightened and run; we are insulted by a rival, are angry and strike. The hypothesis here to be defended says that this order of sequence is incorrect . . . and

the more rational statement is that we feel sorry *because* we cry, angry *because* we strike, afraid *because* we tremble. (James, 1890, p. 449, emphasis in original)

I had discovered that my experience was not unique. Indeed, one of psychology's greatest pioneers had reported just this kind of experience. James's view of emotion is the core of the position that I will be describing throughout this book: that our feelings are the consequences of our actions. They are about our actions, and they are in fact no more or less than knowledge or information about our actions. The way you know that you are angry is through your angry behavior, and the way I know that I am happy is because I smile. The only difference is that I experience my own smile as the feeling of happiness. We know our own minds by observing our own behavior.

Of course, as James pointed out, common sense takes a very different view. According to common sense, feelings are the causes of behaviors, and we commonly use feelings to explain behavior: "I ran from the bear because I was terrified." "You eat because you are hungry." "Enraged by the insult, he couldn't help attacking." "She works so hard because she enjoys her work." "He acts like an idiot because he's in love." (See Figure 1.1.)

Though familiar, ubiquitous, and easy, explanations based on feelings contain a great mystery: We really do not know how feelings could affect behavior. Feelings are not mechanical forces, or fluids that might build up pressure, or any other kind of matter or energy that might cause some physical object to move. So, although clearly feelings do have some intimate, and undoubtedly important, connection with behavior and action, the nature of that connection is not as clear as common sense assumes.

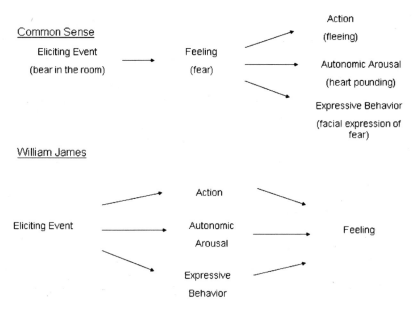

Figure 1.1. Common sense and William James: models of emotion sequence.

The goal of this book is to describe a view of feelings that derives from my experience driving home, from James's theory of emotion, from Gilbert Ryle's philosophical work on the nature of mind, and from many other sources. One of the great benefits of this theoretical perspective is that it dissolves the mystery of how feelings can cause actions. However, this dissolution does not come cheaply, since it involves turning common sense on its head, and common sense is what we all "know" is true until we hear good arguments to the contrary. Consequently, many readers will approach this book with an appropriately high degree of skepticism and will demand some very compelling evidence for such an unlikely idea. As we will see, a large and growing body of research does in fact exist. This research demonstrates that feelings follow from behavior or other underlying processes. The feelings that have been studied include a wide variety of emotions, including anger, joy, sadness, disgust, fear, guilt, and romantic love. Two very large bodies of research have shown similar effects of many kinds of behavior on attitudes and on motives; this research shows that acting as if you believe something leads you to that belief, and acting as if you like something makes you like it. Other research has examined feelings of confidence and pride, and feelings of familiarity, importance, and even realness. Indeed, few if any of those things that we would ordinarily call "feelings" have escaped the research net, and in every case the evidence is that the feelings are the consequences of the behaviors or activities that common sense would identify as effects of the feelings.

After the opening barrage of research (and some theoretical bits tucked in among the facts), I will try to draw together all this into a coherent, overall theoretical statement. The label that seems to make most sense for this position is *self-perception theory*, for reasons that will become apparent shortly. Finally, I will discuss some of the broader implications of this work.

Before getting on to the details of the research work and its theoretical implications, I will briefly sketch the conceptual problems of common sense that generated this research. I will also present a quick overview of the general theoretical position that has emerged from all this research, so that the reader can see where we are headed. Because many of the theoretical ideas have emerged directly from the empirical work, I have postponed until chapter 10 the full, detailed statement of self-perception theory as I now understand it. The final theoretical interpretation that seems to make most sense contains at its heart James's premise that feelings follow and are based on behaviors. As you might expect, though, the final version of self-perception theory is a great deal more complicated.

THE PROBLEMS OF COMMON SENSE

James explicitly contrasts his views with common sense, so common sense is a good place to start. Calling some idea common sense implies that it has always been accepted truth. In fact, however, there is at least some reason to think that our commonsense view of mind and feelings came into existence during the span of recorded history. According to Bruno Snell (1982), some time around 1000 BC to 800 BC, the ancient Greeks "invented" the idea that human beings consisted of two quite distinct things, mind and body (see also Jaynes, 1976). In simple dualism, the world is assumed to contain two kinds of substances, physical and mental. Physical substances are palpable, located in space and time, and observed equally well by anyone who is present. Mental substances are not physical and exist in a kind of "space" that is unobservable, except by the person whose mind it is. Certainly, that dualist view has been dominant and explicit in Western thinking since Descartes (1641/1990). A kind of parody of this dualist view is that mind and body are like a horse and rider. The observable body moves and acts in response to the urgings and commands of the immaterial mind.

The Greeks' explanation of human behavior was closely parallel to their ways of explaining other regularities of nature. The Greeks were animists who explained regularities in nature by assuming that some person or personlike god had been put in charge of things. For example, the Greeks noticed that the sun rose regularly and assumed that there must be a person, whom they named Apollo, in charge of driving his golden chariot across the sky each day. The crops grew during some seasons but not others, so the Greeks imagined there was a person in charge of growth, a person who took half the year off from work.

The Greeks seem to have adopted a similar explanatory strategy to account for the behavior of people. People's actions were explained as due to the presence of a humanlike entity inside, the mind or spirit. The inner mind was ascribed all the qualities that were observable in public actions. In effect, the behavior of people was "explained" by assuming that each person contained another little person. This is obviously not a very promising explanatory strategy, since the only possible explanation for the behavior of the little homunculus inside would be an even smaller homunculus inside the first— then another inside the second, and so on, ad infinitum, like Russian nesting dolls. Since all the Greeks' other animist explanations of nature have seemed inadequate, we should undoubtedly be suspicious of dualism from the start.

Dualism has a number of other logical difficulties. My account of these difficulties is inspired by some philosophical criticisms, especially those of Gilbert Ryle and Ludwig Wittgenstein, but I am not a philosopher and have certainly not captured the subtleties of their philosophical positions, nor have I worried about professional criticisms of their positions. An excellent discussion of Jamesian theories from a professional philosopher's perspective is a book by Jesse Prinz (2004).

THE PROBLEM OF PSYCHOPHYSICAL CAUSATION

Perhaps the most serious of dualism's problems is how the mind might affect the body, or the reverse. The metaphor of horse and rider actually hides the fact that unlike the rider, the mind has no hands to hold the reins or heels to kick the horse-body's sides. The mind is so insubstantial that it seems to be completely the wrong kind of thing to affect the physical body. In fact, when one considers the issue carefully, the effect of the mind from "inside" a physical body is no less mysterious than the claimed "psi" effects of mind on external physical objects. Whether I am moving my fingers or bending spoons and lifting tables, just how my immaterial mind could affect physical objects is unclear.

INTROSPECTION AND THE PROBLEM OF SELF-IGNORANCE AND SELF-DECEPTION

A second problem concerns the ways in which commonsense dualism assumes we know about the minds of others and ourselves. According to dualism, these are two radically different processes. We know about the psychological states of other people by observing and interpreting their actions. We look at what people do in various situations, and we "infer" what their motives, emotions, attitudes, and so forth must have been when they acted as they did. In contrast to these inferences about others, commonsense dualism assumes that we know our own psychological states by a very different route: We just "feel" them directly. This is a kind of direct, unmediated experience of introspection.

The problem with the idea of introspection is that it implies that we should know ourselves with perfect ease and accuracy, whereas we all know that we (or at least many of our friends and relations) are not nearly so self-aware. Indeed, many human attributes can exist only because we are ignorant of our own natures. For example, the type A personality/emotional bully cannot recognize his own anger. The "honest" hypocrite (most are) must not recognize how his own behavior contrasts with his professed standards for others. And perhaps most clearly, the vain person cannot recognize the actual level of his skills and accomplishments.

Of course, the fact that people are not particularly good judges of their own natures is hardly news, and many explanations of self-ignorance have been proposed. Self-perception theory probably provides the simplest, most straightforward: Our knowledge of ourselves is exactly like our knowledge of others, and hence our knowledge of ourselves is subject to all the same problems of inattention, distraction, prejudice, and self-serving misinterpretation. What is not necessary from the self-perception perspective is any elaborate machinery of active repression and defense mechanisms, all humming away in a hidden part of our minds.

THE PROBLEM OF LEARNING HOW TO TALK ABOUT FEELINGS

Wittgenstein (1953) pointed out that it was hardly surprising that we did not know ourselves very well, since it was quite unclear how we could ever learn to correctly name and identify our feelings if they were entirely the product of the intrinsically private introspection of some inner reality. Everything else we talk about has a public, if complex, referent, but supposedly our feelings are of entirely private things that only we can observe. How, then, could we ever learn the proper names of these inner entities and how they relate to the behavior of other people?

Of course, in a general sense, we know how we learn to talk about and understand our feelings: Our parents and other adults teach us how, just as they teach us to talk about and understand everything else in the world. But our parents do not have access to our inner emotional entities. Instead, they know what our emotional states are by observing our behavior, our circumstances, or both (Bem, 1972; Laird & Berglas, 1975). When they see us scowling or observe that a playmate has just taken our favorite toy, they understand that we are angry, and they say something like, "Don't be angry."

The question is how this process could lead us to associate our parents' talk with some inner state or condition, rather than with our behavior or our situation. All the other entities our parents tell us about have some referent in the public world, so why would we make a radically new kind of association for just these words? Furthermore, we would not need to form this new and difficult kind of association. Clearly, if our parents can talk sense about our emotions, the information that they use is adequate. If they use only information from our behavior and our situation, we do not seem to need anything more.

Notice, too, that if we had some interior introspective entities to associate with our parents' naming, we would be unlikely to learn to name these interior entities without error. The errors would arise because, unless our parents are absolutely accurate in interpreting our inner reality every time, there would be a closer association between their naming and the information they are using—our behavior and our situation—than between their naming and our private, internal products of introspection. Thus, if we as children associated the names with the private entities inside, we would in fact be making a mistake, as our parents understood it. We might even expect them to correct us when we talked about any feelings that did not fit their understanding of our behavior or the situation. The net result of this kind of process is that our parents would teach us to ignore the private inner world of introspection when we talk, and instead attend to our actions and their circumstances.

Faced with these problems about feelings and understanding, but simultaneously wanting to preserve the idea of logically private feelings, many people assume that feelings parallel actions in perfect harmony. If so, then perhaps we learn to attend to the feelings because they are more salient and obvious than the behaviors and situational constraints to which our parents are attending. But this solution solves one mystery by replacing it with an even greater mystery: Why would people be constructed so that they have two parallel lives, one public and one private, neither affecting the other, but each nonetheless exquisitely fitted with the other?

The problem of how feelings and behaviors can march together, keeping excellent if not quite perfect step, dissolves if the feelings are about the behaviors. If we feel happy because it is our way of recognizing that we are smiling, or depressed because it is how we feel our body's torpor and our drooping face, then of course they go together. They go together in the same way that your smile goes with my perception of you as happy.

These and a number of other kinds of concerns about commonsense dualism have led to a variety of alternative proposals (e.g., some recent philosophical examples include Churchland, 1988; Dennett, 1991; Searle, 1992). None of these alternatives has won universal acceptance, but at a minimum, the number of alternatives and the effort devoted to developing them signal the degree of discomfort that philosophers still feel about conventional dualism.

SELF-PERCEPTION THEORY

The many logical difficulties with commonsense dualism led philosophers such as Ryle (1949) and Wittgenstein (1953) and behaviorist psychologists such as B. F. Skinner (1957) to propose that in fact no separate realm of mind existed, or indeed could exist. Instead, they argued, our psychological entities consisted only of complex patterns of our essentially public kinds of action and the contexts in which these actions occurred. In this view, feelings are our recognition of these complex patterns of our actions and the situations in which we performed them. The position advocated by Ryle and Wittgenstein is essentially like William James's theory of emotion, but generalized to all kinds of feelings and, in fact, all kinds of self-knowledge. Daryl Bem (1967, 1972) introduced the name *self-perception* for the process of self-observation and interpretation by which our feelings were generated. As he put it, we are in the same position as an outside observer of ourselves, and we must infer our own psychological states from our actions.[1]

Self-perception theory solves all the problems of dualism quite straightforwardly. First of all, we do not need to worry about how feelings may cause behaviors; feelings are *about* behaviors but do not cause them, in the same way that our perceptions of the physical world do not cause that world. Note, too, that it is not that the causal arrow has simply been reversed, because the relationship between behaviors and feelings is not causal, but rather constitutive. We will return to that issue in a moment.

Second, there is no problem about how we learn to talk about our own psychological states because we learn to know ourselves in the same way our parents originally did, and we, too, use our behavior and our situation as the source for our feelings. Finally, we can make mistakes because this process is no more infallible than any other attempt to make sense of things in the world.

BASIC FEATURES OF SELF-PERCEPTION THEORY

Self-perception theory conflicts with common sense in the same way that James's theory of emotion does: by reversing the temporal sequence between feelings and actions. Since self-perception theory conflicts with common sense on an even broader front, it faces even more consistent and powerful skepticism. In order to reduce that skepticism slightly at the beginning, a few essential but often misunderstood features of self-perception theory need to be underlined.

First of all, the process of self-observation and self-interpretation that is implicit in the self-perception label is explicitly assumed to be non-conscious (Bem, 1972; Laird, 1989; Laird & Bresler, 1992; Laird & Crosby, 1974). Like the processes that generate impressions of others (Bargh, 1997; Gilbert, 1989), these self-perception processes are also automatic. The "perception" part of the name should be taken seriously. Good ana-logues to the proposed process are complex perceptual processes, like depth perception (Laird, 1989; Laird & Bresler, 1992). In depth percep-tion, one "immediately" experiences a feature of the world, such as the relative distance of all the objects in it. As we are having these experi-ences of depth, we do not know how we do it, and we do not know what information we use to do it. Similarly, as we all know, we just feel that we are happy, or that we like a political candidate, or that we are hun-gry, and we have no idea where these feelings come from or how they emerge.

Self-perception theory assumes that feelings like these are higher order integrations of various kinds of cues. As with depth perception, the pro-cess of detecting and integrating these cues is automatic and occurs out-side consciousness. The work of self-perception research is to discover the nature of the cues and how they generate experience.

In the case of depth perception, we do know quite a bit about the cues and processes that generate our experience. The experience of depth de-pends on a variety of cues, such as linear perspective, gradients of texture and color, binocular disparity, and motion parallax. A typical experiment to demonstrate the role of these cues involves manipulating one cue while holding the others constant and asking participants to report what they see. Often the result of such a manipulation is an illusion: One sees a two-dimensional line drawing of a cube as three-dimensional.

Typical self-perception research is logically identical. Some behavior that is thought to be a constituent of a feeling is manipulated, and the participant is asked what he or she feels. Harold Kelley (1967) once de-scribed one kind of self-perception experiment as precisely intended to create a kind of feeling-illusion, similar in every logical respect to a per-ceptual illusion. Such feeling illusions have the same logical force as well: If we can create an illusory experience by manipulating a cue, then that cue is probably important in the creation of normal, real-life experi-ences.

Depth perception and the self-perception of feelings are also similar in that, in real life, a multitude of potential cues contribute to the final expe-rience, but no one of these is necessary for that final experience. One can experience depth in an Escher drawing that uses linear perspective alone, or in a picture of a field of sunflowers that contains only texture gradients, or by using binocular disparity or motion parallax on featureless objects.

Similarly, experiments have demonstrated that the experience of sadness can be produced by adopting a sad facial expression or a sad posture (Duclos et al., 1989), or by repeating sad sentences to oneself (Velten, 1968). Of course, both in real-life visual perceptions and in emotional feelings, all or many of these cues are usually available and are combined in some way.

SELF-PERCEPTION AS CONSTRUCTIVE

An important conceptual drift has occurred over the last few pages and needs to be acknowledged. The quotation from William James that began this discussion emphasizes a *causal* connection between behavior and feeling. However, the relationship between behaviors and feelings seems to be constitutive. Feelings are constructed from cues that include behavioral and situational information.

The parallel with depth perception is exact here, too. The relationship between the cues for depth perception and the experience of depth is not causal. Lines converging in the "distance" or different images in each eye do not cause an experience of distance in the same way that the impact of one billiard ball causes the movement of another. Instead, these cues provide the ingredients from which the experience of depth is constructed. That is, the experiences are "built" from the elements of the behaviors.

The difference between a causal and a constitutive relationship will be discussed at length later. One good example involves a load of lumber that was delivered to my house. The lumber *caused* a dented, dead patch of grass on my lawn, but it did not cause the room that was added to my house. The lumber was instead the material from which, assembled in a particular configuration, the house was constructed. Similarly, feelings are constructed out of the experiences of acting in particular ways in particular circumstances.

In sum, self-perception theory holds that our feelings consist of the perception of higher order patterns of our behaviors and the situations in which we are behaving. Neither the process of self-perception nor the cues that enter that process are ordinarily recognizable in everyday experiences. It is precisely the purpose of self-perception research to identify those cues and processes.

SELF-PERCEPTION AS RELATIONAL, NOT CAUSAL

The role of the situation in self-perception constitutes another aspect of the difference between James's view and self-perception theory, a difference that requires emphasis. A major component of the relationship that constitutes feelings is between the behaviors emphasized by James and the social and physical context in which the behaviors occur. A smile in relationship with the arrival of a friend constitutes happiness, but a smile in relationship to the arrival of a relative given to lengthy descriptions of her medical problems may constitute the feeling of anxious boredom. An identical movement of the mouth when the dentist approaches may produce no feelings at all. It appears that the "default interpretation" of emotional behaviors is the feeling of the corresponding emotion, but countless studies have demonstrated that these behaviors can be disqualified by information that defines a different relationship or none at all.

VARIETIES OF CUES FOR FEELINGS

James identified emotional behaviors such as smiling, crying, a slumped dejected posture, or an attack as the source of the cues for emotional feelings. Much of the research described in subsequent chapters supports his view that the important behaviors are overt and easily observed. The behaviors that lead to the more basic emotions such as joy, anger, and fear are especially easy to observe in others. However, for some feelings, such as boredom (Damrad-Frye & Laird, 1989) or familiarity (Jacoby, Kelley, Brown, & Jasechko, 1989), the cues are not overt behaviors. The essence of the self-perception insight is not that all feelings are about overt behavior but simply that they are constituted from and are about some underlying process. That is, they are based on and provide information about the relationship between some activity of the person and its context. Often that activity is some sort of cognitive processing or act. For example, the feeling of boredom is about the inability of the person to keep his or her attention focused where it is supposed to be. The feeling of familiarity, that one has experienced something before, is based in part on the fluency with which the experience proceeds, in comparison to the expected fluency.

In addition to the wide variety of behavioral cues that participate in feelings, there are also cues arising from the situation in which we are behaving. Our understanding of what is common and appropriate in a particular situation may be just as important in generating feelings. For example, people might feel sad if they were attending a funeral, even if the deceased was a stranger, and happy when attending a party, even if they were only observing the festivities from a corner of the room. As noted earlier, self-perception theory assumes that we learn to feel by learning to make sense of the two kinds of information that our parents are using to teach us about feelings: our actions and the situations in which we are acting.

In principle, everyone might use both set of cues equally, but in fact, numerous studies to be described in later chapters make it clear that people differ in which of these two sources is most influential. These individual differences have some interesting relationships with other phenomena. For reasons that will become apparent, we have called the two kinds of cues *situational* and *personal*. People who are more responsive to personal cues are more likely to report feelings consistent with their behaviors, and they are more sensitive to pain; in addition, if they are women, they are more likely to experience premenstrual syndrome. In contrast, people who are less responsive to personal cues instead respond to the situational cues that lead to conformity. It appears that virtually everyone is responsive to situational cues, but that people differ in their responses to personal cues. When in later chapters I refer to people who are more responsive to personal cues, I do not mean that they are unresponsive to situational cues, but only that they respond more strongly to personal cues. People who are identified as more responsive to situational cues are so primarily because they seem to be unresponsive to personal cues.

COGNITIONS ABOUT THE SITUATION, COGNITIONS ABOUT THE BEHAVIOR

A person's understanding of the situation plays a second, very different role. In addition to providing information about how most people would feel in the particular situation, the situation is the usual source of the context for the behavior. These two kinds of information arising from the social situation play different roles in the feeling processes and must not be confused. One kind of information about the situation is about the nature and meaning of the emotional stimulus. For example, at the lowest, perceptual level, William James's bear is only a blob of dark fur ambling into the room; if one has no idea that bears are dangerous, one will not feel fear. Even when you know all about the dangers of the bear in front of you, you will not be afraid if you also recognize how strong are the bars of the cage between you. So, one function of cognitions is to provide the understanding or appraisal of the event that is the occasion for an emotional episode.[2] These are cognitions about the situation that produces emotional behavior.

Equally important are the cognitions about the behaviors and their contexts. A smile in response to a photographer's request that you say "Cheese" is less likely to make you feel happy, and a pounding heart and sweaty palms will be less disturbing if you realize they are the product of too many cups of coffee. In fact, a feeling of happiness is not a direct consequence of the smile, but rather is a product of the relationship between the smile and the context in which it occurs. The default interpretation of a smile appears to be happiness, and the default interpretation of a frown is anger, but both can be disqualified easily. A substantial portion of the literature to be reviewed in later chapters demonstrates the ways in which manipulations of contextual understandings of behavior change its impact on feelings.

EXPERIENCES: THE OBJECTS OF SELF-PERCEPTION THEORY

Any reasonably complex psychological episode may include a variety of distinguishable components, such as the situation, the person's interpretations of the situation, and his or her many reactions to that interpretation, including memories, judgments, feelings, expressive behaviors, physiological responses, and actions. Of this wide array, self-perception theory is directed only at explaining feelings. The theory involves all these other kinds of responses, as they make feelings possible or necessary and are affected by feelings. Yet the theory is not an attempt to explain more than the origins of feelings. As we will see in later chapters, that is more than enough for one theory, both because the task is substantial and because the implications of self-perception theory reverberate widely.

By *feelings*, I mean precisely what the person in the street would mean by feelings. That is, I mean the everyday conscious experiences of anger and joy, liking and disliking, hunger and thirst, sickness and confidence. I mean the kinds of things that people think about when asked, "How do you feel?" and talk about in answer to the question. People may act emotionally without knowing that they are, but it is simply true by definition that they cannot feel without knowing that they feel. Feelings *are* the conscious experience.

Although we all know and talk about feelings easily, there is a complexity that we often overlook. If you were to ask me how I am feeling right now, I can respond readily with "Contented, focused, enjoying the task," but these words are not the feelings. They are only labels for the feelings. They are complex, meaningful labels, but they are descriptions of what I am feeling. The feelings are like any other sensory experience, ultimately impossible to describe (Lambie & Marcel, 2002; Reisenzein & Schonpflug, 1992). These two kinds of knowledge were called "knowledge by acquaintance" and "knowledge by description" by Bertrand Russell (1912). Knowledge by description is what you have when I tell you that "an apple is round, red, and sweet." Knowledge by experience is what you acquire when you taste the apple. Ever afterward you may be able to identify apples by their taste, but you will never be able to describe the taste (except perhaps by the kinds of obscure analogies that wine tasters use). Similarly, to label one's emotional feeling as "angry" is a different thing from experiencing the forward-rushing, tension filled, body-charged, teeth-gritted urge to hurt that is the feeling of anger. The first is knowledge by description, the second is knowledge by acquaintance (which is why I can only allude to it and not truly describe it in this example).

Now that we have separated conceptually the two kinds of emotional processes, it is clear that self-perception theory is concerned primarily with the first, or lower knowledge by acquaintance. The knowledge by acquaintance in turn provides the occasion for the labeling and discussion that make up knowledge by description, which is in its turn the basis of our self-reports. However, the two kinds of knowledge certainly are intertwined; for instance, a label may serve to highlight some aspects of one's "acquaintance experience" and distract from others. Notice, incidentally, that we are ordinarily unaware of the difference between our knowledges of acquaintance and description because we ordinarily take our descriptions of our feelings as adequately complete descriptions. Among highly verbal people, the word is often taken to be sufficient, perhaps precisely because those aspects of the experience that are picked out by the verbal description become the focus, and the ineffable remainder are overlooked.

Three distinct opportunities for inaccuracy in our self-descriptions of ourselves are now clear as well. The first potential problem may occur because we are enacting an emotional pattern of behaviors, but we are unaware of these behaviors as they are going on because we are either distracted or perhaps neurologically impaired. We do not even have an "acquaintance experience" of the behaviors. The second possibility is that we may also in some way apprehend the behaviors sufficiently to have the perceptual "acquaintance experience" but fail to label it correctly or at all. In this case, we may be feeling our behaviors accurately but labeling them incorrectly.

A third possibility for error may creep in between the initial labeling and the actual report to others. For example, participants in experiments are usually eager to be helpful and might report whatever feelings they believed the experimenter wished to hear. These reports might be quite different if they were telling their friends about the experiment later.

METHODS FOR STUDYING FEELINGS

The study of feelings poses some special methodological problems because of these gaps between feelings and final report. The most obvious problems arise because the only way we can tell what someone is feeling is to ask him. The problem with self-reports is, of course, that the person may not report his feelings accurately. In all the self-perception research programs to be discussed in later chapters, the experimenters were very much aware of the danger that participants would be too cooperative and so took various measures to minimize the possibility. Since most of these defensive procedures are specific to the particular research programs, they are best described in the later chapters. However, I would not want to leave any doubt about this issue as you are reading about the research, so I will quickly summarize the kinds of procedures that have been employed.

First of all, the participants were often elaborately deceived about the actual purposes of the research, so that they would not know what they were expected to do. Whenever possible, the experimenter was left in the dark as well, at least about whether a particular participant was expected to do one thing or another. In addition, usually participants were carefully interviewed after the experiment was over to discover whether they had seen through the deception.

In other experiments the manipulations were so cleverly disguised that no participant could perceive their purpose. In some kinds of research the critical variables were autonomic responses such as heart rate and skin conductance that even the most eager-to-please participants could not deliberately control. Finally, many relationships were predicted, and observed, between self-reports of feeling and other variables that participants could not have known their position on, such as whether they were field dependent or not, or could not have changed, such as whether they were overweight. In studies of this sort, some participants were expected to respond in one way, others in a different way, and the experimenter was blind as to which kind of response a particular participant should make. Thus, no consistent pattern of experimenter bias and participant compliance could have produced the observed results. Furthermore, in many of these studies, "faking" correctly would have required the participants themselves to discern very specific and anti-intuitive theoretical predictions about how they should behave. In sum, and as will become apparent as I discuss the actual research, few if any of these results can be explained away as due to participant compliance.

Some perspective on the risks posed by eager participants comes with the recognition that this problem is not unique to research on emotions, motives, or attitudes. For example, when a perception researcher shows participants the Muller-Lyer illusion and asks which line seems longer, the researcher must depend on the truthfulness of the participants' reports.

In fact, self-reports are like any measure of an entity that is not directly observable by the scholar's senses. Confidence in any measure of a complex, abstract entity develops through construct validation. That is, we make theoretically guided predictions about how the underlying entity and its measurement would relate to other measures or events in the world. To the extent that our measures behave in the way that the theory predicted, we gain some confidence in each component, the theory that made the prediction, the theoretical construct that was part of this theory, and the practical measurement of this construct. For example, self-perception theory predicted that women who were more responsive to personal cues would report feeling lowered self-confidence while reading women's magazines (Wilcox & Laird, 2000). When we found that after reading the magazine, the predicted group of women responded to a self-esteem scale with lower scores, we felt more confident about our theory, and also about our measurements of personal and situational cue use and of self-esteem. One such success conveys only a small bit of confidence in the measures, but repeated successes justify increasing confidence.

Certainly, in the case of self-reports of feelings, the construct validation work has been done long ago. Literally thousands of experiments have used self-report measures of feelings and observed the expected relationships. In fact, few, if any, psychological constructs and measures have accumulated greater stores of construct-validational confidence.

Of course, occasionally self-report measurement of feelings may err. A participant may lie to please or confound the experimenter, just as occasionally an intelligence test may fail to identify a good student, or an ohm meter may not measure electrical resistance correctly. It is a hallmark of an adequately validated measure/theory complex that it contains, at least implicitly, the criteria for identifying the occasional exception to its usual good functioning.

Although we have strong theoretical and empirical grounds for relying on self-reports about feelings, we should recognize that self-reports are, of course, distinct from the feelings reported. As noted earlier, there is clearly more to experience than we talk about, and perhaps ever could talk about.

For example, when I look at a painting, I could say that I feel peaceful and enraptured by what I see. My words do not begin to capture all that I am feeling, just as when I say that the picture depicts a three-dimensional landscape, those words do not capture all the experiences that come from the juxtaposition of objects in the three-dimensional "space" of the picture. Experiences of physical space and of feelings are complex and multidimensional (e.g., deRivera, 1977; Ortony, Clore, & Collins, 1988). How much of that complexity we try to capture in verbal reports is, of course, a matter of what our theoretical purpose is.

FEELINGS ARE NOT EPIPHENOMENA

A number of observers have misunderstood self-perception theory and/or Jamesian theories of emotion as assuming that emotional feelings are epiphenomena that have no effect on behavior (e.g., Oatley & Jenkins, 1992). Certainly, the main point of self-perception theory is that the behaviors that commonsense claims are caused by emotion are instead the source of those feelings. But just because the feelings do not cause these particular behaviors does not mean that feelings have no role in behavior. Indeed, feelings seem to have an essential role in the behavior that follows. Just what that role is will, of course, vary from situation to situation, but one major effect is to permit self-control (Laird & Apostoleris, 1996). The nature of these effects will be discussed at length in a later chapter.

Self-perception theory does raise two questions that were obscured by commonsense dualism and its professional counterparts. In commonsense dualism, many behaviors are explained by the presumed causal influence of their antecedent feeling. However, if the feeling follows and is not the cause, then one must ask why the behaviors occurred.

The general shape of the answer to this question follows from asking what feelings *are.* The research indicates that feelings are *about* actions and are really a kind of information. Just as the feeling of distance and the spatial organization of objects is information about the world, feelings of emotion, motivation, and so on are information about one's ongoing behavior and the circumstances in which it occurs. The question of the role of feelings in action then becomes the question of how information might affect behavior. This, too, is a rather knotty question that often has been overlooked or obscured by the assumption that behaviors are caused by mental states.

The best answers to all these questions seem to depend on adopting a somewhat different view of the nature of the human "mechanism." Implicit in the commonsense view of feelings is a model of the human being as a rather simple machine, like a clock or an automobile. At least until recently, automobiles consisted essentially of a set of mechanisms for the transformation of the energy in gasoline into mechanical energy, and the transmission of that energy from the motor to the wheels. The automobile was, in essence, a "one-way" machine in which the flow ran only from the motor to the wheels. This machine had no capacity to monitor its own activities, much less to alter or adjust them to meet new conditions. This latter function was provided by the driver, who decided where to go, observed the road and road conditions, and manipulated accelerator, clutch, and steering wheel to get there. For the first decades of automobiles, the driver even had to adjust the choke and spark-advance to match the engine temperature during starting and, once the car was going, had to decide when to shift gears, based on the speed of the car, and to depress the accelerator more or less depending on the desired speed and the slope of the road.

The parallel between this view of automobiles and drivers and the dualist view of human beings is obvious. Since our bodies demonstrably include many "one-way" processes like muscle contractions, they do not seem able to monitor and adjust the activities of the person. That is the job of the driver/mind.

More modern, complex machines (including at least some aspects of modern automobiles) are quite different and provide a very different analogy. These machines are constructed so that they are constantly altering and adjusting their own functions. The self-adjusting processes of the automobile computer modules include automatic adjustment of spark advance and choke during starting, automatic shifting between gears, and, in many cars, automatic control of speed. Indeed, all that remains for the driver is to keep the car on the road, and "smart" roads and larger computers in the car may soon take over that function as well.

These more complex machines do their magic because they contain control systems that gather and use information about the automobile's actions and its circumstances, so that activities can be adjusted to match circumstances. These are the familiar "negative feedback loops" in which information about the effects of an action, and of any environmental perturbations, is fed back to a mechanism that can in turn adjust the actions.

If we adopt this more cybernetic model of human beings (Carver & Scheier, 1981, 1998; Powers, 1973), then feelings can be seen immediately to be parts of just such a control system. As such, they are absolutely essential to the shaping of subsequent action. This is not a causal role, but rather a cybernetic, control-process role. Feelings are not the forces that produce actions; instead, they are the feedback information about the effects of those actions, information that permits the control and shaping of action. Feelings are like information feeding back to the computer module that the speed is slowing and more gasoline is required. Thus, feelings are not at all like the force of exploding gasoline in the car motor.

In sum, self-perception theory appears to have added some new, apparently difficult questions. We have to give up our easy assumption that feelings are the causes of much behavior, and that feelings act like forces exerting hydraulic pressures that generate action. Instead, we are left with questions about what feelings are, and how they could have any effect. The answers to be proposed in later chapters are certainly not complete, and some must be quite tentative. However, one of the major attractions of self-perception theory is precisely that it raises such questions.

A COMMENT TO THE READER

My goal in this book is to persuade the reader that the self-perception view of feelings is very well supported, by many different strands of research, involving hundreds of individual experiments and observations.

My persuasive goal leads to a mild conflict, because at least three audiences exist and seem to deserve somewhat different arguments. For years I have spoken at other psychology departments and professional meetings about some of this research and the theory that emerges from the research. Some years ago the universal reaction (even in my own department) seemed to be tolerant skepticism—"There goes Laird again, on that crazy self-perception idea." The strong skeptics are still the largest audience. In addition, many nonpsychologists may be unaware of the self-perception perspective but might benefit from knowledge of it. For these two groups, who are not specialists in feelings research, I have included both a relatively large selection of studies and some relatively leisurely descriptions of some key studies.

The second group is social psychologists. My impression is that most social psychologists are aware that many self-perception-like phenomena occur, but they tend to believe that self-perception effects are rare. Following Bem's caution in his early statements, they believe that self-perception takes place only "to the extent that internal cues are weak, ambiguous, or uninterpretable" (Bem, 1972, p. 2). Most social psychologists seem to believe that internal cues are rarely so useless.

Finally, during my recent experiences talking to professional groups, I have encountered a small, but I hope growing, number who are sympathetic to self-perception ideas. Antonio Damasio's (1994, 1999) recent adoption of a variant of self-perception theory has certainly helped. I have been struck, however, that even among this obviously wise and thoughtful group, many are apparently unaware of how much supportive research already exists. My apologies to these last two groups if they sometimes feel an urge to tell me to "get on with it." And now I had best do so.

PLAN OF THE BOOK

I have already described the theoretical structure into which I will fit all this research. At the beginning, I would only ask the reader to keep in mind that rejecting self-perception theory will leave behind a need to account in some other way for the large body of research described here. A wide variety of alternative explanations have been offered for different, small portions of this research. However, at some point, one must question whether a multitude of widely different, often strained, and usually post hoc explanations are preferable to something like self-perception theory. Self-perception theory contradicts common sense but otherwise is an elegant integration of a wide range of unexpected findings.

The largest and most coherent body of research on feelings concerns emotional feelings, and that seems to be the best place to start. Because there is so much research on this topic, it has been divided into four chapters. Chapter 2 concerns facial expressions. It describes many studies in which people were induced to adopt facial expressions and then reported corresponding feelings. Chapter 3 deals with a variety of other emotional behaviors, such as postures, patterns of gaze and breathing, and actions, which have the same effects on feelings as do expressions. Chapter 4 discusses the role of autonomic responses in emotion. The conclusion here is that autonomic activity does affect some emotions, but certainly not all. Chapter 5, on emotions, expands on the implications of individual differences in self-perception processes and describes an integrated view of emotional processes.

Chapter 6 discusses research on the role of behavior in feelings of confidence, pride, and self-evaluation. Standing and sitting tall does make you feel proud (Stepper & Strack, 1993) and confident (Kuvalanka, Grubstein, Kim, Nagaraja, & Laird, 1994)!

Chapter 7 deals with two aspects of motives. The first concerns the extensive research on hunger and eating that demonstrates that feelings of hunger are complex self-perceptions that are based on mixtures of cues from inside and outside one's body. The second topic in the motives chapter concerns the research on intrinsic versus extrinsic motivation. The overjustification effect and other effects of external justifications on productivity and creativity all seem to represent self-perception processes.

Chapter 8 discusses a loosely related group of research programs that have developed quite independently of self-perception theory, but which share its basic insight. This research has looked at various kinds of "cognitive feelings." These are feelings about our mental processes. A familiar example is the "tip-of-the-tongue" feeling that you know something, even though you cannot at the moment remember it. Another is the feeling of familiarity that tells you that you have encountered something before, although you cannot recall when. Feelings of this sort turn out to be based on our self-perception of a variety of features of our remembering processes, such as the ease with which we can begin to process the stimulus object.

Chapter 9 deals with the feelings of liking and disliking, or attitudes. First I discuss the extensive literature inspired by cognitive dissonance theory, which was later reinterpreted by Bem (1967, 1972) as representing self-perception. Although some of this research does not seem to fit self-perception theory, a considerable amount does (Fazio, 1987). Also discussed in that chapter is the foot-in-the-door technique, which may create attitudes, as well as recent work on attitude "creation" through actions.

Chapter 10 is a summary and integration of all the research, organized around four broad questions about self-perception research and theory. The first, and by far the most basic, is simply whether self-perception occurs—does acting lead to feeling? A relatively methodological question follows close behind: Are the effects observed in self-perception research real, or are they perhaps artifacts of the procedures? The most frequently suggested artifactual explanation is some variant of experimenter bias. If self-perception effects occur, and are not due to experimenter bias, two further conditions must be met if we are to adopt self-perception theory. The first is that actions must be not only sufficient to produce feelings but also necessary. We need some evidence that feelings cannot occur without prior actions. Finally, we need some evidence that self-perception processes occur in real life, not just the laboratory.

In chapter 11, I describe more fully a view of human beings that emerges from the research and from Ryle's approach to the problem of mind and body.

If at any time while reading you begin to feel skeptical or distressed by my arguments, I hope that you will pause for a moment and smile, as deeply and naturally as you can. You may find all your negative feelings dissolving into happiness.

NOTES

1. Bem was actually a little more cautious. His explicit statements of self-perception principles assert that we infer our psychological states from our behavior "to the extent that internal cues are weak, ambiguous, or uninterpretable" (Bem, 1972, p. 2). This qualification raises the question of what internal cues might consist of. Bem did not seem to mean that internal cues were the products of introspection, so the basic self-perception position is not seriously changed by this qualification.

2. Appraisal theories have a long and important history in theories and research on emotion (e.g., Arnold, 1960). Such theories seek to identify the properties of events in the world (real, remembered, or imagined) that generate emotional episodes. Appraisal theories are about the processes that inform us that the bear is strong, has large teeth, and has a crabby disposition.

2

Emotional Expressions

Whenever I feel afraid,
I hold my head erect
And whistle a happy tune
So no one will suspect I'm afraid.

The result of this deception
Is very strange to tell
For when I fool the people I fear
I fool myself as well

Make believe you're brave
And the trip will take you far
You may be as brave
As you make believe you are.
> Rogers and Hammerstein,
> "I Whistle a Happy Tune"

As the song makes clear, the experience of mine described in chapter 1 probably was not very special or unusual. James's basic insight was always available to anyone with a little leisure to try on expressions and notice their feelings. In fact, many earlier commentators on emotional processes have also argued that expressions produce their corresponding feelings, not the commonsense reverse. For example, Darwin (1872) observed that the inhibition of the expression of emotion reduced the intensity of emotional experiences. Also in the nineteenth century, Waynbaum (cited in Zajonc, 1985) developed an elaborate theory in which changes in facial muscle contractions were supposed to produce changes in feelings by changing the flow of blood to different areas of the brain. Near the time that James was introducing his theory, Carl Lange (1922) presented a theory that was so similar that James himself endorsed it, with the result that the theory has been known as the James-Lange theory ever since. Indeed, the general "peripheralist" theory of James, Darwin, and the others was so widely accepted in the early part of this century that J. B. Watson despaired of ever overturning it (cited in Winton, 1990).

Despite this widespread acceptance, very little direct experimental evidence for James's theory was developed; in the 1920s, Walter Cannon (1927) attacked James's theory with vigor and some marginally relevant research. Cannon's assault was so successful that little or no research appeared again until the 1960s. Cannon's critique, which will be discussed in chapter 4, was directed almost entirely at the role of autonomic arousal in generating feelings. When Jamesian research reappeared, it was first directed at arousal, but by the mid-1970s it also included the role of expressive behavior. The largest and most consistent body of evidence in support of James's theory concerns facial expressions and is the focus of this chapter.

THE THEORETICAL CONTRAST

James's theory differs from common sense in the direction of the connection between feelings and behavior. Common sense assumes that the causal arrow runs *from* the feeling to expressive behavior, as well as to arousal and action. In contrast, James's theory assumes the connection is the reverse, from behavior to feeling (see Figure 2.1). Thus, the basic test of any Jamesian theory is to manipulate a behavior and then observe the resulting feelings. This is the "empirical fulcrum" that permits the comparison of James and common sense. If James's theory is correct, the feelings should change with the behavior.

Experiments like these are strong, critical tests for James and self-perception theory. If changing behavior does change feelings, then self-perception theory may still not be correct. But if behavior failed to affect feelings, then James and self-perception theory almost certainly would be wrong. So, the first question is whether changing behavior really does lead to changes in feeling.

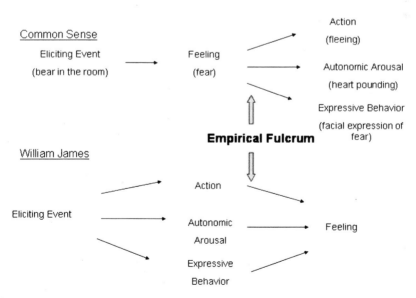

Figure 2.1. The empirical fulcrum for comparing common sense and James's theory of emotion.

MANIPULATING EXPRESSIONS DIRECTLY

My first experiment on this question was essentially an attempt to see if other people would have experiences like the one I had while driving home that day (Laird, 1967, 1974). Early on, I did ask a number of my friends to adopt facial expressions and then tell me what they felt. The results were encouraging, but then again, friends are supposed to encourage you in such moments. After all, when I asked people to smile, and then asked them how they felt, they probably could guess what kind of answer I was looking for. To reduce the likelihood that subjects were just being cooperative, the procedure and purposes of my experiment had to be much better disguised by an elaborate cover story.

The subjects were recruited for an experiment on "electromyographic (EMG) measurement of facial muscle activity." When they arrived at the laboratory, they were told about the small electrical impulses generated by muscle activity, and that we would be examining the effects of looking at different kinds of pictures on this "EMG activity." The supposed recording machine was an old, actually useless piece of apparatus, but it looked persuasively scientific. Silver-cup recording electrodes appeared to be attached to the machine. The subjects were told that during the study I would record their facial muscle activity while they looked at photographs.

While I was attaching the electrodes to their faces, I explained that we needed two kinds of recordings, from muscles that were relaxed and from muscles that were contracted. Therefore, on different trials they would be asked to contract and relax various muscles, and then maintain this position for the 10-second duration of the trial. Actually, of course, these contractions and relaxations would be the way in which I would produce the facial expressions.

Then, almost as an afterthought, I mentioned that there was one kind of error in our electrical measurements that we needed to factor out statistically, and that was the effect of moods on brain activity. I explained that ordinarily we would have measured emotions directly, but we did not have any more channels on the polygraph, so we were doing it indirectly, by asking them to report on their mood during each trial. So that they would feel free to report changes in feelings for which they would have no explanation, they were told, "We all have moment-to-moment fluctuations in mood that we ordinarily don't pay much attention to, but in this experiment they may be important, so be careful to notice how you are actually feeling during each trial, and then afterward tell us." These reports were based on rating scales that asked them how strongly they felt various emotions.

Two kinds of trials were run in this experiment. In one, the subjects were asked to contract the muscles between their eyebrows, by drawing their eyebrows down and together, and to contract the muscles at the corners of their jaw by clenching their teeth. This produced a kind of intense frown. In the other kind of trial, the subjects were asked to contract the muscles under the electrodes on their cheeks, by drawing the corners of their mouth back and up to produce a smile.

Notice that in the subjects' minds, the EMG was the important measurement in the experiment, and the important manipulation was the kind of picture that they looked at during each trial. The actual experimental manipulations, the contractions of facial muscles, had been presented as simply a means for obtaining the correct kinds of EMG measurements. The measure of emotional feelings had been almost dismissed, as a way to get rid of a small source of error.

To ensure that the subjects were persuaded by this charade, they filled out a "funnel" questionnaire at the end of the experiment that asked increasingly pointed questions, up to the point of asking directly whether the muscle contractions affected their emotional feelings. Some subjects did recognize that they had adopted emotional expressions, and some reported noticing that these expressions affected their feelings. The last group were, of course, reporting exactly what I had hoped would happen, but to be fastidious, I excluded them from the final analyses.

In this procedure, the experimenter obviously could not be blind to the subject's facial position, since the point of the experiment was to induce a natural-seeming expression. Instead, an attempt was made to measure any potential effects of the instructions or the behavior of the experimenter (me). Two subjects were scheduled for each experimental session, and only one was assigned, randomly, to have his or her face manipulated. The other was the "observer" subject. The two subjects were seated next to each other, with a screen between them so that they could not see each other. Both could see the experimenter at all times. The observer did everything the experimental subject did, except contract and relax facial muscles. If the experimental subjects' emotional feelings were being affected by aspects of the experiment other than the facial expressions, then the observer subjects would be expected to show similar effects. However, they did not.[1] The observer subjects' feeling reports were the same in either expression. The observer subject control has been called by Fridlund (1994) the "pseudoexperimental control" procedure. He recommended it as a particularly strong method for ensuring that experimenter demand is not responsible for any apparent effects of any kind of manipulation, including facial expressions.

On the other hand, the results for the experimental subjects were exactly what James would have expected. When subjects were in the smile position, they reported significantly higher levels of happiness, and when they were in the frown position, they reported significantly higher levels of anger. On the average, the events for this group of 60 subjects were like those I had experienced in my car: Adopting facial expressions of emotion led to the corresponding emotional feelings.

ARE EXPRESSIONS SUFFICIENT TO PRODUCE FEELINGS?

This result was replicated, with some variations, in a number of other studies. Many of these involved weaving together the effects of expressions on
feelings with other kinds of self-perception phenomena and will be discussed more fully in later sections. The portions of these studies that were
replications of this first one were very similar in basic design and results
(e.g., Duclos & Laird, 2001; Duclos et al., 1989; Duncan & Laird, 1977, 1980;
Edelman, 1984; Kellerman & Laird, 1982; Kellerman, Lewis, & Laird, 1989;
Laird & Crosby, 1974; MacArthur, Solomon, & Jaffee, 1980; Rutledge &
Hupka, 1985; Wilcox & Laird, 2000; for a more complete review, see Laird
& Bresler, 1992). In all these, subjects were induced to adopt facial expres-
sions and then reported corresponding emotions.[2]

A somewhat different, but conceptually identical, technique for manipulating expressions was used in a number of more recent studies by Levenson,
Ekman, and their colleagues. Ekman and his colleagues have developed a
very precise system (the Facial Action Coding System [FACS]; Ekman &
Friesen, 1978) for identifying emotional expressions by coding the movements of individual facial muscles. In a series of studies (e.g., Levenson,
1992; Levenson, Carstensen, Friesen, & Ekman, 1991; Levenson, Ekman, &
Friesen, 1990; Levenson, Ekman, Heider, & Friesen, 1992), they instructed
subjects how to contract the muscles identified by the FACS to form specific
expressions of six emotions. In each of these studies, the corresponding emotional feeling was induced. In some of these studies, the subjects were aware
of the emotional nature of their expressions, but in others they were not.

In the Levenson et al. studies, specific patterns of autonomic activity
were also produced by the facial expressions. The theoretical significance
of those results will be discussed in a number of places later in the book.

In sum, a large family of studies provides a substantial body of evidence that the minimum self-perception result does occur: Manipulation
of expressive behavior does produce corresponding changes in feelings.

Exaggerating and Minimizing Expressions

A second strand of research employed a quite different methodology.
Rather than trying to directly create the expressions, the goal in these
studies was to modify the natural, ongoing expressions of emotion. In one
example of this approach (Lanzetta, Cartwright-Smith, & Kleck, 1976),
subjects were asked to endure a series of uncomfortable electric shocks.
On some trials they were asked to intensify their expressive reactions to
the shock, on others to inhibit them. During each shock and pretense trial,
recordings were made of the subjects' skin conductance. (Skin conductance normally rises much higher after painful or unpleasant events than
after nonpainful events.) After each trial, the subjects also were asked how
painful the shock had been.

The intensity of the shocks had the expected effects: Subjects reported
that the more intense shocks were more painful, and their skin conduc-

tance rose higher. Their behavior had similar, although smaller, effects: If subjects acted as if the shock was more intense, they reported more pain and their skin conductance was higher. If they acted as if the shock was mild, then their pain reports and their skin conductance reflected their actions. Thus, in these studies, feelings of pain seem to have been due at least in part to the subjects' facial expressions of pain, at least when they were receiving actual shocks (Kleck et al., 1976).

A number of other studies of this general form were carried out, with consistent results (e.g., Kraut, 1982; Vaughan & Lanzetta, 1980, 1981; Zuckerman, Klorman, Larrance, & Spiegel, 1981). For example, in one study the subjects were induced to exaggerate or minimize their facial expressions in order to fool a supposed audience (Kleck et al., 1976). As we would expect, minimizing their facial expressions produced less intense feelings, and exaggerating them made the feelings more intense. In sum, it is quite clear that if people minimize their expressive behavior, they report feeling less intensely, and if they exaggerate their expressive behavior, their feelings are more intense. A somewhat similar procedure for inducing facial expressions also asked participants to communicate to an audience. In this case, the participants looked at photographs of happy or angry faces and then were asked to communicate as clearly as possible to some observers what the person in the photograph was feeling. The result in two studies was that the communicators reported feeling what they were trying to express (Kleinke, Peterson, & Rutledge, 1998).

EXPERIMENTER BIAS?

All the studies mentioned thus far involved techniques for minimizing the possibility that the experimenter's expectations and behavior, rather than the expression manipulations, had induced the subjects to report appropriate feelings. Nonetheless, some small amount of uncertainty remained, and indeed some variant of experimenter bias is the most frequently proposed alternative explanation of these studies (e.g., Capella, 1993; Fridlund, 1994).

At least three conceptually independent kinds of research provide strong counterarguments to the experimenter bias possibility. One, described earlier, is the use of the pesudoexperimental controls. Both in my first study (Laird, 1967, 1974) and in Rutledge and Hupka's (1985) replication, observer participants were exposed to the experimenter's behavior but did not show any change in feelings to match the feelings of the participants whose faces were manipulated.

A second phenomenon that cannot be explained by experimenter bias is the effect of facial manipulations on autonomic responses. Both the autonomic patterning found by Levenson et al. (1990) and the skin conductance results in the Lanzetta et al. (1976) and Kleck et al. (1976) studies show that facial expression manipulations affect autonomic response, even though people are unaware of their autonomic response levels and are unable to influence them. Consequently, the subjects in these studies could not have been producing the autonomic effects to please the experimenters.

These results do have a second, important implication in that they add a major complication to a Jamesian theory of emotional experience. In the simple version of James's theory depicted in Figure 2.1, no causal arrows connect expressive behavior and autonomic responses. Inhibiting or exaggerating one's expressive behavior would not be expected to produce changes in autonomic responses. Obviously, some addition to the theory is required to account for these results. I will take that issue up in chapter 5. For the moment, the important point is that manipulating facial expressions does produce corresponding change both in emotional feelings and in some other aspects of emotional response that are not susceptible to conscious control.

Particularly Well-Disguised Manipulations

Another response to the experimenter bias possibility was observed more recently, in a number of especially well-disguised replications. The first were two studies by Strack, Martin, and Stepper (1988). In this research, subjects were recruited for a study of the best techniques for teaching writing to people paralyzed below the neck. The supposed experimental question was whether it was better for the subjects to hold a pencil in their mouths with the lips tightly clamped around it, or with the lips drawn back. The latter position (see Figure 2.2) produces an expression like a smile, whereas the former produces an unpleasant, disgustlike expression. The subjects spent some time trying to write in these expressions and then judged a series of cartoons for their funniness.

The results were just as expected: The subjects who viewed the cartoons in the smilelike expressions judged them to be funnier and to evoke more amusement than did subjects who viewed the cartoons in the other expres-

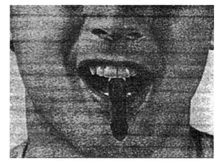

Figure 2.2. Unobtrusive manipulation of facial expressions. *Source:* Strack, F., Martin, L. L. & Stepper, S. (1988). Inhibiting and facilitating conditions of the human smile: A nonobtrusive test of the facial feedback hypothesis. *Journal of Personality and Social Psychology 54,* 768–777. Published by APA and reprinted with permission.

sion. None of the subjects in this research recognized that the "writing positions" created expressions of emotion, or that the purpose of the research involved their emotional feelings. In an elaboration of the Strack et al. procedure, Soussignan (2002) found that more intense, "Duchenne" smiles produced stronger feelings of happiness than did less intense, and arguably less genuine-seeming, smiles.

Another ingenious manipulation of facial expressions was performed by Larsen, Kasimatis, and Frey (1992), who attached golf tees to their subjects' foreheads, between the eyebrows. Under the guise of studying "divided attention," they asked their subjects to perform a number of tasks while manipulating the golf tees with their forehead muscles. On some trials the participants were instructed to make the tips of the tees touch, which they could only do by drawing their eyebrows down and together. The effect was to create an expression like sadness. On comparison trials they kept the tees separated. One of the other tasks involved rating the sadness of pictures that had already been found to elicit some sadness. However, when the golf tee manipulation had produced a sad expression, the subjects rated these pictures as significantly sadder.

A third, extensive series of studies showed the effects of another subtle manipulation on emotional feelings (Zajonc, Murphy, & Inglehart, 1989). In these studies, subjects were induced to pronounce various sounds that required adopting an approximation of a facial expression. The best known example in the United States is undoubtedly the "ee" sound, used by photographers who ask their subjects to say *cheese* before the picture is clicked, thereby producing a smile. Another was the German sound "ü," which is pronounced somewhat like the English sound "eu," and produces an expression very much like disgust. When subjects were saying "Ü," they reported much less pleasant feelings than when they were, for example, saying "ee." Once again, the subjects were completely unaware of the purposes of the experiment. A similar result, using the same techniques, was obtained with native Japanese speakers (Yogo, 1991).

In these three kinds of research, the effects of expressions on feelings are very unlikely to have been due to subject awareness. These results, in company with all the procedures used in the other studies to minimize this possibility, leave us more than reasonably confident that expressions genuinely do produce feelings. Some additional, more complicated grounds for ruling out experimental demand will be discussed later.

HOW SPECIFIC ARE THE EFFECTS OF EXPRESSIONS?

One of the perennial questions about emotional processes is whether they should be seen as representing discrete, and perhaps basic, emotional processes (e.g., Izard, 1977), or whether they should be seen as continuous dimensions (e.g., deRivera, 1977; Feldman-Barrett & Russell, 1998; Watson & Tellegen, 1985). For example, emotions certainly possess valences—they are positive or negative, good or bad. Some theorists have argued that this is the key feature of emotions (e.g., Frijda, 1986; Ortony et al. 1988; Reisenzein & Schonpflug, 1992). In support of this idea is the fact that factor analytic approaches to emotional experience invariably produce pleasantness/unpleasantness as the first factor. The same factor structure emerges whether the analysis focuses on reports of feelings or on perceptions of faces (Russell & Bullock, 1985). On the other hand, distinctive clusters of emotions can be identified, even among the unpleasant emotions (e.g., Shaver, Wu, & Schwartz, 1992). Distinctive facial expressions also exist and are reliably distinguished by members of a wide variety of cultures (e.g., Ekman, 1992a).

Although the discrete and dimensional approaches to emotion are often seen as rivals, both can be and probably are true (e.g., Davidson, 1992; Duclos et al., 1989). No one would doubt, for example, that dimensions such as height and weight can be used to describe people, even though the people are individuals. Furthermore, as Osgood, Suci, & Tannenbaum (1957) demonstrated many years ago, judgments of virtually any kind of object yield dimensional structures in which evaluation is the first factor.

Whatever the answer to the question of the ultimate nature of emotional phenomena, the controversy does raise a critical question about the interpretation of the studies discussed thus far. In all these studies, two expression conditions were used, such as a smile and a frown, or exaggerating or minimizing an expression. If a third condition was included, it was a neutral expression (Duncan & Laird, 1977). Thus, all these conditions differ linearly on pleasantness. Consequently, differences in reported happiness or anger might reflect only differences in pleasantness, not specific effects of expressions on correspondingly specific feelings (Winton, 1986).

If the effects were dimensional rather than discrete, self-perception theory would be seriously challenged. Self-perception theory holds that we know ourselves in essentially the same way that we know others. Since it is apparent that we distinguish discrete facial expressions in others, and use them to make discrete judgments about the emotional states of these others (Ekman, 1992a), we should be doing the same thing for ourselves.

Fortunately, as the reader will have guessed from this elaborate buildup, the results clearly support the discrete, specific interpretation. Our first study (Duclos et al., 1989) used to examine this issue expanded the number of expressions to four; most important, all four were negative expressions: anger, fear, sadness, and disgust. Four more recent studies (Flack, Laird, & Cavallaro, 1999a; Flack & Martin, 2004; Flack, Laird, Cavallaro, & Pelletier, 2000; Flack, Laird, & Cavallaro, 1999b) included as part of their designs a replication of these aspects of the Duclos study. All these emotions, as well as a number of others, were measured. In all four studies, the results were very specific. For every emotion, the highest rating occurred in its corresponding expression. People were saddest when in a sad expression, most afraid in the fear expression, most angry in the anger expression, and most disgusted in the disgust expression. These results demonstrate that the effects of facial expressions are specific and do not simply reflect variations in pleasantness.

The pattern of results in these four studies will not fit any single dimension, such as pleasantness. However, the pattern does fit a two-dimensional scheme that emerges from factor analyses or multidimensional scaling (MDS) of both faces and feelings (e.g., Feldman-Barrett & Russell, 1998; Russell & Bullock, 1985) or hierarchical cluster analysis of emotion names (Shaver et al., 1992). In both MDS and factor analytic results, the four negative emotions are distinct, but some estimate of "distance" can be obtained. For example, in Russell and Bullock's scaling of pictures of faces, anger and disgust are relatively close to each other, whereas fear and sadness are much farther apart. In the Shaver et al. study, disgust is part of a subcluster within anger. Consistent with this proximity of anger and disgust, in all four of these studies, the disgust expression increased anger feelings almost as much as disgust feelings. Similarly, in the anger expression, disgust feelings were elevated almost as much as anger. However, these spillovers between anger and disgust did not reflect a general increase in negative feelings, since sadness and fear were not elevated in either of these expressions.

In addition to this unexpected "spread" of the effects of the closely related anger and disgust expressions to each other, two other unexpected results were observed. The fear expression produced a significant increase in ratings of surprise, which none of the other expressions did. This effect was very consistent with the scaling studies (e.g., Russell & Bullock, 1985) in which the closest emotion to fear is surprise. In addition, the sad expression produced significant reductions in reports of happiness, interest, and agreeableness. Since these three lie opposite to sadness in the circumplex model, it makes sense that a sad expression should both increase sadness and decrease happiness, interest, and agreeableness. Angry and fearful expressions and feelings are not directly opposite to happiness in the dimensional schemes, and neither angry nor fearful expressions caused reductions in happiness. Therefore, it was not just that any negative expressions would diminish happiness.

In sum, the overall pattern of results in all five studies was even more consistent with other research on emotional expressions and feelings than we had expected. Both in that research and in our results we see a variety of distinguishable facial expressions and emotional experiences. Both expressions and experiences vary in their similarity and the organization of their relationships. In this study the impact of the expressions on the experiences nicely replicated this organization.

Similarly specific effects of expressions on feelings were also found by Levenson et al. (1990) and by Hess, Kappas, McHugo, Lanzetta, and Kleck (1992). Clearly, the effects of facial expressions on feelings do not just reflect variations in pleasantness. Instead, the production of facial expressions of specific emotions leads to experiences that fit those expressions precisely. When people are induced to look angry, they feel angry, not sad or afraid. When they are in a sad expression, they feel sad, not angry or afraid, and so on. Note, however, that the results are also entirely consistent with the dimensional schemes that array emotional phenomena on the dimensions of valence and arousal (e.g., Feldman-Barrett & Russell, 1998).

EXPRESSIONS AND EMOTIONAL COGNITIONS

A particularly subtle possible interpretation of the results described thus far was proposed by Reisenzein (1994; Reisenzein & Schonpflug, 1992). He distinguishes experiences of emotion from judgments or beliefs about emotional experiences. He then suggests that perhaps the manipulations of expressive behavior affect only the judgments about the experiences, not the experiences themselves.

This idea has some plausibility because, clearly, when subjects in self-perception experiments report their experiences, they are in some sense reporting judgments about those experiences. The parallel with object perception is close here. When I ask you what color the apple is, you have a direct experience, what Russell called "knowledge by acquaintance," that includes the color as well as the apple's shape, size, and so on. But when you say "red," this is a judgment about the way the color experience of the apple is best described. This is the same point made by Lambie and Marcel (2002) and discussed in chapter 1. Three different things, then, can be distinguished: the experience or feeling, the judgment about that feeling, and the verbal report of the judgment. If we assume for the moment that the report accurately reflects the judgment, or what Lambie and Marcel call "awareness," then it is still possible that the awareness is affected by the expressions while leaving the phenomenology or preverbal experience unchanged.

Actually, once we consider this cascade of processes, at least one more becomes apparent. The experience or feeling that is unverbalizable, or perhaps preverbal, is a global, unified, and not obviously analyzable unit. In the case of the apple's color, we know that the experience of redness is actually based on a comparison of the wavelength of the light reflected from the apple to the wavelengths of light reflected from the background. This comparison at least begins with ganglion cells in the retina. At this lowest level, then, information is extracted from the sensory arrays that will ultimately lead on to experienced qualities of the world. However, this lowest level information is not at all accessible to awareness, even though it is one of the ingredients that constitute experience.

So there seem to be four levels of organization of information in play here. In the example of the apple, the lowest level is the activity of neurons "reporting" the relationship between the wavelengths of light reflected by apple and background. Then there is the experience of redness that is experientially immediate and direct, typical knowledge by acquaintance. Then there are the judgment and finally the verbal report of the judgment.

Like the experiences of redness and depth, emotional experiences must be based on lower order cues that are themselves not easily experienced. The same four levels are identifiable. At the lowest is the sensory information from stretch receptors in the muscles about what they are doing. Somewhat higher is an integration of this information, and information from the context to form the knowledge by acquaintance of anger or joy. Then there is the judgment about how to label these, a judgment that includes, of course, more than just pairing the sound of the word with the experience, since the meaning of the label is included as well. Finally, there is the report of the label (and its meanings).

Where in this cascade of processes would we expect the manipulations of expressive behavior to play their role? To a considerable extent, the answer seems to depend on whether people in self-perception experiments are aware of their expressive behavior and consciously recognize its emotional import. If I adopt a smile and think to myself, "I am smiling," then you ask me about my emotional state, my answer might well reflect judgmental processes. I probably would think, "I am smiling, and therefore judge that I am happy." But that is precisely the kind of process that all the experimenters have been at great pains to prevent occurring. The reason for keeping the participants in these studies in the dark about the nature and purpose of the manipulations is to prevent judgmental processes from affecting the final reports.

Most of the experimenters, including me, did not work so hard to keep participants in the dark because of this judgment/experience issue. We were simply trying to avoid one particular kind of judgment process, in which the participant thinks, "The nice experimenter seems to want me to say I feel happy, so I will." But without intending to, we also designed experiments that make the judgment explanation relatively unlikely. The manipulations of expressions seem to be working by supplying information at the lowest level of the four I have discussed. The expression manipulations do, of course, affect judgments and verbal reports of judgments, but they do so only by way of first affecting the preverbal phenomenology of emotion that the judgment reflects.

EMOTION, MEMORY, AND JUDGMENT

If the feelings produced in self-perception experiments are like any other kind of feelings, then we should expect that feelings produced by manipulating expressive behavior should function in the same way that experiences induced by more conventional means do. Because emotional episodes are so complicated, showing this similarity is a little trickier than it first looks. We would not be impressed, for example, to find that feelings induced by some self-perception procedure affected other aspects of emotional response. Instead, to compare the effects of expression-generated experiences with naturally occurring experiences, we need to find an arena in which emotional feelings have been shown to affect something else that is not another usual component of an emotional episode. Fortunately, a number of studies on the impact of emotional states on memory and judgment show such effects.

A great deal of research in the last decade or so has demonstrated that emotional processes can affect cognitive processes such as memory and judgment. If expressions are affecting emotional feelings as self-perception theory suggests, then manipulations of expressions should affect memory and judgment in the same way.

The most common kind of relationship that has been found between emotional state and memory is "mood congruence." In these studies, subjects are first induced to experience some emotional feelings and then are asked to recall material with emotional content (Blaney, 1986; Bower, 1980). A great many techniques have been used to induce emotional states, including hypnotizing subjects, giving subjects presents, rewarding or punishing them, or inducing experiences of success or failure. Emotional states have even been manipulated by playing sad or happy music. Presumably these techniques produce emotional effects that are typical of everyday life.

In the mood and memory studies, once the emotional state is established by whatever means, the subjects are asked to recall various kinds of events. The routine finding in this kind of research is that people are better able to recall emotional material that is consistent with their emotional state at the time of recall, as compared with inconsistent material.

If expressions are creating normal emotional experiences, then the same kinds of interactions between expression manipulations and the content of memory should occur. Four studies have demonstrated such effects.

In the first of these studies (Laird, Wagener, Halal, & Szegda, 1982, Study 1), subjects first read two passages with emotional content. Half the subjects read two humorous stories by Woody Allen, and half read two anger-provoking editorials from the *New York Times*. After a brief intervening task, the subjects were induced to adopt either a smile or a frown expression, by an adaptation of the technique described earlier in this chapter. Then the subjects were asked to reproduce as completely as possible one of the selections they had read. When their reproduction was finished, they were positioned in the other expression and asked to recall the other passage. (Orders of expressions and passages and their combinations were all counterbalanced.) Judges blind to the subjects' experimental conditions later scored the recalled material for numbers of elements included.

The subjects who had read the Woody Allen stories recalled significantly more material when their recall occurred in a smile expression than a frown, whereas the subjects who had read the editorials recalled more in a frown expression. A typical mood-congruence effect had occurred.

Actually, the results were a bit more complicated because this mood-congruence effect occurred only in a part of the sample. The subjects who showed the mood-congruence effect on memory were those whose feelings were affected by their expressions. Subjects in identical expressions whose feelings were not affected did not show any mood congruence. Thus, clearly the effects on memory were not produced directly by the expressions. Instead, the effects on memory were produced by the feelings that were generated by the expressions.

In a second study (Laird et al., 1982, Study 2), as part of an apparently unrelated task, the subjects heard a number of emotional sentences, such as "Oh, be careful!" and "That really makes me mad," each spoken by a different person. These sentences expressed emotions of happiness, sadness, fear, and anger. Later, and unexpectedly, participants were asked to recall as many sentences as possible. Different groups of subjects tried to recall the sentences while in happy, angry, sad, and fearful expressions. Consistent with the first study, subjects recalled more of each type of sentence while they were in a congruent expression.

These two studies demonstrated that emotional feelings affected the ability to recall emotional material that was not personally relevant. A third study (Laird, Cuniff, Sheehan, Shulman, & Strum, 1989) looked at the effects of expressions on recall of personal history. Subjects were asked to remember incidents from their own lives while they maintained expressions of happiness, anger, and sadness. On each personal recall trial, the subjects were given a card with a neutral word on it, such as *cat* or *tree*. The subjects' task was to remember an event from their own lives that was connected to the cue word. Once they had identified an event, they were to write a very brief description of the event, which they were told was just to serve as a reminder to them later. The cards were collected after each trial. The subjects recalled two experiences in each of the three expressions and in a neutral expression. After they had completed the eight recall trials, there was a 10-minute intervening task, and then the cards were returned, after being shuffled, and the subjects were asked to describe their emotions during the experience, using a series of rating scales, such as "happy," "angry," "surprised," and so on. When these ratings were completed, the subjects were asked to describe their facial position on each trial. As is typical in these experiments, the majority of subjects could not identify their facial positions as expressions.

Compared with the experiences in the neutral condition, the experiences recalled in the smile condition were significantly happier. The experiences recalled in the anger condition were also significantly angrier than those recalled in the neutral condition. These experiences did not differ on any other negative emotion ratings, such as fear or sadness, indicating that this effect was not due to differences in pleasantness. Thus, for these two expressions the expected mood-congruence effect occurred and was specific to the kind of expression. In the sad expression, the experiences recalled did not differ on any emotion dimensions. This is not an unusual result in research on mood congruence and memory, in which sad memories often do not show the same effects as other kinds of memory. A possible explanation is that sad memories are encoded differently from other kinds of memories because they are less likely to be rehearsed (e.g., Isen, 1990).

Simone Schnall (Schnall & Laird, 2002) found a similar effect of expressions on feelings that extended beyond the time that the expressions were being maintained. She also found that a sad expression and sad feelings did not have the same effect as other expressions.

In these four studies, the impact on memory of manipulating expressions of emotion was identical with the effects of other kinds of emotion manipulation. Thus, these results suggest that expression manipulations "work" by creating typical kinds of emotional experiences.

A related phenomenon is the effect of emotional feelings on judgments. When people are induced to feel an emotion, this feeling can serve as information about its apparent object (Schwarz & Clore, 1988) or can more directly "infuse" the judgment process (Forgas, 1995). If expression-induced feelings are like feelings that arise from other sources, then the same effect should occur. A number of studies demonstrate such effects. The best example is a study by Martin, Harlow, and Strack (1992) in which subjects were asked to read a story about a social situation in which a friend failed to do something he had promised the narrator. After reading the story, the subjects rated how they would have felt if they were the narrator, on scales measuring anger and tolerance-understanding. Half of the subjects read the story and made their judgments while they held a pen in their teeth in the way described earlier that produces a kind of smile. The other half of the subjects responded while they were clenching their teeth tightly onto a folded piece of paper towel, producing an angerlike expression.

As predicted, the subjects who read the story while in the pen-smile position were significantly less angry and more tolerant than the other subjects. Their judgments about the story had been affected by their facial expressions.

A kind of mirror-image effect was also demonstrated with facial expression manipulations (Convoy & Laird, 1984). In this study, subjects were manipulated into smile or frown expressions and then asked to make up stories in response to pictures like those in the Thematic Apperception Test (TAT). The emotional content of the stories was rated by judges blind to the expression condition. The stories created while the subjects were smiling were rated as significantly happier and less angry than the stories created while the subjects were frowning.

Facial expressions also induce people to make different kinds of judgments about the emotions of others (Wagener & Laird, 1980b). When smiling, people attributed more happiness to pictures of others than when frowning.

In sum, a wide variety of studies have demonstrated that experimentally manipulated facial expressions affect memory and judgment. These effects parallel the effects of other kinds of emotion manipulations and indicate that expression manipulations produce the same sorts of emotional effects as, for example, succeeding and failing, listening to music, and perhaps even undergoing hypnosis. Thus, these results argue against Reisenzein's speculation that expressions do not affect emotional experience itself. These studies also add to the array of findings that show that changing expressions does change emotional experience, as James and self-perception theory had predicted.

ARE THE EFFECTS OF EXPRESSIONS "BIG ENOUGH" FOR SELF-PERCEPTION THEORY?

In a meta-analysis of some of the research on the effects of facial expressions on feelings, Matsumoto (1987) obtained an effect size of $r = .343$. He observed correctly that this is a "moderate" effect size, and then he raised the question of whether it could bear the theoretical weight that was being loaded onto these expression effects. This effect size implies that about 18% of the variance in feelings during these experiments is explained by the effects of expressions. Does this experimental effect size account for enough of what is going on to justify adopting a Jamesian or self-perception view?

We should recognize that the background logic of these experiments is somewhat inconsistent with the whole idea of effect sizes. The purpose of these experiments is to show what *can* occur in specially contrived experimental circumstances, not to model actual real-life emotional episodes. Recall that the point of these experiments was to test whether there was any plausibility to the proposed link from expressive behavior to feelings. So, any demonstrable effect is sufficient to add some credence to Jamesian self-perception theories, since the opposing theories would predict no effects at all. Leaving aside the question of whether effect sizes are at all appropriate in this case, let us consider the answer to Matsumoto's size question.

Evaluating the observed effect size of .343 depends on two quite different issues. One is how seriously we should ever take effect sizes of this magnitude; the second is how to understand this particular example. In a well-known book on meta-analysis, Rosenthal (1991) provides an answer to the first question. He argues that an effect size of this order is indeed important and deserves to be taken very seriously. It is certainly more than large enough to license some substantial theoretical work. In fact, it is just about the same size as the effects observed in Rosenthal's famous research on experimenter bias; therefore, it appears to warrant as much confidence in self-perception theory as in the evidence for experimenter bias.

The second question concerns the particular effects in these experiments. For a number of reasons, the experimental effects seem likely to underestimate what happens in everyday life. Perhaps the most important of these reasons is that the expression manipulations are inevitably very crude. To disguise the purposes of these experiments, the procedures for manipulating expressions all produce approximations to real expressions. To the extent that the manipulated expressions do not match the subjects' own natural expressions, the magnitude of the effects would be underestimated. Consider, for example, the kinds of expressions that are produced by asking people to hold a pencil in their mouth or to pronounce the sound "ü." They certainly have some of the features of a natural expression of happiness or disgust, but equally clearly the "expressions" are only approximations. Insofar as they do not produce the complete, natural expression, we would expect the intensity of subjects' experiences to be reduced.

A second problem is that even when the experimenter tries to "create" a full-fledged expression of emotion, these expressions may not match the subjects' own natural expressions. This problem was brought home to me during a debriefing session after one of these experiments, when I asked a subject how the facial positions had affected him. During the experimental manipulations he had readily adopted a frown and a smile that seemed very natural to me, so I was surprised by his response that the "contortions," as he called them, were extremely strained and uncomfortable. Apparently to avoid offending me by this comment, he simultaneously gave me a smile that I experienced as very warm and friendly. But it was in fact a tiny fraction of the kind of smile that I had just posed him in. The corners of his lips barely moved, and yet it seemed like a nice warm smile. Puzzled over this, and talking with him about my puzzlement, I realized that his natural range of expressive movements was very small. However, I had "adapted" to this range of movement very rapidly, so that I understood what his expressions "meant" in that the little lip twitch was a warm, friendly smile. This kind of adaptation and sense making seems highly analogous to the way in which we all can rapidly adapt to regional accents in speech, so that we only notice the meaning of what is said. These variations in the range, and perhaps style, of people's expressive movements are a second major potential source of error in the expression manipulation experiments.

A third factor that may diminish the size of the effects is the subjects' understanding that they are in an experiment in which variations in emotional feelings are not expected or even appropriate. A subject in my first experiment described this problem very well when he said during debriefing, "I don't know why, but when my jaw was clenched and my brows down, I couldn't help myself, I found my thoughts wandering to things that made me angry." Subjects often report during debriefing that they were surprised at the effects of the expressions, and probably as a result at least some subjects are reluctant to report their changing, and apparently irrational, feelings.

A fourth interference with the effectiveness of the expression manipulations is the effect of some subjects' emotional states when they arrive at the experiment. Subjects who are already feeling strong emotions, such as anger or sadness, or in a few cases apprehension about participation in a psychology experiment, are much less able to change the feelings, or perhaps to notice any changes in their feelings.

Finally, the magnitude of the expression effects is certainly reduced by all the things that interfere with any experiment. Subjects who are exhausted, disinterested, distracted, or trying too hard to outwit the experimenter are all unlikely to show these or any other experimental effects. Unlike the first four, this factor is common to all experiments and deserves no special status in our argument. It is the kind of thing that contributes to the fact that almost no psychological experiments produce truly large effect sizes (and therefore why an effect size of .343 is considered by most psychologists to be more than enough on which to build a theory).

After considering some of the factors that might enhance or diminish the magnitude of the expression effects, we are left with no firm conclusion. A good argument can be made that the experiments underestimate the effects. I think that anyone who has run such an experiment and experienced firsthand the problems of any of these methods would opt for that choice. Still, we who run these experiments also have reason to kid ourselves, and the factors on the other side are important, too. Perhaps the place to leave the issue for now is that we seem to have adequate grounds, including an adequately large effect size, to continue in the theoretical development and research. Let us see where it takes us.

One other point needs to be made here. Some Jamesian emotion theories have focused entirely or primarily on the effects of expressions on feelings (e.g., Izard, 1990; Leventhal, 1980; Tomkins, 1962; Zajonc, 1985). These theories are often called *facial feedback* theories. For these theories, the issue of the effect size of expressions is critical, since the theory assumes that all emotional feelings are generated by facial expressions. In contrast to these theories, self-perception theory explicitly assumes that facial expressions are only one source of feeling. In the next two chapters I will describe a variety of other kinds of information that contribute to emotional feelings. Self-perception theory would predict that the effects of any one kind of behavior, including expressions, on feelings would not be as strong as the combined effect of the variety of information sources that function in real-life emotions. Two studies looked at the combined effects of facial expressions and emotional postures and found that the two kinds of cues do indeed combine to produce stronger feelings than either does alone, as self-perception theory would have predicted (Flack et al., 1999a, 1999b).

Actual emotional episodes, especially those with strong feelings, include many other kinds of cues as well. In addition to a scowl and an angry posture, rage would include increased arousal, altered breathing, changes in pitch and timbre of voice, and perhaps both verbal and physical assaults. All these would probably combine to increase the intensity of the experience. Recently we demonstrated that adding tone of voice to posture and expression produced a small additional increment in the intensity of feelings (Flack, Cavallaro, & Laird, 1997).

In sum, the effects do seem to be adequate to justify further theoretical investment. The current state of the evidence probably does not support a firm conclusion about the potential power of a combined manipulation, but certainly the effects are large enough so that we cannot dismiss them.

ARE EXPRESSIONS NECESSARY FOR EMOTIONAL EXPERIENCE?

I have discussed a great many studies that show that expressions are sufficient to produce emotional feelings: If people are induced to adopt expressions, they will feel the corresponding emotion. This is the first, essential step in the empirical testing of self-perception theory. If expressions did not produce feelings, then we could dismiss self-perception theory instantly.

However, self-perception theory makes a stronger claim. The claim is not quite that expressions are also necessary for feeling, because there are a multitude of emotional behaviors, and probably no one of them is necessary. However, self-perception theory does predict that reducing the amount of expressive behavior will at least reduce the intensity of emotional feelings.

A few studies of expressions do show this expected, even required, effect. For example, one common paradigm has asked participants to inhibit as well as exhibit expressive behavior (e.g., Gross, 1998; Gross & Levenson, 1993, 1997; Kleck et al., 1976; Kraut, 1982; Vaughn & Lanzetta, 1980, 1981; Zuckerman et al., 1981). In these studies, the reductions in feeling due to inhibiting are often as large as the increases produced by expressing.[3]

We (Laird et al., 1994) induced participants to inhibit their expressive behavior by a different ruse. We attached electrodes to their faces, explaining that the electrodes were highly subject to movement artifacts. Therefore, on the trials in which we were recording from those electrodes, it was important that they not move their facial muscles. As a comparison, on other trials we told participants we would record from their fingers, so they should not move their hands. Then the participants watched brief segments of funny movies. Inhibiting their facial expressions did reduce the participants' enjoyment of the movies.

In a more recent study, Sandi Duclos (Duclos & Laird, 2001) explored the effectiveness of deliberate inhibition of expression on feeling. In contrast to the many studies of college students, the participants in Duclos's study were adults recruited from a mainstream church who were unacquainted with recent psychology and who were very dubious about the potential benefits of controlling their expressive behavior. Nonetheless, inhibiting expressive behavior was quite effective in reducing the intensity of both sadness and anger.

The inhibition procedures used in Duclos's study were designed to mimic those used in the behavior therapy technique of systematic desensitization in treating anxiety disorders. In systematic desensitization, clients are taught to relax all their skeletal muscles and then to contemplate the objects of their anxiety while maintaining the relaxation (Wolpe, 1958). The muscular relaxation prevents the feelings of anxiety, as self-perception theory would predict; as a result, the association between stimulus and anxiety is weakened and eventually disappears. Relaxation techniques are also successful in the treatment of anger (Hazaleus & Deffenbacher, 1986). The success of systematic desensitization therapy demonstrates, in a very practical way, that feelings depend on expressive behavior occurring first.

The evidence that expressions are necessary for emotional experience is certainly less extensive than the evidence that they are sufficient. However, a reasonable number of studies, as well as many therapeutic examples, show that preventing expressive behavior does reduce feeling. In later chapters I will present more such evidence with regard to various other combinations of behavior and feeling.

INDIVIDUAL DIFFERENCES IN THE EFFECTS OF EXPRESSIONS

I have described a rich variety of experiments demonstrating that when people are induced to adopt expressions of emotion, they report feeling that emotion, or reflect in some other way the presence of such a feeling. William James and self-perception theory have been regularly and reliably confirmed in these studies. Now it is time to introduce a major qualification to these results. Some people do feel happier when smiling and angrier when frowning, but some do not. These differences, which are consistent and stable, are related to many other kinds of behaviors and properties of people. Ultimately, as we will see, these individual differences simultaneously strengthen the Jamesian and self-perception explanations and restrict the simplest, basic empirical prediction of these theories.

I began to suspect the existence of individual differences in the effects of expressions during my very first experiment (Laird, 1967, 1974). Although the overall effects of the expression manipulations were clearly significant, these effects seemed to be contributed by a portion of the subjects. These subjects would often report quite strong swings in their feelings from one expression condition to the next. We also found that if people felt happy when in a smile, they were also very likely to feel angry when frowning (Duncan & Laird, 1977). Another group of subjects appeared to be completely unaffected by any of the expression manipulations.

The simplest explanation for these differences was random variation and error. Perhaps I was just looking at a continuous range of responses created by chance, and attending to those at the extreme ends of the distribution. To test this possibility, Melvin Crosby and I (Laird & Crosby, 1974) ran a study in which we repeated the expression manipulation procedure on the same subjects, on two occasions separated by a few days to a week. If the differences were due to random variation, then we would not expect the same random events to occur to the same individuals on two occasions—their responses on the two days should have been unrelated.

Instead, we found that there was substantial (and significant) consistency across the two experimental sessions. If a subject responded to the expression manipulations on their first session, then he also was likely to respond on the second session a few days later. The differences in response seemed to be due to some property of the person that lasted at least for a few days. Charlie Bresler (Bresler & Laird, 1983) later replicated this basic result with up to five different experimental sessions, distributed over as long as a month, and found that responses were stable over at least that span of time.

The simplest and least theoretically interesting explanation of these differences was that the unaffected subjects represented failures at manipulating expressions. If we did not manage to match a subject's idiosyncratic smile or frown on one occasion, we might well miss it on the second. To explore this possibility in the Crosby study, we asked subjects a few questions about their emotional experiences in everyday life. If the differences in the effects of expressions were related to other aspects of their emotional life, then it would strongly suggest that the differences reflected something about the people and were not produced by experimental error.

The nature of these differences was suggested by the basic assumption of self-perception theory, that we know ourselves in essentially the same way that we know others. In perceiving others, there are only two kinds of information that we might use (Laird & Berglas, 1975). The first would be a person's actions, especially his facial expressions. The second would be the situation that he was in. For example, we might know someone was happy because we could see he was smiling or because we knew the person was at a party (and we know that most people at parties are happy).

These two kinds of information are usually consistent—most people smile at parties. But occasionally the two kinds diverge, such as when someone arrives at a party still scowling after a quarrel on the doorstep with his or her companion or is insulted while there. When information from behavior conflicts with information from the situation, observers would have to base their judgments on one or the other. According to self-perception theory, individuals must make the same kind of choices for themselves. When their behavior conflicts with the situation they are in, they must rely on one or the other.

Of course, the standard expression manipulation procedure is designed to produce just such a conflict between the situation and the person's actions. The situation is that the subjects are in an experiment, in which they are performing an apparently innocuous and unemotional task. This situation implies that the subjects should feel no emotion, except perhaps boredom or mild apprehension about the strangeness of the situation. In contrast, the subjects' manipulated expressions imply that they should feel an emotional experience. Thus, the subjects must choose between the situational information and the information from their behavior.

Based on this analysis, we suspected that the individual differences reflected how much subjects responded to cues from their behavior or from the situation. To explore this possibility, one of the questions we asked subjects was how easily they could move from a situation in which one emotion was appropriate to a new situation in which another emotion was appropriate. An example would be having an argument with one person and then going directly into a conversation with another. We imagined that subjects who responded most strongly to situational cues would find this no problem. When the situational cues changed, their feelings would change as easily. In contrast, changing expressive behavior seemed likely to be slower and more inert. Thus, we predicted and found that subjects whose feelings were consistently affected by their expressions reported more difficulty in changing situations than those who were not so affected.

A second question was suggested by the apparent difference between the ways in which information from the situation and from behavior would be processed. As James had first emphasized, information from behavior seems to be processed in much the same way as other sensory or perceptual information. In contrast, the idea that "most people at a party are happy, and therefore it is appropriate for me to be happy now, too" seems much more like a judgment. The question consisted, then, of asking subjects whether they felt their emotional experiences were more like a sensation or perception or more like a judgment. As predicted, the people who consistently responded to the expression manipulations were significantly more likely to describe their emotional experiences as like sensations.[4]

The relationships between the subjects' responses to questions and to the expression manipulation procedure indicated that we were dealing with a "personality variable." That is, these theoretically consistent differences seemed to reflect an enduring property that we might expect to find expressed in a variety of other situations and activities.

In the chapters to come, a variety of these individual difference results will be reported, and their theoretical implications are important. Because I will be discussing these connections so often, it is helpful to introduce a set of brief labels for the differences. I have referred to one kind of information as arising from the situations in which people find themselves. This kind of information I have called, unimaginatively, *situational* cues (Laird & Berglas, 1975). Situational cues consist of information about what most people would be feeling in a particular situation; these are not norms about what one *should* feel, but rather information about what everyone *would* feel.

The other kind of information arises from the person's own behavior, such as her facial expressions. As will become apparent in later chapters, this information seemed to extend beyond simple behaviors and to include anything that is distinctively true of the person. This includes especially his or her actions, as well as the consequences of the actions and things like physical appearance. We were tempted to call these cues *personal,* but at the time we were inventing these labels, research on personal and situational causal attributions was very popular, and the potential for confusion seemed too great. Consequently, we called these cues from behavior and the person's properties *self-produced* (Laird & Berglas, 1975). This is a clunky, unsatisfactory label, and more recently we have reverted to our original idea and have taken to calling these cues *personal* again. As a quick rule of thumb, situational information would let you draw conclusions about a person's feelings without actually observing the person, as long as you knew what situation he or she was in. In contrast, personal information requires that you observe the particular individual and his or her actions and properties.

Many of the studies already described included a systematic look at the role of these individual differences. Most commonly, the subjects' response to personal cues was determined in a separate procedure, in which their expressions were manipulated and their feelings assessed. Usually we have administered two pairs of trials, each pair consisting of a smile and a frown. Subjects who report feeling happier on the smile trial and angrier on the frown trial in both pairs of trials are assigned to the personal cue group.

In virtually every study in which we have looked for individual differences, we have found them. For example, in the studies on the effects of expressions on memory, mood-congruent memory was observed only in those subjects who were more responsive to personal cues. In these memory studies, the subjects' expressions were manipulated twice. During one set of expression manipulations, the subjects were asked to recall material and so on. During the other, their feeling responses to the personal cues of their expressions were assessed. Only those who felt happy when smiling and angry when frowning also showed mood-congruent memory.

As noted earlier, the fact that mood-congruent memory occurred only in the personal cue subjects was useful in defining the nature of the effect. Since all subjects had received identical expression manipulations, the expressions themselves could not be the source of the effect. Instead, the active ingredient must have been the feelings these expressions engendered.[5]

Similar qualifications on some other cognitive effects were also observed. For example, the effects of the judges' expressions on judgments of the emotional feelings of others occurred only in subjects who were more responsive to personal cues (Wagener & Laird, 1980b). Similarly, only the subjects who were responsive to personal cues showed the effects of expressions on the kinds of fantasies created in response to TAT-like pictures (Convoy & Laird, 1984). Like the memory results, these individual differences also indicate that emotional projections onto other people and into fantasy products are produced by the feelings, not the expressions themselves.

RELATIONS WITH OTHER PSYCHOLOGICAL VARIABLES

The idea that people differ in their focus on themselves or their situation is widespread in psychology. A similar "person versus situation" emphasis is contained in such well-known personality measures as extroversion/introversion (e.g., Eysenck, 1970),internal versus external locus of control (Rotter, 1990), private and public self-consciousness (Carver, Antoni, & Scheier, 1985), and self-monitoring (Snyder, 1974) and body consciousness (Fenigstein, Scheier, & Buss, 1975). In a number of studies (e.g., Bresler & Laird, 1983), we have looked at whether these measures were related to subjects' response to personal cues in the expression manipulation procedure. None of these measures have been found to be related. From time to time people have suggested that men and women might differ in their responses to personal and situational cues. We routinely include participant gender as a factor in our analyses and have rarely found any main effects or interactions involving gender.

In retrospect, the explanations for the lack of relationships have always been reasonably clear. For example, introversion refers to how much one wants to be alone and is comfortable being alone. That is certainly not like the extent to which one's feelings are based on one's behavior. Similarly, self-monitoring asks explicitly how much one deliberately adjusts one's actions to fit social expectations, but responding to situational cues is entirely nonconscious. Public self-consciousness is very much the same as self-monitoring, whereas private self-consciousness concerns how aware you are of your feelings, but not how those feelings arise. Perhaps the closest of these measures is body consciousness, especially private body consciousness, which measures how sensitive you are to relatively subtle variations in bodily state. In some studies, we have found that private body consciousness paralleled response to personal cues in predicting a third variable. For example, in a study of the tendency to misinterpret the bodily cues of fatigue as sadness, only subjects who were more responsive to personal cues showed this confusion (Bresler, 1984). Although body consciousness was not related to response to personal cues, it did independently predict whether subjects would confuse fatigue and sadness.

Two other experiments, both studies of taste sensitivity, showed the same parallel prediction between the two measures (Hopmeyer & Stevens, 1989; Stevens, Dooley, & Laird, 1988). If people who are more responsive to personal cues or are high in body consciousness are more tuned in to sensations from their bodies, they might also be more sensitive to other sensations. To test this, subjects were asked to taste a series of concentrations of sucrose. The degree to which subjects are sensitive to sensory changes is expressed as the slope of the psychophysical function relating chemical concentration to taste intensity. As predicted, subjects who were more responsive to personal cues produced significantly steeper psychophysical functions, as did subjects higher in body consciousness. However, once again, responses to personal cues and body consciousness were not themselves significantly related.

Similar differences in sensory sensitivity occur for pain as well. Participants who were more responsive to personal cues detect cold pressor pain more rapidly and tolerate less of it (Genov, Pietrzak, Laird, Bemis, & Fortunato, 2000). Differences in susceptibility to premenstrual tension also seem to reflect these differences in sensory acuity (Schnall, Abrahamson, & Laird, 2002).

The parallel between self-perception and sensory/perceptual processes emphasized in both the theory and these last results suggested another measure that might be related: field dependence/independence (Wapner & Demick, 1991). The basic procedure used to measure field dependence, the Rod and Frame Test, is conceptually perfectly parallel to the expression manipulation procedure. In this test, the subject is seated in a completely dark room, in which the only things he can see are a luminous rectangle, the frame, and inside it a luminous rod. Both the rod and the frame can be independently rotated, and in a typical experimental trial, when the subject first sees them, both have been rotated so that they are not vertical. The subject's task is to rotate the rod so that it is vertical.

In this situation, there are two conflicting kinds of information that the subject can use to adjust the rod. One is the frame. In our built world, rectangles are everywhere—buildings, windows, doors, walls of rooms, and so forth, and all of them are aligned to be vertical and horizontal. Thus, the frame provides clear and ordinarily reliable information about what constitutes vertical. The second kind of information comes from the subject's vestibular and proprioceptive systems that identify vertical by the effects of gravity. The point of the test is to put in conflict these two ordinarily reliable and consistent sets of cues, from the environment and from one's body.

In the Rod and Frame Test, subjects consistently rely on one or the other of these two conflicting kinds of information. Some align the rod most closely with their bodies, whereas others align the rod with the frame. Those who respond to the frame are called field dependent because the frame defines an external "field." Those who ignore the frame and rely on the cues from their bodies are called field independent.

The parallel between field dependence and response to personal cues is probably obvious. In the measurement procedures for both, two kinds of information are available, from the situation and from the person's own bodily activities. These two sets of cues ordinarily agree, but when they do not, people consistently use one or the other. We might expect, therefore, that subjects who responded to the personal cues of the expression manipulation would also be field independent on the Rod and Frame Test. That is indeed the case (Edelman, 1984). Another measure of field independence is the Embedded Figures Test. Subjects who respond to personal cues in the expression manipulation procedure also score significantly higher (more field independent) on the Embedded Figures Test (Duncan & Laird, 1977).

Are field dependence and response to personal cues the same variable traveling under different names? At this point the answer is unclear. The answer will depend on whether measures of the two do distinguishably different work. That is, are there occasions when one measure predicts some other phenomenon and the other measure does not? In only one study have both been used to predict some third phenomenon. In a study by Edelman (1984) of the determinants of obesity, which will be described in more detail in the later chapter motives and desires, both the Rod and Frame Test and the expression manipulation procedure were used as predictors. In this study, the expression manipulation provided better prediction, but the increase was not significant. So, the question of the independence of the two measures is unanswered at the moment. The two bodies of research, on Field Dependence and on self-perception, have not yet been brought into close enough contact.

The relationship with Field Dependence adds some complications to our interpretation of the observed individual differences in response to personal cues. However, these results do add some additional confidence that the differences in how people respond to the expression manipulation procedure are related to other psychological processes.

SUMMARY

A very large number of studies have demonstrated that changing a person's facial expressions will produce corresponding changes in emotional feelings. A number of kinds of data indicate that these effects are not at-

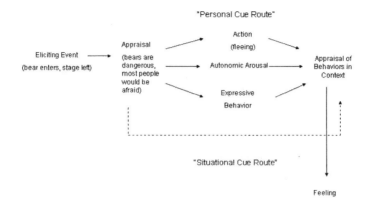

Figure 2.3. Self-perception model including individual differences in personal and situational cue response.

tributable to experimental demand, but we will see in chapter 5 that there are other data and arguments that will strengthen this conclusion. The effects of expressions on feelings also are large enough to justify further theoretical elaboration. However, they do not occur in all people. Instead, consistent, reliable differences in the effects of expressions on feelings have been observed. When induced to smile and frown, some subjects consistently report feeling happy and angry, but others do not. These differences seem to reflect the kinds of information that people use in constructing their feelings. Some people are most affected by "personal cues" from their own behavior, whereas others rely primarily on the normative information from the social situation, or "situational cues." See figure 2.3.

The question of whether expressions are necessary for emotional feelings to occur is already complicated by the fact that people who are relatively unresponsive to personal cues do not, of course, "need" expressions. A further complication is the fact that expressions are only one among a variety of potential cues for emotional feelings. None of these is probably essential. Still, reducing or preventing facial expressions clearly does diminish emotional feelings.

In the next chapter I will explore a number of other kinds of personal cues that contribute to the experience of emotion.

NOTES

1. Rutledge and Hupka (1985) employed the same sort of observer-subject control, with similar lack of effects in the observers, as well as similar effects of the expressions on the manipulated subjects.

2. In some of these studies, only certain groups of participants were expected to show the effects, and in every case did so. Groups predicted to show no effects of expressions on feelings also behaved as predicted.

3. Gross and his colleagues in particular often fail to observe reductions in reported feelings and instead find effects on measures of autonomic arousal and memory (Richards & Gross, 2000). Why his results are different from many others is unclear, but two candidate explanations occur to me. One is that his measures of feelings are often relatively brief and unspecific, so perhaps they do not capture feelings very precisely. The second is that perhaps his effects were obscured by the fact that he does not separate his participants into those who are more or less likely to be affected by their own expressive behavior. I will discuss that issue further in chapter 5.

4. Rutledge and Hupka (1985) used the same questions, with a slightly different response format, and failed to find any relationship between facial feedback effects and scores on the questionnaire. However, they did find that subjects identified as more responsive to situational cues responded more strongly to situational cues in their paradigm.

5. Mood-congruent memory probably occurs among people who are more responsive to situational cues, when mood is manipulated by other means.

3

Postures, Gaze, and Action

Don't sigh and gaze at me
People will say we're in love!
Rodgers and Hammerstein,
                    "Oklahoma"

Of course, the song from "Oklahoma" is really about the lovers discovering they are in love, as two of my colleagues, Jim Lewis and Joan Kellerman, and I found out. Jim Lewis and I were sitting one day in the university coffee shop. Jim was a bit older than most graduate students, and both of us were feeling very paternalistic as we looked around at the scattering of undergraduate students. One of us remarked that a nearby couple really seemed to be in love. Then our shared interest in self-perception theory kicked in, and we looked at each other with dawning enthusiasm. Self-perception theory says that we know our own feelings in the same way and from the same kinds of cues as outside observers might know about our feelings. Here were Jim and I, outside observers, "knowing" somehow that this couple was in love. If self-perception theory was correct, then the way that we knew they were in love might be the way the couple themselves knew that they were in love! That is, the cues we were using to identify their loving might well be the source of their own feelings of love.

We began to examine their behavior carefully. Fortunately, we did not embarrass them or ourselves, because they never noticed. They were oblivious to everything in the room except each other. In fact, as we watched, we realized that the only distinctive thing they were doing was gazing into each other's eyes. We were too far away to hear what they were saying, and they were not holding hands or doing anything else we could see, except holding one of those long, unbroken mutual gazes that is characteristic of lovers, and no one else.

GAZE AND LOVE

The next step was to see what would happen if we induced the gazing in the laboratory (Kellerman et al., 1989). Pairs of opposite-sex strangers were recruited and asked to gaze into each other's eyes for 2 minutes. At the end of the 2 minutes, they were put in separate rooms and asked to describe how they felt about their partner. As a comparison condition, we asked different groups of participants to gaze at each other's hands. This meant that they were equally focused on each other, but on a different part of the body. It occurred to us that perhaps being gazed at might be enough, as if the partner's undivided attention was sufficient to make us feel special and thus attracted to a person with such good judgment. Alternatively, the self-perception process might not require that the other gaze back. Perhaps it would be enough if one partner gazed, no matter what the other partner did. To explore these possibilities, in two additional kinds of pairs, the two partners did not do the same thing. One would gaze at his or her partner's eyes, while the partner gazed at her or his hands. A fifth condition examined what would happen if the gazing was given a different meaning. In this condition, a participant was told that the experiment was really concerned with eye blinking. The participant was recruited as a confederate of the experimenter and told to count the partner's eyeblinks during the 2-minute span. These "eyeblink" participants were always paired with another participant in either the eyeblink or the eye gaze condition, so that the eyeblink participants were always sharing a mutual gaze with their partner, but thought of it quite differently. With this eyeblink condition, we were essentially inducing a behavior like that of lovers but then "disqualifying" that meaning. Instead, we gave it a meaning external to the situation and without implications for the partner's feelings.

The participants' ratings of their partners consisted of two groups of adjectives. One group described the partner's attributes, such as "admirable" and "responsible." High scores on this measure indicated liking or respect for the partner. The second group of adjectives described the participant's own feelings about the partner, as "attracted to him or her" and "excited." These clusters were combined to create measures of liking and of romantic attraction.

The gaze conditions had a significant effect on both of these measures. When participants shared mutual gaze, their scores on the two measures were significantly higher than when either or both looked at the hands. Notably, neither being gazed at nor gazing by oneself was sufficient to induce increased attraction. The two participants were more attracted to each other only when they shared the gaze.

The eyeblink condition, in which the participants performed the objectively identical gaze but understood it in a different way, produced less attraction than the "gaze" condition, although the difference was significant only on the measure of romantic attraction. Thus, it seems clear that the participants needed to share mutual gaze, but it was also essential that the gazing not be "explained away" by some other purpose. (This "explaining away" is a standard kind of misattribution effect, which will be discussed at length in the next chapter.)

After all the discussion of individual differences in the preceding chapter, the reader might well be wondering if there were differences in the effects of gaze on feelings. Joan Kellerman pursued this question in a second study (Kellerman et al., 1989). This experiment was an improvement in a number of ways over the first. In this experiment, the measures of participants' feelings were questions taken from a standard measure of Liking and Loving that is used in a large amount of research (Rubin, 1973) on romantic relationships. The items are similar to those developed by Hatfield and Sprecher (1986) in the Passionate Love Scale. In addition, each participant responded to these measures both before and after the gaze conditions, so that actual change could be measured. The study included an expression manipulation procedure to assess response to personal cues. Finally, and perhaps most important, the experimental conditions included orthogonal manipulation of both gaze and situational cues intended to be romantic.

The study also employed a deceptive cover story to disguise its real purpose. The participants were told that the experiment was on extrasensory perception (ESP) and all the actual experimental procedures were described as "tuning exercises" that might enhance ESP performance. The need for the participants to be strangers was easily fit into the cover story, and the gazing conditions were supposed to increase ESP. The dependent measures were described as necessary because "how you feel about your partner might easily affect success at sending or receiving thoughts." The expression manipulation procedures were also supposed to "tune" ESP. Judging by the participants' reactions when the deception was revealed, this cover story was the all-time favorite of our participants—they were extremely disappointed during the debriefing when they were told the true nature of the experiment.

After the gaze trial, the participants were separated to respond to the second set of loving scales. To maintain the illusion during the experiment, they also performed a brief ESP sending and receiving task. (There was no evidence of successful transmission of thoughts.)

Only the mutual eye gaze and mutual hand gaze conditions were run in this experiment. Half of the participants in each of these conditions were run in a normal, spare, brightly lit experimental room. The other half were run in an identical room next door, which was dimly lit, had more comfortable, casual furniture, and had romantic music playing during the gaze conditions.

The gaze conditions had the same effects as in the first experiment: Participants reported significantly more liking and especially loving when sharing mutual gaze. However, this effect occurred only among the participants who were identified in the expression manipulation procedure as more responsive to personal cues. That is, only people who felt angrier when frowning and happier when smiling also felt more romantically attracted when gazing. The other participants, assumed to be more responsive to situational cues, were unaffected by the gaze conditions.

The room differences were situational cues, and as we expected, the situational cue group was affected by these differences. The situational cue participants who did their gazing in the (slightly) more romantic room reported significantly more liking and loving for their partners. Surprisingly, the personal cue participants showed the same effect. They, too, felt more romantically attracted to their partners if the experiments were run in the more romantic room.

In the personal cue group, the two kinds of cue, gazing and room style, did not interact. Instead, each contributed independently to the intensity of the participants' final experience. The effects of situational cues suggested that our earlier view—that the two kinds of cues were alternatives—might be mistaken. Our experimental procedures have usually put the two kinds of cues in opposition, so that participants had to respond to one or the other. By forcing our participants to choose, we seem to have distorted the true nature of the differences between people. Here in the gaze study, in which the personal cue participants could respond to both, they did so. Thus, it seems as though the differences among people are in how much they respond to personal cues, and presumably everyone uses situational cues except when they conflict with personal cues. I will return to this issue at various points in the next few chapters.

Although men and women often seem to differ in their responses to romantic behaviors and situations, we observed no differences between the two sexes in either of these gazing studies.

In sum, these two studies added love to the other emotional feelings that had been shown to be affected by manipulations of expressive behavior. They also expanded the definition of the behavior. For example, in the first study it was apparent that it was not enough for the participant to gaze alone; the participants had to share the gaze with a member of the opposite sex. Thus, the experiences were dependent on the participants' own behavior *in relation to the behavior of the other*. As described in that paper (Kellerman et al., 1989), the gazing behavior essential for feelings of love was like a dance, in which the partners moved together.

Subsequently, Williams and Kleinke (1993) replicated the gaze effects of the previous two studies and extended these effects by adding touching as another variable. Of course, touching is one of the things that people in love very often do. Although it is not quite as distinctive as mutual gaze, touching does seem to be a good candidate to contribute to the experience of love.

Half of the participants in the study gazed into each other's eyes, and the other half gazed at each other's hands. Half of the participants in each gaze condition were also asked to hold hands. In this study, individual differences among the participants were also examined, but on a quite different dimension: whether the participants were high or low on the Romantic Beliefs Scale (Sprecher & Metts, 1989).

Once again, gaze affected feelings for one's partner, but only among participants who were high in romantic beliefs. High romantic participants who shared mutual gaze reported greater romantic attraction to each other and more positive moods; they were also more willing to return for another experimental session with their partners.

Touch had similar effects. Among high romantic participants, those who touched reported more positive moods, fewer negative moods, and a greater willingness to return with their partner. The effects of touch on romantic attraction did not reach significance. Although it would have been nice to see the last measure produce the expected results, the overall pattern is nonetheless very consistent. That is, touching seems to be another expressive behavior that contributes to the self-perception of a feeling, in this case, attraction to another person.

Williams and Kleinke (1993) also obtained measures of the participants' heart rate and blood pressure. Compared with the baseline at the beginning of the experiment, gazing increased both systolic and diastolic blood pressure. Touch did not affect blood pressure measures, but it did affect heart rate. The finding that engaging in an expressive behavior produced changes in physiological response is consistent with the work by Lanzetta and Kleck and their colleagues (e.g., Lanzetta et al., 1976) and by Levenson et al. (1990), which was discussed in the preceding chapter. These studies show that when people are induced to adopt facial expressions of emotion, their physiology changes as well.

As noted earlier, this kind of result reassures us that participants' responses on the self-report measures are not due to compliance, since even the most compliant participant could not readily affect his or her heart activity. At the same time, however, this kind of result raises questions about the mechanisms by which feelings are produced, both in these experiments and in real life. We have to consider the possibility that the route from expressive behavior to feelings is indirect. That is, the expressive behavior might affect autonomic responses, which in turn produce the feelings.

However, the pattern of heart activity reported by Williams and Kleinke does not fit any easy mediational hypothesis. For example, because blood pressure responses were affected only by gaze, the parallel effects of touch on feelings cannot be explained by blood pressure mediation. And because the heart rate measure was affected only by touch, heart rate could not mediate the effect of gaze on feeling. Williams and Kleinke discuss a number of explanations for these results that are specific to the dynamics of gaze and touch, independent of the romantic context. These explanations seem to be the best fit to the pattern of their results, but they certainly seem to rule out the possibility that the autonomic responses mediated the effects of gaze and touch on feelings.

In sum, three different studies have demonstrated that inducing people to adopt long, unbroken mutual gaze with a member of the opposite sex is sufficient to produce increased feelings of romantic attraction. Also contributing to the feelings of attraction are touching and being in a more romantic environment. This research adds two new expressive behaviors, gazing and touching, to those shown to influence feelings. It also adds a new feeling, romantic attraction, to the list of feelings that have been shown to fit the self-perception paradigm.

The opposite gaze behavior, avoiding another person's eyes, has a very different meaning: It is an expression of guilt or shame. If people were induced to avoid someone else's gaze, then self-perception processes should lead to increased guilt. To test this hypothesis, we (Schnall et al., 2000) recruited participants for a study of interviewing style. A pair of participants appeared for each experimental session, but one participant was in fact a confederate of the experimenters. After the confederate had been assigned, apparently by chance, to be the interviewer and the real participant the interviewee, we surreptitiously asked the interviewee to serve as our confederate. We explained that we wanted to test the impact of different gaze styles on the behavior of the interviewer. Randomly, our "confederate" was asked either to make as much eye contact as was comfortable or to avoid eye contact as completely as possible while being interviewed. Afterward the participants were asked to describe their feelings during the interview, in order "to control for the impact of these feelings on the interview."

As we expected, the interviewees who were avoiding the gaze of the interviewer reported significantly greater feelings of guilt than did those who were gazing back. A variety of other feelings, such as anger, fear, sadness, and happiness, were also assessed; the only differences were in guilt. Furthermore, as we would expect by now, these effects occurred only among those participants identified as more responsive to personal cues in the expression manipulation procedure.

Thus, we have seen that two different kinds of gaze pattern produce feelings of two very different emotions. Prolonged mutual gaze produces feelings of romantic attraction, whereas avoidance of gaze leads to feelings of guilt.

POSTURE AND EMOTIONAL FEELINGS

Probably the most distinctive expressive feature of happiness is the smile. In contrast, the facial expression of sadness is much less distinctive. Instead, the most striking expressive behavior of sadness is the slumped, curled-up posture. Self-perception theory would certainly expect that postures would play the same role in producing emotional feelings as any other kind of expressive behavior.

In a number of studies, Riskind (Riskind, 1983, 1984; Riskind & Gotay, 1982) asked participants to adopt erect, confident-appearing postures or slumped, and perhaps dejected-seeming, postures. In the slumped postures, participants were more susceptible to learned helplessness and feelings of stress and perceived more stress in others as well (Riskind & Gotay, 1982). The slumped, contracted posture also affected accessibility of memories, making pleasant memories less accessible and unpleasant memories more available (Riskind, 1983). In a third posture study reported in this paper, participants in slumped postures who were then exposed to experiences of success and failure produced a more complex pattern of results. Riskind interpreted these results as indicating that success and failure information was not processed in the same way if the participants were in the slumped postures. However, over the five studies reported in the three papers, the general result was clear: The slumped posture made people feel sad or depressed. This interpretation does not quite account for some small anomalies in the results, but it seemed worth further exploration.

Sandi Duclos (Duclos et al., 1989) asked participants in her study to adopt one of three postures. In the "sad" posture, participants were asked to slump down in a chair, with their head dropped against their chest and hands limp in their laps. The "angry" posture consisted of sitting erect in the chair, leaning slightly forward, with hands clenched tightly into fists and raised as if to strike. The "fear" posture consisted of leaning back in the chair, with the hands raised in front of the face, palms forward, and the face slightly averted. These postural manipulations were disguised as part of a study on body muscle tensions and cognitive processing, and the few participants who recognized an emotional purpose for the study were, of course, removed from the subsequent analyses.

After the participants had held the posture for 30 seconds, they filled out a mood rating scale describing their feelings, as well as a measure designed to maintain the cover story deception. Following the posture manipulations, the participants were also run through the expression manipulation procedure to determine their responses to personal cues.

As predicted, each posture increased its corresponding emotional feeling, and only its own feeling or closely related feelings. The sad posture increased sadness but not anger or fear; the anger posture increased anger (and disgust) but not sadness or fear; and the fear posture increased feelings of fear (and surprise) but not anger and sadness. These effects occurred only among those participants who were identified by the expression manipulation procedure as more responsive to personal cues.

The pattern of results fits precisely those obtained with facial expression manipulations, including the additional unpredicted results of anger manipulations on feelings of disgust, and the effects of fear manipulations on feelings of surprise. Both of these, as I discussed in the previous chapter, were unexpected and yet entirely consistent with a great deal of data on the relative similarities and differences among emotional expressions and feelings.

These results do not necessarily resolve the question of how best to understand Riskind's results. It is entirely possible that postures have more than one kind of effect, but what these results do make clear is that postural information can play the expected role in self-perception processes leading to emotional feelings.

Recently Bill Flack and others have replicated these results with postures (and with expressions) both with normal participants (Flack et al., 1999a) and with outpatients diagnosed as suffering from schizophrenia and depression (Flack et al., 1999b). In this second study, participants adopted four postures, the three from the Duclos study and an erect, supposedly happy posture. This happy posture had no discernible effect when compared with a neutral control, but all the other postures had the expected distinctive effects. The failure of the "happy" posture seems most likely due to the fact that there really is no distinctively happy posture. In this condition, participants were asked to stand erect, with their heads high, but that does not seem to be an especially happy posture rather than, for example, confident or simply attentive.

The posture manipulations in these studies were always disguised, and as usual, participants who saw through the deception were dropped from the analyses. However, as with the studies manipulating facial expressions, some slight risk remained that some participants were complying deliberately. Stepper and Strack (1993) devised an especially clever way to manipulate postures that no participants could see through. The study was described as examining the effects of different "ergonomic working positions" on performance. The participants were assigned to work either at a normal-height desk or at a desk that was lower the level of their chair. The latter required that the participants bend forward into a slumped position, which was intended to mimic in some degree the posture of sadness. After working in these positions for a short time, participants were asked to report their feelings of pride. Participants who had worked in an upright position reported significantly higher feelings of pride.

In two studies, we (Laird, Kuvalanka, Grubstein, Kim, & Nagaraja, in press) studied the closely related effects of postures on feelings of confidence. In the first study participants were asked to read a persuasive speech into a video camera while they were in erect, natural, or slumped standing postures. After completing their speech, they answered a number of questions about their performance, which included a measure of how confident they had felt while making the speech. In the slumped posture, they reported significantly less confidence. The second study was very similar except that the participants were seated and asked to solve difficult anagram problems. Their postures were manipulated by the Stepper and Strack (1993) technique of changing the height of their work surface. When they finished working on the problems, they were asked how confident they were of their answers. Again, the slumped posture produced significantly less confidence. Notably, however, in each of these studies the effects of posture occurred only among those participants who were identified as more responsive to personal cues.

Berkowitz (1990, 1994) describes two studies in which a part of an angry posture produced the expected effects on feelings. The behavior manipulated in these studies required participants to clench their dominant fist (vs. a relaxed hand) while recalling emotional events from their lives. The clenched fist produced significantly higher ratings of anger, but only when the memory was of an angry episode. The clenched fist reduced the intensity of sad feelings during the recall of sad experiences.

In sum, 11 different studies have manipulated postures and observed changes in feelings of depression, anger, fear, sadness, confidence, and pride. These are all, of course, "sufficiency" studies, and although the evidence is less substantial than for expressions, it seems clear that adopting emotional postures is sufficient to create emotional feelings. All these studies also contain procedures to minimize the potential impact of experimenter bias.

The primary missing components of the posture research are conditions that would permit inferences about the necessity of these cues. Loving without gazing seems likely to be a feeble experience, and sadness without a slumped posture seems likely to be less painful, but we have no evidence for these intuitions. We also have no evidence that these effects take place outside the laboratory, although many of the manipulations seem to have modeled real life reasonably well.

RESPIRATION AND FEELINGS

One of the standard channels of recording during "lie detection" is breathing. Changes in respiration are thought to reflect increases in emotionality of one sort or another. Surprisingly, however, very little research has looked at this aspect of emotional behavior. One exception to this oversight is the work of Susana Bloch and her colleagues (Bloch, Lemeignan, & Aguilera, 1991). In this research, participants were induced to breathe in patterns previously identified as characteristic of different emotions. As the participants continue to breathe in these patterns, they report feeling the corresponding emotion. In a somewhat more elaborate methodology, Pierre Philippot and his colleagues (Philippot, Chapelle, & Blairy, 2002) have also demonstrated that adopting the breathing patterns characteristic of an emotion induces that emotional feeling.

VOCAL BEHAVIOR

The tone of our voice is notorious for revealing our feelings, even at times when we would rather not be so open. Volumes of research demonstrate that in fact a variety of paralinguistic features of speech, such as pace, amplitude, and pitch, do convey information to observers about the speaker's emotional state (see Banse & Scherer, 1996; Johnstone, Van Reekum, & Scherer, 2001; Kaiser & Scherer, 1998; Scherer, 1986). Following the by-now-obvious logic of self-perception theory, we would expect that if people were induced to adopt the paralinguistic speech properties of an emotional state, they would report corresponding feelings.

At least five studies have demonstrated such effects. In two studies, Elaine Hatfield and her collaborators (Hatfield, Hsee, Costello, & Weisman, 1995) induced people to read passages while using the pace, pausing, rhythms, and other speech characteristics of five emotions. In each case, the result was emotional feelings that matched the speech patterns. Similarly, in a third study, emotion-like variations in the pitch and speed of speech produce corresponding changes in emotional feelings (Siegman & Boyle, 1993). For example, participants asked to speak in a loud, harsh tone reported feeling more angry, whereas when speaking in a soft, low tone, they reported feeling more sad. Bill Flack has replicated this basic procedure with both normal and psychiatric patient populations (Flack et al., 2000; Flack et al., 1999a).

The research on vocal expressions of emotion is certainly preliminary and sparse, but it does support the general point of self-perception theory. With admittedly modest confidence at this point, we can add vocal expressiveness to facial expressions, postures, and gaze as expressive behaviors that function as determinants of emotional experience.

EMOTIONAL ACTIONS

Many emotion theorists, starting with Darwin, have emphasized the survival value of emotional patterns of behavior (e.g., Plutchik, 1980). Much recent research has been concerned with identifying the distinctive character of emotion-related actions (e.g., Frijda, 1986; Frijda, Kuipers, & ter Shure, 1989). Thus, the relative dearth of self-perception studies on emotional actions is at first glance surprising. However, a few studies do exist.

Flight and Fright

One study (Bandler, Madaras, & Bem, 1968) is a perfect experimental analogue of James's famous example of the bear. James suggested that we see a bear, flee, and then are frightened. In this experiment, participants were induced to flee, and then a measure reflecting fear was obtained.

The study participants were told that the study concerned pain perception, and they were asked to press their hand onto a plate that delivered painful electric shocks. They received these shocks under two conditions. In one, they were told to remove their hand as soon as they felt the shock; in the other, they were asked to hold their hand on the plate for the duration of the shock. Thus, in one condition the participants were "escaping" the shock, whereas in the other they did not. After each shock they were to judge its intensity. Actually, all the shocks were exactly the same intensity; consequently, the participants received much more shock in the no-escape condition, in which they endured the whole shock. However, the participants' judgments were exactly the reverse. They felt the shocks they had escaped were more intense than the ones they had endured.

Why this paradoxical result? Pain perceptions of this sort consist of two conceptually distinguishable parts, the sensory information and the fear of the painful stimulus. Apparently, the participants had interpreted their escape behavior as indicating that the shock was more severe and scary, just as James would have predicted.

A conceptually similar study (Zimbardo, Cohen, Weisenberg, Dworkin, & Firestone, 1969) gave participants some painful electric shocks and then asked the participants to continue receiving the shocks. The act of agreeing to receive more shocks led the participants to rate the shocks as less painful.

Sins of omission are often seen as less serious than sins of commission, apparently because choosing to do something is a more positive response than simply failing to do something. In a test of this bias in judgment, Fazio, Sherman, and Herr (1982) asked participants to divide neutral cartoons into funny and unfunny categories. Half indicated the funny cartoons by performing a vigorous action, like blowing a whistle, and the other half of the participants indicated the unfunny cartoons by the same action. Then the participants rated the cartoons again. Their vigorous actions affected their subsequent judgments, so that those who indicated which cartoons were funny by the vigorous action reported the cartoons were funnier, while the vigorous-unfunny group reported the cartoons were less funny. In contrast, passive, nonactions did not change opinions about the cartoons.

This same effect—that vigorous action has stronger implications for attributed attitudes than does nonaction—has also been observed in studies of inferences about the attributes of others (e.g., Fazio, 1987). The fact that the processes are so parallel, and that they involve an effect that is not immediately obvious, emphasizes the parallels between self-perception and other perception.

Beliefs About One's Actions

Most of the studies I have reported thus far have examined the impact of ongoing actions as they are being performed. However, self-perception surely includes memories for past actions as well. In fact, an intriguing set of manipulations was developed by Salancik (1974) from a self-perception perspective. He asked people to rank order lists of reasons for action, and the lists differed in their attitude relevance. The simple act of ranking the items in the lists then changed people's attitudes to fit the kinds of items they had been considering during the ranking process. A particularly relevant application of this technique to emotions explored the reasons for love. Seligman, Fazio, and Zanna (1980) reasoned that love was more intrinsic, whereas liking was less intrinsic and perhaps more extrinsic. They asked dating couples to rank lists of either intrinsic or extrinsic reasons for their dating. For example, a reason from the intrinsic list was "I go out with . . . because we have a good time together." A reason from the extrinsic list was "I go out with . . . because my friends think more highly of me since I began seeing her/him." After the ranking, the participants responded to Rubin's (1973) Liking and Loving Scales. Ranking a list of extrinsic reasons for dating one's partner reduced loving scores and anticipated likelihood of marrying, relative to both controls and people who rated intrinsic reasons. Apparently, thinking about these relatively unromantic reasons for dating was enough to undermine (temporarily, the authors assure us) feelings of love.

Symbolic Action

In an intriguing program of research, Manfred Clynes (1977) asked people to press with their fingers to express a variety of emotions. The patterns of pressure that they generated were then averaged over a number of trials to remove random variations. Clynes discovered that these averaged patterns of pressure for each emotion were similar across different people and distinctive to the particular emotions. Apparently there is a kind of common symbolic "language" of pressure that all his participants understood.

In the next step, Clynes asked participants to repeatedly press out the pattern of an emotion. As they did so, they eventually found themselves feeling the emotion they were expressing. Note that this is, in itself, a kind of self-perception task in which an action—pressing patterns of an emotion—creates the corresponding feeling. Obviously, these patterns are not themselves natural features of an emotional episode. They may perhaps be metaphoric expressions, or they may, as Clynes argues, be minimal forms of patterns that actually do underlie natural emotional episodes. In either case, performing these metaphoric or minimal forms seems to be sufficient to induce the experience.

Self-Disclosure and Deceit

In the movie *Sex, Lies, and Videotape*, a man and woman who are virtual strangers agree to exchange very personal confidences, and the audience knows immediately that they are about to have an affair. From a self-perception perspective, revealing confidences is an action that is typical of lovers, so self-disclosure is likely to lead to attraction. A great deal of research has demonstrated that people who disclose themselves are liked by the audience, but only a few studies have looked at the effect on the discloser. However, as both the movie and self-perception theory would predict, when people are induced experimentally to disclose themselves to another, they report greater attraction to that person (McAllister, 1980; Schlenker & Trudeau, 1990).

The movie plot contains the opposite effect as well. The heroine's husband has been having an affair with her sister, and the constant deceptions both must practice seem to be eroding both the husband's and the sister's love for the heroine. The implication of the movie is that lying is incompatible with loving.

One of Clynes's studies (Clynes, Jurisevic, & Rynn, 1990) demonstrates the incompatibility of loving and lying in the context of his finger pressure technique. The participants were asked to press out patterns of love that would ordinarily have made them report feeling love. On some trials, they simultaneously committed a trivial lie, and on others they told the truth. On the lie trials, the participants reported significantly lower levels of loving than on the trials in which they told the truth. As a comparison, anger feelings were unaffected by lying.

The self-disclosure studies showed the effects of actions on how participants felt about the people to whom they disclosed. The act of hiding something about oneself might also make you feel differently about what you have hidden, since hiding and revealing imply something about the object of these actions. To test this idea, Michael Fishbein (Fishbein & Laird, 1979) first administered to participants a confusing battery of tests of preferences as an excuse for giving each of his participants the same number, which was their "score." The participants were not told anything about the meaning of their score or what the tests were supposed to measure, so all they knew was a number. Then the participants were asked to wait in another room with a confederate who was described as another participant who would be taking the test shortly. As if as an afterthought, half the participants were asked not to reveal their score to the confederate. The other half were told to try to find an occasion to mention it, which all did. Thus, one group was hiding and the other revealing their score. As the final step in the experiment, the participants were separated from the confederate and in the midst of some distracter questions were asked to evaluate their own performance on the test. Participants who had concealed their scores rated their performance significantly less positively than participants who had revealed their score. Here, then, the act of concealing or revealing something about themselves had led them to an evaluation of themselves.

Catharsis and Anger Expression

Much the largest body of research on emotional action has focused on anger and its expression in action, including speech. The purpose of this research was not to support self-perception theory, however. Instead, the research revolved around the idea of catharsis. From the perspective of common sense and many psychological theories, the idea of catharsis makes reasonable sense. Commonsense theories assume that emotional feelings are the forces that drive emotional behavior, so clearly, bottling up these forces might have unexpected and undesirable results. The feelings forcing one toward aggression may build up until, like steam under pressure, they burst forth in a bout of aggressive behavior that is extreme, ill-timed, or inappropriate. Far better to "cathartically" release these feelings of anger and aggression, perhaps vicariously through reading about or watching performances of aggressive acts, or indirectly through violent sports.

The idea of catharsis has been used to explain and justify aspects of our culture such as violent movies and TV, so naturally catharsis has been the subject of considerable research. In studies attempting to show the effects of catharsis, participants are characteristically encouraged to express angry feelings, usually verbally. If catharsis is at work, they should subsequently report feeling less anger and act less angrily. Unfortunately for the catharsis hypothesis, the result is almost invariably the reverse. Participants induced to say and do angry things then report feeling more, not less, anger (e.g., Ebbesen, Duncan, & Konecni, 1975; Kahn, 1966; Kaplan,

1975; Mallick & McCandless, 1966). For example, Bushman, Baumeister, and Stock (1999) angered their participants and then gave them a punching bag to work off their anger. The punching *increased* the amount of subsequent aggression, even in a group that had been given very positive information about the good effects of catharsis.

After an exhaustive review of the anger and catharsis literature, Tavris (1984) concluded, just as self-perception theory would have predicted, that acting angrily increased anger feelings and future angry actions. Berkowitz (1993) points out that the best evidence is that aggressive stimuli incite aggressive behavior, and that angry acts and statements are aggressive stimuli. Thus it is not surprising that acting angrily increases, rather than decreases, anger.

Saying How You Feel

Another body of research demonstrates the impact of verbal expressions of feeling on the subsequent feelings. This research uses a technique developed by Velten (1968) for inducing mood states. In this technique, the participant reads aloud a long series of sentences that express a particular emotional state, most commonly sadness. After saying sentences such as "I feel so hopeless" and "It is so gloomy today" for a while, the participants report feeling very sad. This is hardly surprising, and a number of people have suggested that the effects might be mediated by the participants' expectancies. However, in a meta-analytic review, Larsen and Sinnett (1991) show that the effect is substantial even when the procedure is sufficiently disguised so that expectancies are unlikely to have produced the effects. They also report significant effect sizes for dependent variables that are less amenable to conscious, expectation-driven control, such as memory retrieval. In sum, it appears that saying emotional things makes you feel emotional, as self-perception theory would expect.

Two studies by Daryl Bem (1965, 1966) take a different approach to emotions. Participants were first "trained" to associate a colored light with telling the truth. Then, in a separate procedure, they were induced to make statements while the truth light was on. If they said a cartoon was funny with the truth light on, they thought that it really was funnier (Bem, 1965), and they believed their descriptions of their own past behavior (Bem, 1966). In both of these cases, participants felt whatever their verbal behavior implied, as long as they also made their statements in a context in which they had learned to tell the truth.

Another of Bem's (1965) studies involves a subtle effect of behavior. He showed participants cartoons that they had previously rated as neither funny nor unfunny and asked them to now assign them to one of two categories, labeled "very funny" or "very unfunny." The effect of assigning the cartoons to one or the other of these extreme categories was to change the way they were rated in a later series of judgments. The participants seemed to have accepted their own judgments as reflecting the actual funniness of the cartoons (see also Fazio et al., 1982).

A great deal of other research also demonstrates the effects of action on feelings. However, this research has focused on the liking/disliking dimension of feelings and so will be discussed in the chapter on attitudes.

In sum, a scattering of studies have examined emotional actions and found the expected effects on emotional feelings. This shortage of research on emotional action only defers to subsequent chapters the building of a strong case for the role of action in self-perception. The absence of research on actions and emotions is balanced by the dominance of action manipulations in all the research on feelings other than emotions.

SUMMARY

In this chapter we have added to the stockpile of research that fits the Jamesian, self-perception view of emotions. To the abundant research on facial expressions, discussed in the previous chapter, we have added postures, gaze, appearance, breathing patterns, tone of voice, and emotional actions. All these have been shown to be sufficient to influence emotional feelings as self-perception theory would predict. We not only feel angry if we frown but also feel sad if we sit in a slumped posture or talk in a slow, low voice; loving if we exchange mutual gaze with another, touch, or exchange confidences; and afraid if we escape a potential threat. Many of these studies involved manipulations that are unlikely to have provided opportunities for experimenter bias. None have been directed at the "necessity" question, and indeed in most cases many other sorts of cues are normally available, so we would not expect postures, gaze, and so on to be necessary. Finally, none of this research looked at real-world situations, although it seems very plausible that in real life gazing leads to loving, depressed postures lead to sadness, and expressions of anger lead to more, not less, anger.

4

Autonomic Arousal and
Emotional Feeling

During an intense emotional episode, often the most striking bodily events are the changes in visceral responses. Especially during anger or fear, the autonomic nervous system produces a dramatic group of changes in bodily activity. The heart beats more rapidly and intensely, and respiration increases, whereas the activity of the digestive system is reduced. Glucose is released into the bloodstream from the liver, and blood flow is directed away from the viscera and skin to the muscles and the brain. Cannon (1936) called these responses the *fight-or-flight* response and pointed out that they had the effect of preparing the organism for intense physical activity, to flee or to do battle.[1]

In keeping with the rest of his theory, James of course argued that these bodily changes were the source, not the results, of emotional experiences. In fact, although James's original theoretical statements and examples included expressive behavior and actions at least as often as visceral responses, with time the emphasis shifted increasingly to the viscera, so that many people understood him to be claiming that these visceral, autonomic changes were the entire source of emotional experiences.

Despite James's shift in theoretical emphasis, the evidence is perhaps weakest, and certainly the most confusing, for this part of his theory of emotion. Some bodies of evidence support James and self-perception theory very strongly. However, other bodies of evidence are considerably less consistent. A number of reviewers have looked at this evidence and have been skeptical (e.g., Cotton, 1981; Manstead & Wagner, 1981; Reisenzein, 1983). However, I think the evidence is not as inconclusive as these reviewers have believed, and in this chapter I will describe the sense it seems to make.

CANNON'S CRITIQUE

James's shift in emphasis toward autonomic activity and visceral changes probably resulted from the combining of his theory and that of Carl Lange. Lange (1922) proposed that the events that instigated an emotion, such as seeing a bear, produced immediately a series of changes in peripheral blood flow and pressure, and that the perception of these blood flow changes was the experience of the emotion. Lange's theory was like James's in emphasizing the role of peripheral factors, but unlike James's in assuming that the only important peripheral changes were changes in blood flow. Lange also made the theory seem more obscure by focusing on blood flow changes rather than the full range of emotional responses, including expressions and actions.

Despite the dissimilarity between their theories, in his later writings James (1890) also emphasized visceral changes. This was certainly a strategic error, since it opened his theory to the criticisms of Walter Cannon (1927). These criticisms were far more effective than they deserved to be. Cannon's criticisms were directed primarily toward the notion that the experience of emotion was the perception of *visceral states*, by which he meant changes in autonomic arousal. His five objections to James's theory were as follows:

1. Animals that had been surgically treated so that they could not receive any feedback from their viscera still showed normal emotional behaviors, such as a cat hissing and lifting a paw to strike when confronted with a barking dog.
2. Visceral responses were not sufficiently differentiated to account for the wide variety of emotional experiences. Heart rate, blood pressure, and so forth all tended to just be stronger or weaker, and to move in unison, up or down. Cannon argued they could not provide the variety of different feelings such as fear, anger, or disgust.
3. The viscera are too insensitive to provide adequate feedback. There are relatively few sensory nerves in the viscera, and as we all know, we have little sense of what is happening with our liver, stomach, or even heart, so it seemed we really could not have very many sensations from them.
4. The viscera respond too slowly to account for the rapid onset of emotional experiences. The viscera may take half a second or more to respond to autonomic stimulation, whereas emotional feelings often seem to appear almost instantaneously.
5. His final argument was most directly contradictory to a Jamesian/ self-perception theory: that artificially produced arousal of the viscera did not produce corresponding emotional experience. An injection of epinephrine produces many of the same physiological symptoms as emotionally produced arousal, but people who received epinephrine injections do not report feeling emotions.

These criticisms (perhaps coupled with Cannon's Nobel Prize reputation) seemed sufficient to persuade everyone that the perception of visceral changes could not be the source of emotional experiences. Of course, at best the point could only have been that visceral changes could not be the *only* source, since these criticisms concern only the activity of the viscera.[2] However, since the Jamesians had drifted toward thinking only about visceral activity, the effect of these criticisms was to discredit James's theory in most people's eyes—hence, the fact that I was taught as an undergraduate that James's theory of emotion was an example of a great psychologist's lapse in judgment.

In fact, these criticisms are not nearly as powerful as they seemed, as has been noticed by various psychologists over the years (e.g., Allport, 1924; Hebb, 1958; Tomkins, 1962). The first argument is perhaps the silliest, since this experimental demonstration has absolutely nothing to do with James's theory. James was explaining the origins of emotional experience, and no experiment with animals was likely to reveal anything about experience, at least unless the animals could talk and report their feelings.

Furthermore, James would have predicted exactly the same results of this kind of experiment (see Figure 4.1). The prediction of James's theory becomes clear if one considers the sequence of events for the surgically altered cat in the experiment. The cat sees a dog, and according to James, automatically three kinds of response begin to occur. The cat begins to hiss and arch its back, which are expressive behaviors. The cat begins to prepare for the action of attacking the dog, perhaps lifting a paw and exposing its claws. And the autonomic nervous system responds to produce increased heartbeat and

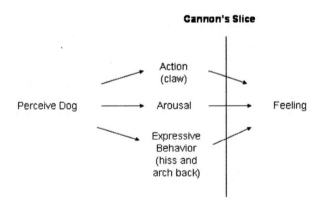

Figure 4.1. James's model of Cannon's deafferented cat, and why it behaved as James would have predicted.

changes in blood flow away from the digestive organs and toward the muscles. Notice that in James's view, the hissing and showing of teeth that Cannon observed would have been expected to occur simultaneously with the autonomic responses, both having been initiated by the recognition of the rival. The next step, according to James, was that the cat might perceive its hissing and teeth baring, its aggressive actions, and its autonomic arousal, and hence feel anger. Clearly, if the cat could not perceive the last of these three, its experience might have changed, but since it is a cat, we cannot ever know. But if cat feelings are anything like human feelings, then James (and self-perception theory) would expect that the hissing is part of the source of the feelings, not an indication of the existence of those feelings.

The points about the speed, distinctiveness, and sensitivity of visceral response were better taken. Autonomic reactions do take a relatively long time to develop completely. Furthermore, the autonomic effects on the viscera do appear to be very similar for all emotions. Note, however, that the failure to detect differences among emotions could have been a result of the low resolving power of the physiological instruments of the time. Cannon had no way of knowing whether quite distinctive changes might not be discovered with better technology, as they have been (e.g., Levenson, 1992; Levenson et al., 1992; G. E. Schwartz, Weinberger, & Singer, 1981). More important, as Cannon himself recognized and as previous chapters have demonstrated, the qualitative differences among emotions might have been determined by the very distinctive expressive behavior. The expressive behaviors also occurred rapidly enough to initiate emotional feelings that might then reach their full flower when the autonomic responses had built up as well.

Only the last of Cannon's points was really persuasive. He was referring to research directly intended to test James's theory. Maranon (1924) injected a number of people with epinephrine, which produces many of the visceral symptoms of emotion. His results were a good example of the complexity of the typical results of research on arousal. Two thirds of his subjects either reported no emotional effects or described feelings "like an emotion" but clearly different. About a third of his participants reported something like genuine emotional feelings. A similar variety of responses was observed by Landis and Hunt (1932). This array of results can look good or bad for James's theory, depending on the theoretical screen through which you are looking. If one is a believer, then the fact that anyone at all reports feeling an emotion after being injected with a chemical, while sitting in a laboratory, is impressive. If one is a skeptic, one instead sees the glass as half empty and wonders what happened to all the other subjects.

The first major response to Cannon's critique came 35 years later, when Stanley Schachter and his associates (Schachter & Singer, 1962; Schachter & Wheeler, 1962) proposed a compound "cognitive-physiological" theory that met all of Cannon's criticisms and preserved part of James's theory.

Their theory also explains the inconsistencies in Maranon's results in a way that Maranon would have appreciated (Cornelius, 1991).

Like James, Schachter argued that autonomic arousal did mediate part of the experience of emotion, but unlike James, Schachter thought that arousal mediated only the intensity of emotional experience—the difference between annoyance and anger, or contentment and joy. He proposed that the quality of emotional experience was mediated by the person's cognitions (beliefs) about which kind of emotion was appropriate to the circumstances. So, in a typical emotional episode, the sight of a bear approaching would automatically produce autonomic changes such as increased heartbeat, blanching, shutting down of digestive processes, and so on. These autonomic changes would be experienced as an intense emotion, and the particular kind of emotion—fear versus anger, for example—would be determined by the person's understanding of the situation. A kind of parody of the processes involved would be something like: (a) "I am intensely aroused, so I must be feeling some powerful emotion," and (b) "I see a bear, I know that people being approached by bears feel fear, so my emotion must be fear." (I must add immediately that no one, especially Schachter, ever thought that anyone actually consciously experiences such a thought process. This is just an example of the kind of unconscious cognitive processing that Schachter argued occurred. If these processes ever took place consciously, which they never do, then they might be something like this.)

Notice that Schachter explicitly agreed with Cannon's point concerning the lack of differences among autonomic responses and capitalized on this point to propose that arousal mediated the intensity of *all* emotional experiences. Schachter (1964) also pointed out that the early onset of emotional feelings could be due to the presumably quick cognitions. As the autonomic responses build up, we might assume the intensity of experience builds as well. Finally, Schachter explained that Maranon's mixed results occurred because the subjects had cognitions about their arousal that interfered with their potential emotional experiences. Maranon's subjects had been coworkers and acquaintances who knew they were being injected with epinephrine and also knew what its effects would be, so their cognitions were that no emotion was appropriate. Schachter's expectation was that if people were injected with epinephrine but did not know what the drug or its effects were, they would feel stronger emotions.

People suffering an attack of "coffee nerves" experience the basic effect that Schachter was predicting. An external, nonemotional, chemical source has produced a pattern of bodily changes that are similar to those of a strong emotion. When the coffee makes individuals' hearts pound and their palms sweat, they may experience these bodily events as anxiety, just as some of Maranon's subjects may have experienced the effects of the epinephrine injections. But when the coffee drinkers realize the source of their "nerves" is too much coffee, they usually feel better. The coffee drinker might even say that he was feeling "as if I was anxious," as many of Maranon's subjects also said.

As a test of this theory, Schachter and Singer (1962) conducted an experiment in which the subjects' arousal levels and cognitions were independently manipulated. The subjects believed they were participating in an experiment on the effects of a chemical called "Suproxin" on vision. They were given an injection and then asked to wait for the drug to take effect. Actually the injections were either of a neutral saline solution or of epinephrine. Epinephrine injections act quite quickly, so the epinephrine-injected subjects were in fact aroused during the waiting period.

During the waiting period, all subjects were exposed to two different kinds of situations, produced in part by a confederate of the experimenter who was introduced as another subject also waiting for the Suproxin to take effect. In the "euphoria" condition, the confederate began to act increasingly giddy, cracking jokes, climbing the furniture, rolling up paper and shooting it into the wastepaper basket, and trying to recruit the real subject to his antics. In the "anger" condition, both the subject and the confederate were asked to fill out a questionnaire about their life experiences that contained a series of increasingly insulting questions. The confederate surreptitiously kept approximate pace with the real subject on the questionnaire and punctuated his responses with increasingly angry comments, until finally he slammed his pencil down and left the room.

During both situations the subjects were observed, and the amount and intensity of their emotional behavior were judged. At the end of the "waiting period" they provided self-reports of their feelings. The basic logical shape of the experiment was to create four combinations of conditions, in which subjects were exposed to either a happy, euphoric situation or one that would provoke anger, and either they were aroused by an adrenalin injection or they were not.

Schachter and Singer's (1962) anger and adrenalin-injected condition actually included three subgroups. One was simply ignorant of any possible effects of the injections. A second, the "epinephrine-misinformed" group, was told that the Suproxin injection might cause emotion-irrelevant side effects such as a headache or itchy hands. These two groups behaved similarly and are conflated in the discussion of the effects of epinephrine in the next few paragraphs. The third group was told what the actual effects of the adrenalin injection were; the impact of this accurate expectation will be discussed extensively later.

If Schachter's theory was correct, then in the ignorant and the misinformed groups, the epinephrine should have increased the intensity of subjects' emotional feelings in both euphoric and angry situations. The predictions in regard to emotional expressive behavior are actually a bit more ambiguous. James might have argued that since these behaviors are normally generated at the same time as arousal, expressive behaviors should not be increased either directly by the arousal or indirectly by way of the feelings. However, it is easy to imagine systems in which increasing arousal also increases expressive behavior and action. That certainly was

Schachter and Singer's assumption, since they did expect to find differences in expressive behavior as well.

This study was justly famous for its clever design and its unexpected and dramatic predictions, and because it inspired a great deal of follow-up research. Most people remember the results as confirming Schachter's predictions, that increased arousal increased the intensity of both emotional experiences. In fact, the results were not quite as neat as predicted, and the best results were observed on the measures of emotional behavior. Compared with the saline control group, the epinephrine-injected groups acted significantly more angry and reported feeling more anger. Not all individuals in the epinephrine-injected group showed increased heart rate, and Schachter and Singer made some plausible, if post hoc, adjustments of the subject groups. After these adjustments the epinephrine and placebo groups did differ significantly in the amount of euphoric behavior they produced. However, their reports of euphoric feelings remained stubbornly similar.

In a similar study (Schachter & Wheeler, 1962), the same pattern emerged. Injections of epinephrine or of an epinephrine antagonist affected how much people laughed at humorous film clips but did not affect reports of feelings of mirth.

Despite the mild disappointment regarding the feelings of happiness, Schachter's studies seemed to confirm his half-Jamesian theory of emotion, and Schachter's theory was widely cited as correct. The results of follow-up research were not actually so positive. Reviewing the next two decades of research inspired by Schachter's work, Reisenzein (1983) suggested that none of the four general types of research that evolved as further tests of Schachter's theory provided strong support. The first of these four types of research consisted of attempts to increase arousal directly by administration of chemicals, as Schachter and Singer had done. A second explored the opposite effect, of drugs such as beta-blockers that reduce adrenergic arousal. A third group explored the effects of physical conditions that might be expected to affect a person's access to arousal cues. The fourth group—the largest and most consistently supportive group of studies—consisted of studies of misattribution of arousal. Each of these groups of studies deserves closer attention.

Note that the first of these groups tests whether artificial arousal is sufficient to increase emotional feelings, the following two test whether arousal is necessary, and the last group contains both kinds of explorations. Note also that the issue of experimenter bias rarely arises in discussions of the arousal research, probably because it is assumed that autonomic responses are outside of conscious control.

CHEMICALS INCREASING AROUSAL

For practical reasons, many of the studies that followed Schachter did not use epinephrine. However, at least two studies did use epinephrine, and these produced results that raised some questions about Schachter's theory.

In these studies (Marshall & Zimbardo, 1979; Rogers & Deckner, 1975), subjects were injected with adrenalin and placed in conditions that should have aroused euphoria or at least happiness. Instead, participants reported increased negative emotions. In company with similar effects with a different, hypnotic manipulation of arousal (Maslach, 1979), these results led Marshall and Zimbardo, as well as Maslach, to propose that arousal had a "negative bias" and was experienced as unpleasant, even when the situation and its attendant cognitions implied a happy experience.

Other studies manipulated arousal by other kinds of drugs, such as ephedrine or caffeine, that have less powerful effects than epinephrine. The results have been mixed at best (Manstead & Wagner, 1981; Reisenzein, 1983, 1994). These studies vary on a multitude of dimensions, so any conclusion about the differences between the studies that do and do not support Schachter's theory must be tentative. However, it does appear that the studies that have reported increases in emotional feelings after arousal manipulations have been those in which the target feelings were anxiety, fear, anger, or romantic love, whereas other feelings, including happiness and sadness, were unaffected by arousal (Laird & Bresler, 1990).

An additional complication in these studies is that the meaning of drug effects is often unclear. All these drugs were used in Schachterian experiments because they produce peripheral changes that mimic autonomic arousal, but they may also have effects in the central nervous system. For example, there is little dispute that caffeine in substantial doses causes peripheral arousal symptoms, such as increased heart rate, sweating, and flushing, and it also produces anxiety feelings (Newman, Stein, Tretlau, Coppola, & Uhde, 1992). The question is whether the anxiety is mediated by the peripheral symptoms or whether the two are produced in parallel, with the caffeine causing the anxiety directly by its effects in the brain. (In the case of epinephrine, this explanation is less probable, because peripheral epinephrine is not thought to cross the blood-brain barrier, and epinephrine is metabolized very rapidly, so that the effects probably all occur peripherally.)

Another manipulation produces complex physiological effects and elicits changes in feelings that may be due to autonomic arousal. In this technique, called the *hypoglycemic clamp*, blood glucose is experimentally lowered by a continuous injection of insulin into the veins of normal volunteers. The resulting hypoglycemic state produces increases both in autonomic arousal and in unpleasant emotional feelings belonging to Thayer's (1996) tense arousal factor (Gold, MacLeod, Frier, & Deary, 1995; Hepburn, Deary, Munoz, & Frier, 1995; McCrimmon, Frier, & Deary, 1999). Since the effects of the hypoglycemic state are complex, the mood effects may well be produced by some other mechanism than self-perception. Nonetheless, in the absence of an articulated alternative, we may take these effects as some support for Schachter's model.

In sum, the studies in which arousal was manipulated with drugs are best described as "not inconsistent" with Schachter's theory or the predictions of James and self-perception theory. Some studies support the theories, but others do not. These studies also suggest that, at a minimum, Schachter's original view must be qualified: Increases in arousal intensify only some feelings, such as anger or fear, and not all feelings, as Schachter had proposed.

CHEMICALS REDUCING AROUSAL

A second body of work concerns the effects of drugs intended to reduce arousal. Most of the drugs used in this kind of research are administered for clinical purposes, and relatively few studies are experimental tests on normal subjects. However, one of Schachter's early studies was just such an experiment. Schachter and Wheeler (1962) administered epinephrine to one of their experimental groups, but another group received chlorpromazine, which Schachter and Wheeler describe as an epinephrine antagonist. The chlorpromazine group did exhibit a drop in amused behavior. However, this result suffers from the same problem that was noted in regard to drugs that increase arousal, namely, that chlorpromazine may very well work in the brain, rather than just changing the amount of peripheral arousal. Indeed, most antianxiety drugs are assumed to work centrally, in ways that are irrelevant to self-perception theory.

Beta-Blockers and Anxiety/Fear

One class of drugs is an exception to the uncertainty about central versus peripheral effects. The beta-adrenergic blocking agents are specifically presumed to work peripherally in the body *outside* the central nervous system. These drugs act by interfering with the action of adrenalin at the peripheral neural sites, where adrenalin produces the characteristic visceral arousal symptoms. If Schachter is correct, then these antiadrenergic drugs that act peripherally should effectively reduce anxiety, anger, and perhaps other emotions.

Once again, the evidence seems to be contradictory. In laboratory studies of the effects of beta-blockers, the effects seem to be difficult to demonstrate (Reisenzein, 1994). However, extensive reviews demonstrate successful practical uses of beta-blockers for some kinds of anxiety disorders (Noyes, 1985) and also for reducing performance anxiety (Dimsdale, Newton, & Joist, 1989). Despite the mixed results with experimental populations, little question remains that beta-blockers are effective treatments for reducing anxiety in clinical populations.

The beta-blocker results are less susceptible to the argument that they might affect the brain directly rather than by way of the peripheral symptoms. All beta-blockers are presumed to work peripherally, but they vary in their lipid solubility, with more lipid-soluble compounds being more likely to penetrate the blood-brain barrier. If beta-blockers were working directly on the brain, then more lipid-soluble types should be more effective. However, in both reviews, by Noyes (1985) and by Dimsdale et al. (1989), lipid-insoluble compounds were just as effective as soluble versions in reducing anxiety, suggesting that the effects were primarily peripheral.

Beta-Blockers and Anger/Rage

Beta-blockers have also been used to control anger and aggression (Mattes, 1985; Volavka, 1988). One of the best studies (Ratey et al., 1992) was a very well-controlled double-blind study of the effects of nadolol, a particularly lipid-insoluble and hence peripheral-acting beta-blocker. As Schachter would have predicted, the beta-blocker treatment significantly reduced aggression.

In sum, in a wide variety of studies, beta-blockers have reduced anxiety and aggression, and these effects seem to be due to the peripheral actions of the drugs. The weaker results in experimental studies may be due to the brief administration and often small doses employed (Noyes, 1985). The different results are probably not due to any differences between clinical and nonclinical populations, since many of the studies of the effects of beta-blockers on skilled performance did employ "normal" people who wished to reduce performance anxiety. Beta-blockers do seem to be effective for this purpose.

Beta-Blockers and Sadness/Depression

A different kind of emotional effect of beta-blockers has also been observed. These drugs are most frequently prescribed for the treatment of hypertension because one of their effects is to prevent the increases in blood pressure that are otherwise produced by adrenergic arousal. One of the common side effects of beta-blocker treatment is sadness and depression (Rosen & Kostis, 1985). This result is consistent with the fact that sadness is a low-arousal emotional state. Once again, one must be cautious in interpreting these effects, since they could be produced centrally. They do seem to occur equally with the peripherally acting beta-blockers, therefore suggesting that chronic drug-produced reductions in arousal level may lead to sadness and depression.

In the end, the results with respect to beta-blockers are not quite as neat as we would have liked, but they are generally supportive of Schachter's (and James's) expectations. Certainly they are much more supportive than the studies that sought to increase arousal through drugs. The results suggest that removing cues from visceral arousal does reduce the intensity of some emotional experiences. Few, if any, of these studies have examined emotions other than anxiety and rage, so this literature is consistent with the idea that arousal contributes to the experience of those emotions. The evidence also suggests that lowering arousal levels may increase a third emotion, sadness.

Finally, none of this research on chemical alterations of arousal levels has considered a factor that may explain the sometimes weak or inconsistent results: individual differences, especially in people's response to personal versus situational cues. A few studies, to be discussed later, have found that the effects of arousal occur only among people who are responsive to the personal cues from their bodies. If so, then many failures to find effects in unselected populations would be expected, where whatever impact the arousal manipulations may have had on the personal cue participants might be obscured by the lack of response of the situational group.

PHYSICAL/MEDICAL MODIFICATIONS OF VISCERAL CUES

A third set of studies has examined the effects of physical conditions that affect visceral activity or feedback.

Spinal Cord Injury

The most cataclysmic interference with autonomic feedback occurs when people suffer injury to the spinal cord and lose feeling in part of the body. Without sensations from the body, people cannot feel the effects of autonomic arousal, such as a pounding heart or butterflies in the stomach. Thus, individuals with spinal cord injuries would be expected to feel less intense emotions.

The first study of this sort was conducted by Hohmann (1966). Hohmann interviewed people who had suffered spinal cord injuries about the changes in their emotional experiences and found that they reported less intense feelings of the high-arousal emotions of fear, anger, and sexual excitement. They reported no loss of intensity of low-arousal emotions such as sentimentality.

The amount of sensation lost following a spinal cord injury is proportional to the height of the injury in the spinal cord. At the extreme, people whose injury occurs in the cervical area lose almost all sensation from their bodies, whereas people whose injuries are lower in the spine retain more sensations from their bodies. One would expect, then, that the degree of loss of emotional intensity would be correlated with the height of the injury, and that was also observed by Hohmann.

This study was replicated with more elaborate measures and controls by Chwalisz, Diener, and Gallagher (1988). Their results are considerably weaker than Hohmann's, although they did find that higher level lesions were associated with diminished anger and some loss of intensity in general. They also found that some emotions, including joy, love, sentimentality, and sadness, increased in intensity. Note that none of these are high-intensity, high-arousal emotions, and so these increases are not inconsistent with Jamesian theories, if we assume that only fear, anger, and romantic attraction are high-arousal emotions. Chwalisz et al. conclude, "What our results do suggest is that autonomic feedback could play a small role in emotional intensity" (p. 826).

A third study appeared to be even less supportive of the Schachter-James self-perception predictions, but in fact it is irrelevant. In this study (Bermond, Nieuwenhuyse, Fasotti, & Schuerman, 1991), people with spinal cord injuries were exhaustively interviewed, and no consistent postinjury decreases on their measures of experience were reported. However, none of these measures were actually direct measures of emotional feelings. In-stead, one group consisted of descriptions of bodily symptoms, such as "my blood pressure went up." Considerable research suggests that even uninjured people are unable to report accurately on such items (Pen-nebaker, 1982), so it is not surprising that these reports were inaccurate. The second group of items consisted of descriptions of situations, such as "There was a sense that I had no control over the situation" (p. 204). This latter group of items was endorsed significantly more often after the injury, but again these are not reports of feelings. Instead, they are reports of the kinds of situations that tend to produce feelings. Thus, the Bermond et al. (1991) results are not really parallel with Hohmann's and do not really bear on the Schachter theory one way or the other.

A fourth study (Lowe & Carroll, 1985) is described so briefly that it is difficult to be sure what the data were like, but the authors describe their results as showing no change in emotional intensity after injury and there-fore consider that they were not supportive of Hohmann or Schachter.

The "score" on these four studies would seem to be one "yes," one "maybe," one "don't know," and one qualified "no." That is certainly a fa-miliar pattern of mixed results, but we should probably not take any of them, including the positive ones, too seriously. All four of these studies suffer from a major problem: To a considerable extent, they rely on current judgments about how emotional experiences *now* compare with the same experiences *before* the injury. In all studies, the time between injury and re-port was a number of years, or even decades. The result, as Chwalisz et al. (1988) note, is a real danger of memory biases. For example, Ross (1989) has shown that people are extremely poor at judging which aspects of themselves have changed or remained the same, even over much shorter periods of time. Instead, people seem to judge themselves to have changed or remained the same depending on whether their lay theory about the at-tribute predicts change or stability (e.g., Nisbett & Wilson, 1977; Ross, 1989). Consequently, in all these studies, we cannot be confident that the subjects were reporting actual changes in their emotional life, rather than their beliefs about what should have happened.

One solution would be a more experimental test of emotional intensity that examined the current emotional responses of spinal cord–injured people to emotional stimuli. At least one such study exists. Jasnos and Hakmiller (1975) studied male subjects who differed in the level at which their injury had occurred. All were shown slides of nude women, injured women, and clothed women and were asked to describe their "thoughts and feelings." These descriptions were later rated blindly on a 5-point scale to "best describe the most intense level of emotion indicated by the protocol." The results paralleled Hohmann's in that the higher a subjects' lesion, the lower his rated emotional intensity was on the nude slides. There were no differences on the slides of injured women.

Once again, these results are consistent with Schachter's theory but also equivocal. For example, increasingly high lesion levels also make sexual activity more difficult; thus, reduced sexual feelings might reflect anxiety, reluctance, or resignation.

In sum, the studies of spinal cord injuries are inconclusive and leave ample room for "half-full" versus "half-empty" disagreements. Indeed, in the case of spinal cord injuries, the glass seems a bit less than half full. Clearly, the effects of spinal cord injuries on the intensity of emotional feelings are not dramatic, and after spinal cord injury, people can have quite normal and satisfactory emotional lives.

This is what would have been predicted by self-perception theory, though of course the theory should not take much credit for the inconclusive data. Still, self-perception theory is less discomfited by the weak results of these studies than would be many other Jamesian theories that place more weight on autonomic arousal. In previous chapters we have seen a great deal of evidence that the final emotional experience is an integration of a multitude of kinds of information—from facial expressions, postures, and actions, as well as from the situation. Following spinal cord injury, people would still have access to facial expression feedback and situational cues. We have seen already that people who are more responsive to personal cues also respond to situational cues when there are no conflicting personal cues. Hence, people with spinal cord injuries might either respond immediately to situational cues or learn to rely more heavily on situational cues after the injury. The increased intensity of the descriptions of emotional situations observed by Bermond et al. (1991) is consistent with the possibility that people learn to rely more heavily on situational cues after spinal cord injury.

One clear implication of these studies on spinal cord injury is that the capacity to experience autonomic arousal is not absolutely necessary in order to have normal emotional experiences. However, these studies certainly leave open the possibility that many people might use these cues, in company with others, to generate their emotional feelings.

Pure Autonomic Failure

A somewhat less catastrophic medical condition may provide a somewhat "purer" test of the role of arousal cues in feelings. Pure autonomic failure (PAF) is, as the name says, a failure of the autonomic nervous system with the result that arousal responses can no longer occur. Pure Autonomic Failure characteristically occurs in adults in their 30s and 40s and is not thought to involve any central nervous system damage. While doubtless troublesome, PAF certainly does not produce the degree of life disruption that spinal cord injuries do. Thus, it provides a relatively straightforward test of the role of arousal in emotional experience. Since the disorder is rare, samples are small, but the results are entirely consistent with Schachterian and Jamesian theories. These people seem to have dramatically diminished intensities of emotional experience. When asked how much they agreed with the statement "I no longer feel emotional," the PAF group did not overlap with normal controls in the strength of their endorsement. They also had much lower scores on the Hamilton Anxiety Scale (Critchley, Mathias, & Dolan, 2002).

Caution is certainly appropriate in interpreting these results for at least two reasons. One is simply the general uncertainty attached to the interpretation of any life-changing disorder. The second is that PAF sufferers might have sustained some damage to the central nervous system that simply has not been identified yet. Nonetheless, the results appear on face value to be especially strong support for the necessity of arousal for intense emotional experiences, particularly of anxiety and distress.

Panic Disorder

A second medical phenomenon, panic disorder, more clearly suggests a role for autonomic arousal in emotional experiences of some people. In panic disorder, people report attacks of intense fear that occur without any apparent cause. A number of studies have found that people who suffer from panic disorder are also much more likely to suffer from mitral valve prolapse, a heart disorder that causes symptoms such as heart palpitations, shortness of breath, and dizziness. These symptoms are similar to those that accompany fear, and a number of authors (see Crowe, 1985, for a review) have suggested that the physical symptoms of mitral valve prolapse may cause feelings of panic in some people. Since many people who suffer from panic disorder do not have mitral valve prolapse, that cannot be the whole explanation of panic disorder. However, if this is the mechanism for some panic disorder, then it is an example of visceral symptoms generating emotional experiences.

A similar but more general mechanism has been described in some other cases of panic disorder, whereby people appear to have "mistaken" the bodily symptoms of exercise or hypoglycemia for fear (Ottaviani & Beck, 1987). Mechanisms like these might account for some additional proportion of people who suffer from panic disorder, although once again this does not seem to be the whole story. A third possibility is a kind Pavlovian conditioning of arousal symptoms that then appear catastrophically (McNally, 1990). Interestingly, all the various theories of panic disorder seem to assume that the first step is the appearance of physical arousal symptoms, sometimes even in sleep—symptoms that are not responses to threats but are mistakenly experienced as fear.

One of the standard diagnostic procedures in panic disorder also represents a very clear example of externally produced arousal leading to feelings of anxiety. In these "physiological challenge" procedures, people are given various treatments that produce autonomic arousal, including sodium lactate, norepinephrine, caffeine, and CO_2/O_2 mixtures. Most people who do not suffer from panic disorder react unemotionally to these challenges, but panic sufferers experience panic attacks (Woods & Charney, 1988), demonstrating that the arousal symptoms have indeed caused the panic.

In sum, the literature on panic disorder is consistent with self-perception theory approaches in two ways. First of all, the prevailing explanations of panic disorder all make sense only if something like self-perception theory is correct. That is, they assume that panic disorder arises in people who, for one reason or another, are subject to arbitrary "autonomic storms." The essentially nonemotional arousal is then experienced as an emotion, anxiety. These are, of course, only theoretical explanations, so while they are consistent with self-perception theory, they certainly do not constitute empirical evidence for it. However, the second important feature of this literature is empirical and perfectly consistent with self-perception theory: The physiological challenge procedure consistently demonstrates that inducing arousal causes terror in those who suffer from panic disorder.

AN INTERIM SUMMARY

The research reviewed thus far in this chapter is not as consistently supportive as that in the preceding two chapters, but overall it is still reasonably supportive. The weakest body of evidence comes from studies in which various chemical or drug manipulations of arousal were expected to increase the intensity of emotional feelings. Certainly, Schachter's original idea that arousal mediated the intensity of all emotional experiences must be given up. But the evidence in the drug manipulation studies does show that some emotions—anger and fear—are increased by drug manipulations. In certain select groups, such as people suffering from panic disorder who are exposed to physiological challenges, these effects are very strong. Peripherally acting beta-blockers also seem to produce reliable, powerful reductions in emotional experiences of anger and anxiety in populations and contexts where anger and anxiety are particularly problematic.

The relatively weak and sometimes inconsistent results from laboratory manipulations of arousal contrast strikingly with the quite powerful results in certain more practical contexts. Why would people who suffer from panic disorder so reliably respond to the physiological challenges, and people who have problems with anxiety and anger be effectively treated by beta-blockers, when none of these manipulations work as well in the usual laboratory contexts? I think the answer lies precisely in the fact that people who suffer from panic disorder or from problems with anxiety and anger are especially selected. Recall that I have already talked about a great deal of research demonstrating that people differ in how strongly they respond to personal and situational cues. If the theorists of panic disorder are correct, only people who are responsive to personal cues should be afflicted. If you experience an essentially random "autonomic storm" and are unresponsive to personal cues, your arousal cues would have little meaning for you. At most, you would probably find unexpected sweating and butterflies in your stomach as mildly interesting, or as something to mention to your doctor when next you meet. On the other hand, if you do respond to personal cues, you would experience your arousal as clearly emotional, an emotion that seems to come from nowhere and to be uncontrollable and literally terrifying.

Similarly, people would use beta-blockers to treat anxiety and anger only if their feelings are too intense and inappropriate, driven, we might imagine, by excessive autonomic response. In short, people became members of the target groups only because they were responsive to personal cues. In contrast, in the experimental studies we can assume that the participant groups contained roughly equal proportions of those who were and were not responsive to personal cues. Mixing together people who are affected by arousal cues and those who are not is an excellent recipe for obtaining mixed and inconsistent results.

The overall pattern of the evidence does seem to lean heavily toward the view that autonomic arousal contributes to the experience of some emotions, particularly fear, anger, or rage, although some uncertainty remains. Fortunately, we do not need to remain in this unsatisfactory state, since the final body of evidence is much stronger and more consistent in showing that increasing arousal increases feelings, and decreasing arousal reduces feelings.

MISATTRIBUTION OF AROUSAL

The research reported thus far all involves some more or less uncommon and often technological manipulation of arousal. In misattribution research the arousal is produced by natural processes, and the "trick" of the research is to change the person's understanding of the origins of that arousal. The result is that subjects report experiences that are consistent with how they understood their arousal to have been caused. Their feelings no longer reflect the real source of their arousal.

There are two ways in which arousal may be misattributed. In one, the arousal naturally produced by an emotional stimulus is attributed (incorrectly) to something else, and the result is that the person feels the emotion less strongly. In the opposite effect, a naturally produced arousal is misattributed to a new emotional context, and the result is that the second emotional experience is more intense. Both of these effects have been observed repeatedly, in hundreds of studies.

Emotional Arousal Misattributed to Nonemotional Causes

Most people erroneously recall the Schachter and Singer (1962) study as showing that epinephrine increased feelings of both anger and euphoria. They probably misremember these results because the study did produce some other dramatic effects on feelings of both anger and happiness. These involved the group of subjects who were told what the consequences of the adrenalin would be. In that study, you will recall, three groups of subjects were injected with epinephrine. The groups differed in what they were told about the effects of the injections. One group was told nothing, and a second group was misinformed about the effects. The third group was told accurately what the effects would be—pounding heart, sweaty palms, flushing, and so forth. This "informed" group had received equal amounts of epinephrine, and Schachter and Singer checked the heart rates to ensure that the arousal was equal. However, the informed subjects reported significantly *less* intense emotions than the other epinephrine groups, and in fact less intense feelings than the saline control subjects.

The informed subjects seemed to have discounted the effects of the injection, as if they were saying to themselves, "I have been given an injection that will make my heart pound, and therefore these bodily events have nothing to do with my emotional feelings." (Again, I must add the disclaimer that this kind of imaginary dialogue does not actually take place in anyone's mind and is instead a model of the nonconscious processes that are hypothesized to occur.)

The most striking feature of these results is that the informed subjects' scores were lower than even the saline-injected controls. Presumably, the saline controls naturally produced some arousal; for example, in response to the insulting questionnaire, they reported feeling moderate anger. Since the informed subjects reported feeling significantly less anger, the discounting apparently had affected both arousal due to the epinephrine injections and the subjects' own naturally occurring arousal. Thus, it appeared that naturally produced arousal could be "discounted away" if it was misattributed to an injection.

Misattribution and Fear/Anxiety

Nisbett and Schachter (1966) followed the lead provided by Schachter and Singer's informed subjects in a subsequent study of pain. Nisbett and Schachter argued that part of the experience of pain is fear, and that the intensity of fear experiences is in part due to arousal. Thus in this study, they asked subjects to endure an increasingly intense series of electric shocks until the shocks became too unpleasant. All subjects were given a pill that they were told would either increase arousal or have side effects that were irrelevant to arousal. Half of the subjects in each of these groups were told that the electric shocks would be intense, and the other half was told the shocks would be mild. The expected misattribution effect occurred in the mild shock group, whose fear presumably was not too severe. The mild fear subjects who were induced to "misattribute" their natural arousal to the pill endured significantly more intense shock levels.

Schachter's misattribution studies were followed by a multitude of other misattribution studies, in which subjects were induced to attribute their natural arousal to various pills and procedures, such as white noise, strange rooms, and the lights or ventilation of a room (for reviews, see Ross & Olson, 1981; Reisenzein, 1983). The feelings that were successfully reduced by these procedures include anxiety, anger, cognitive dissonance, and the discomfort of social comparison (Tesser, Pilkington, & McIntosh, 1989).

The results were not, however, entirely consistent. For example, Storms and Nisbett (1970) increased reported sleep success in a group of insomniacs by inducing them to misattribute their arousal at bedtime to a pill. Others produced opposite effects.(e.g., Kellogg & Baron, 1975).

These inconsistencies and many others like them led Ross and Olson (1981) to propose a theory to explain when such effects occur. They pointed out that misattribution depends on the relative strength and clarity of subjects' understanding of the true source of their arousal, in relation to their belief in the plausibility of the misattribution "source." If, for example, subjects were very well aware of the effects of the true source, misattribution would be less likely to occur. On the other hand, the more plausible the fictitious source of arousal, the more likely that misattribution would occur.

Olson, both by himself (1988) and in conjunction with Ross (Olson & Ross, 1988), tested predictions of this model by inducing participants to misattribute the arousal of speech anxiety. Speech anxiety is a particularly good test of the analysis because three previous studies (Cotton, Baron, & Borkovec, 1980; Singerman, Borkovec, & Baron, 1976; Slivken & Buss, 1984) had failed to find misattribution effects, in studies that failed to meet Ross and Olson's criteria. In the three studies reported by Olson and Ross that did meet their criteria for an effective manipulation, successful misattribution and reduction of anxiety did occur.

Misattribution and Cognitive Dissonance

One of the phenomena in which misattribution has been most frequently and consistently demonstrated is cognitive dissonance. Cognitive dissonance theory (Festinger, 1957) proposed that when people found themselves acting in a way that was inconsistent with their beliefs, they would experience an aversive motivational state, known as cognitive dissonance, and would be motivated to reduce this state. For example, in many experiments, people would be induced to write or speak an argument that was contrary to their true beliefs. They would then be assumed to be experiencing the unpleasant feelings of cognitive dissonance.

Dissonance theory presumes that the arousal of cognitive dissonance is like the arousal of other unpleasant feeling states, such as anxiety or fear. If dissonance is like other negative, aversive states, we might expect that dissonance would be accompanied by arousal, and indeed it is. After a person makes counterattitudinal speeches or statements, arousal indices are raised (e.g., Cooper et al., 1978; Croyle & Cooper, 1983). Presumably this arousal leads to the unpleasant feelings of dissonance and therefore could be misattributed "away." In a number of studies, research participants made counterattitudinal speeches and then were led to attribute their arousal to a pill or other actually neutral characteristics of the situation. When dissonance-produced arousal was misattributed to other neutral features of the experiment, participants did not change their attitudes (Losch & Cacioppo, 1990; Zanna & Cooper, 1974).

In sum, a substantial number of studies have demonstrated misattribution of arousal involved in dissonance, so that people do not feel the need to change their attitudes. These studies argue strongly that arousal does play a role in the experience of dissonance.

Stepping back a little further, misattribution techniques have consistently reduced anxiety, fear, and cognitive dissonance. This pattern is the same as we have been seeing throughout this chapter—that arousal seems to be an important contributor to the experience of fear, anger, and some related unpleasant emotions, and if the arousal is disqualified as a contributor to an emotional feeling, the feeling is diminished.

INCREASING AROUSAL THROUGH MISATTRIBUTION

The opposite effect of misattribution has been observed at least equally as often. In these studies, naturally occurring arousal produced by exercise or an emotional stimulus is misattributed to a different emotional stimulus, and it produces a stronger second emotional feeling as a result. (Note that, of course, the logic of these studies is exactly like the research that manipulated arousal through epinephrine or other drugs. The only difference is that in these "misattribution" studies, the arousal is produced by some more common, everyday life event, not a drug.)

In one program of research, Zillmann (1983) induced arousal in a particularly interesting way. He began by asking subjects to peddle an exercise bicycle until they were breathing hard and their heart rate was elevated substantially. Zillmann reasoned that immediately after exercising, subjects would certainly be aroused, as evidenced by breathing and heart rate, but that the subjects would also realize very clearly the source of their arousal. After a considerable amount of time, they would no longer be aroused. Yet at some intermediate time, they might still be somewhat aroused; because the more obvious symptoms of their exercise had died down, they would no longer recognize that the exercise was still affecting them. At that point, their exercise-induced arousal could be misattributed to another source.

In a series of studies, subjects have been exercised, and then with short, moderate, or long delays, they have been confronted with an emotion-inducing situation. For example, in one study subjects were confronted with a confederate who angered them, and they were given an opportunity to retaliate. The consistent finding is that subjects in the middle group act and report feeling stronger emotional feelings (see Zillmann, 1983, for a review). Those in the long delay group have no arousal remaining; those in the short delay condition have presumably plenty of arousal but are also very clear about its source, namely, the exercise. Zillmann has also demonstrated "excitation transfer" from exercise to sexual attraction.

A second large group of misattribution studies have focused on sexual attraction. Berscheid and Walster (1974) proposed a Schachterian arousal theory of passionate love: that the feeling of passionate love was rooted in the experience of arousal in the presence of an appropriate love object. A series of studies have tested the misattribution implications of this idea. In the first of these, Dutton and Aron (1974) arranged to have male subjects meet an attractive female confederate just after they had crossed one of two bridges over a river. One of these bridges was low and wide; the other was high, narrow, and shaky. Crossing the latter was expected to have induced some fear in the men, which would in turn produce arousal that could be misattributed to their feelings about the woman. The attractive confederate had given all the men her phone number, ostensibly so they could find out more about the study. The dependent variable was the proportion of men who called her later, for a date. As Dutton and Aron had predicted, more men who had crossed the high bridge called. In a second study, men who were aroused by the threat of electric shock also were more attracted to a female stranger.

A number of studies have followed that confirm this general finding (White & Kight, 1984; White, Fishbein, & Rutstein, 1981) for feelings of passionate love and for the closely related feelings of erotic attraction (e.g., Zillmann, 1983). When people have been aroused by fear, anger, or physical exercise, they then report being more strongly attracted sexually or romantically.

The opposite kind of misattribution result has also been observed with romantic attraction. In this study, male subjects met an attractive woman confederate who engaged in behavior that had been previously shown to produce increased attraction. Half of the subjects, however, were led to attribute their arousal to a "vitamin" that would make them feel "excited, aroused and a little flushed" (p. 437). These subjects reported significantly less attraction to the confederate (McClanahan, Gold, Lenney, Ryckman, & Kuhlberg, 1990). In this study, misattribution was used to "explain away" the arousal of romantic love and hence reduce feelings of attraction.

A meta-analysis of 21 studies of misattribution and "romantic attraction" found an average effect size of $d = .27$, which is "moderate" and was confirmed by a further study by the authors (Foster, Witcher, Campbell, & Green, 1998). Both the analysis and the study added a new principle to the equation: that even when participants were aware of the true source of their arousal, the arousal still affected their feelings. Or, to put it the other way around, it was difficult to entirely "misattribute away" all the impact of arousal. The "emotional illusion" remained despite the knowledge that it was an illusion. This result seems analogous to how in the Muller-Lyer illusion the two lines seem resolutely different in length, even after both have been measured.

In sum, a large number of misattribution studies have demonstrated that leading people to attribute natural arousal to emotions increases the intensity of feelings, and leading people to attribute natural arousal to something other than emotions leads people to have less intense emotional feelings. The emotions that have been studied include the by-now-familiar pair of anger and fear, and also two new additions, cognitive dissonance and sexual attraction/passionate love. Note, too, that both sufficiency and the weak form of necessity have been demonstrated. If people are prevented from being aroused, or their arousal has been misattributed to a neutral source, then they feel less strong emotional feelings.

Individual Differences

After the frequent discussion of individual differences in the previous chapters, their absence is striking here. Studies of the effects of arousal on feelings rarely have examined individual differences. The misattribution literature provides one piece of evidence of an individual difference connection with other self-perception effects. Joan Duncan (Duncan & Laird, 1980) asked subjects who were mildly afraid of snakes to approach a real snake. Subjects were given a placebo pill and were told that it would make them feel either tense and jittery or calm and relaxed. Notice that these two instructions focus on some of the symptoms that are presumably the constituents of the experience of fear.

Two opposite effects of this placebo/misattribution manipulation were observed, depending on whether subjects were more or less responsive to personal cues. Subjects who were less responsive to personal cues simply accepted the instructions (situational cues) at face value and displayed the conventional placebo effect: If told the pill would make them calm, they reported less fear and were more willing to approach the snake. If told the pill would make them tense, they reported more fear and avoided the snake. The subjects who were more responsive to personal cues showed the opposite effect. When told the pill would make them more relaxed, they reported greater fear and avoided the snake; when told the pill would make them tense, they were less afraid. This latter effect is, of course, the standard misattribution of arousal.

Apparently, these personal cue subjects unconsciously used the pill instructions as a context for their own feelings, as if they were saying to themselves, "The pill is making me more relaxed, but I am still very tense, so I must be even more afraid than usual." (Yet again, the warning seems necessary: No one ever consciously says these things. They are models of the kind of process that is presumed to be taking place entirely outside of consciousness.)

This study represents another example of the phenomenon noted earlier, that subjects who are more responsive to personal cues do respond to situational cues as well. In this study, the situational cues were not the direct basis of the personal cue groups' feelings but did serve as a context in which their personal cues of natural arousal were interpreted.

In sum, this study demonstrated that people who are responsive to personal cues from facial expressions also responded to personal cues from arousal. In contrast, subjects who were unresponsive to personal cues from their expressions also ignored their natural arousal cues and accepted the placebo message directly.

Recently Alex Genov, Robb Pietrzak, and others from our lab have explored the relationships between arousal and feelings as a function of response to personal cues, in three different settings. In two (Genov et al., 2000; Pietrzak et al., 2001), we measured various aspects of arousal, including heart rate, skin conductance, and variously skin temperature and/or EMG. In the first of these studies, emotional responses were instigated by the cold pressor task, which consists of holding one's arm in ice water until (remarkably rapidly) the pain becomes too unpleasant to tolerate. In the second, emotional reactions were induced by asking participants to imagine as vividly as possible that a romantic partner was unfaithful. In both cases, the basic manipulation produced substantial increases in arousal measures, and these increases were identical among people who did and people who did not respond to personal cues in the expression manipulation procedure.

The striking difference between the two groups was in the relationship between their arousal responses and their feelings of pain or of anger and betrayal. Among the participants who were unaffected by personal cues, there was no relationship at all, whereas among those who were affected by personal cues, arousal and intensity of feeling were substantially correlated.

This correlation might have occurred for three reasons, of course. Our preferred alternative is that the personal cue group "used" their arousal cues in determining their emotional feelings, whereas the arousal cues were irrelevant to situational cue group. However, it is certainly possible that the causal arrow could have gone the other direction, or even that both arousal and feelings were produced by some third factor among the personal cue group.

The resolution of this uncertainty requires that the arousal be manipulated so that the causal nexus is clear. That was the purpose of a third study, in which Alex Genov (2000) used the Zillmann exercise paradigm to induce arousal states in his participants and then measured the effects of this arousal on their feelings while watching frightening movies. The results were slightly complicated, but clearly the induced arousal increased the intensity of feelings among the personal cue group and not among the situational cue group. And again in this study, heart rate and reported intensity of fear were significantly, positively correlated among the personal cue group but slightly negatively correlated among the situational cue group.

These four studies indicate that arousal cues affect feelings in the same people who are affected by other emotional behaviors, and that these effects probably occur by the same mechanisms. Of course, four studies constitute a modest basis for drawing conclusions, but this is all the evidence there is, one way or another, and it is at least consistent with the expectations of self-perception theory.

SUMMARY

The evidence for the role of autonomic arousal in experience is certainly not as straightforward and consistent as the evidence for the other components of emotional feelings. After Schachter and Singer's strong early theoretical statements, a disappointed critical reaction to these somewhat confused results is hardly surprising. One of Schachter and Singer's major points seems to have been seriously overstated: Autonomic arousal does *not* appear to be a component of all emotional feelings. Nonetheless, the actual array of data is really quite persuasive in showing that in some people, some emotional feelings are derived from cues arising from their autonomic activity. In particular, increasing arousal by epinephrine, hypnosis, ephedrine, caffeine, high temperatures, and exercise has been quite reliably shown to increase anger and fear and their close relations, such as rage and anxiety. Reducing arousal through beta-blockers reduces anxiety and anger. At least in the misattribution literature, a third unpleasant feeling has also been shown to involve arousal, the feeling of cognitive dissonance. These results all fit reasonably well the view of Marshall and Zimbardo (1979) and Maslach (1979) that arousal is a component only of negative emotions. However, the misattribution research has added a fourth, positive, feeling to this group. This is the cluster of emotional feelings that includes romantic attraction, passionate love, and erotic stimulation. Finally, there is at least modest evidence that a fifth emotion, sadness, has been associated with decreases in autonomic arousal.

This pattern of results actually fits both common sense and other emotion research far better than the Schachter and Singer assumption. In describing their own emotional experiences, people often do describe arousal symptoms, but only for exactly these emotions: anger, fear, and passion (Rime & Giovanni, 1986).

A substantial body of research using factor analyses or multidimensional scaling has shown that many features of emotions can be represented in a two-dimensional space (Feldman-Barrett & Russell, 1998). Different researchers have given the dimensions somewhat different names, but one of the two dimensions always is good versus bad, and the second is something like aroused versus unaroused. In these studies anger and fear, and romantic love or sexual attraction, are among the highly aroused emotions, and sadness is the least aroused. However, many other emotions, including happiness, are neither aroused nor unaroused and seem to be determined far more strongly by other factors (see Figure 4.2).

Overall, then, the pattern of the results seems to have been just what we should have expected (Laird & Bresler, 1992), rather than the broader expectations of Schachter and Singer. Emotional feelings that are conventionally thought to involve bodily symptoms of arousal are the same emotions that scaling studies identify as strongly defined by an arousal dimension. It is precisely these feelings that are influenced by arousal manipulations.

What exactly is the role of arousal in emotional experience? Apparently arousal serves as one of a number of cue sources that generate some emotional experiences. Arousal is sufficient to increase anger, fear, passionate love, and their close relations. Arousal is also necessary in the somewhat weak sense that some cue sources are required. An absence of arousal will reduce the intensity of those same emotional experiences.

Adults

Figure 4.2. Circumplex of relationships between emotion judgments.
Source: Russell, J. A., & Bullock, M. (1985). Multidimensional scaling of emotional
facial expressions: Similarity from preschoolers to adults. *Journal of Personality
and Social Psychology, 48,* 1290–1298. Published by APA and reprinted with
permission.

NOTES

1. The autonomic nervous system does not function in nearly as simple a fashion as this description implies. Indeed, there is some reason to question whether
the term *arousal* is sensible at all. The various facets of the arousal response sometimes move together, but at other times one will rise while another drops (Lacey &
Lacey, 1958). For the bulk of this chapter I will follow the tradition of talking about
"arousal," but at the end I will address this issue again.

2. Cannon did consider the role of postural and expressive behavior and in the
course of his discussion granted the basic self-perception kind of effect that has
been described in the previous chapters. However, he hypothesized a mechanism
in his thalamic theory that could account for these effects without compelling him
to adopt a real self-perception position.

5

Theoretical Summary on Emotion

In the first chapter I identified four important questions about the evidence for self-perception theory: (1) Are behaviors sufficient to produce emotional feelings? (2) Is the sufficiency evidence adequately free of experimenter bias? (3) Are behaviors necessary, as well as sufficient, for the occurrence of emotional feelings? (4) If behaviors are necessary and sufficient for feelings in the laboratory, are they also necessary and sufficient in the real world? We are now in a position to answer those questions directly, at least with regard to emotional feelings.

ARE BEHAVIORS SUFFICIENT TO PRODUCE EMOTIONAL FEELINGS?

The first was the sufficiency question: Is emotional behavior sufficient to produce corresponding emotional feelings? In the previous three chapters, I have reviewed a very large amount of evidence showing that when people are induced to act as though they feel an emotion, they report feeling the way they have acted. For many feelings, a number of different kinds of behaviors have been studied. For example, in different experiments anger has been shown to be produced or intensified by frowning, angry postures, clenched fists, increases in arousal, and free verbal expression of anger. Similarly, fear has been produced by facial expressions, arousal, escaping actions, and fearful postures; romantic attraction is increased by sharing mutual gaze, touching, sharing confidences, increases in arousal, and being in romantic surroundings.

In sum, most of the obvious behavioral features of a number of emotional feelings have been studied, and in every case they have been shown to generate those feelings. These studies cover a wide range of emotional

88

feelings, including anger, fear, happiness, sadness, disgust, guilt, and romantic love. The behaviors manipulated have included facial expressions, postures, gaze, tone of voice, breathing patterns, overt actions, and autonomic arousal. Clearly, inducing people to act emotionally does lead to emotional feelings, as James and self-perception theory predicted. Emotional behaviors do seem to be "sufficient."

The concept of sufficiency deserves a little more examination. Three versions of sufficiency can be identified, varying in how "strongly" they reflect James's original ideas and self-perception theory. The weakest version is that behavior is sufficient to increase already ongoing feelings, but it cannot initiate feelings. A slightly stronger version is that behavior can initiate feelings, but the effects are broad and unspecific, such as just generally good or bad feelings. Finally, the most specific version is that the effects of behaviors are, as James originally argued, to produce specific emotional experiences: Specific behaviors produce specific feelings.

Note that these three kinds of sufficiency are ordered, so that any evidence in support of the most specific will count as evidence for the two less specific versions. On the other hand, any studies that are designed so that they bear only on the weakest version will be mute regarding the stronger versions. Inevitably, therefore, evidence for the strongest version is less common than for the weaker versions. For example, to demonstrate real specificity of effects, more than two kinds of behavior must be manipulated, and more than two kinds of feelings including those that match the behaviors must be measured. With one or two kinds of behavior, the results might be reflecting only an effect on global positive or negative feelings. Although more difficult to develop, evidence for the strongest version of sufficiency exists, and seems substantial—at least to my admittedly biased eyes.

First of all, both expressions and postures have been shown to have very specific effects on feelings that cannot be explained by simple variations in pleasantness (Duclos & Laird, 2001; Duclos et al., 1989; Flack et al., 1999a; Flack et al., 2000; Flack et al., 1999b; Levenson et al., 1991; Levenson et al., 1990; Levenson et al., 1992) and also on memories (Laird et al., 1989; Laird et al., 1982; Schnall & Laird, 2002). In addition, the pattern of confirming and disconfirming results of tests of Schachter's theory of emotion (Schachter & Singer, 1962) actually supports indirectly the strongest version of the bodily feedback hypothesis. Although Schachter had assumed that increasing arousal would strengthen all emotional experiences, the evidence is that arousal strengthens only fear and anger (and their close relations) and romantic, passionate attraction. These three are the specific emotions that folk theories and scaling studies both identify as high in arousal. Furthermore, even among these emotions, some physiological distinctions are identifiable (Levenson et al., 1991; Levenson et al., 1990; Levenson et al., 1992). Other emotional feelings, such as sadness and happiness, are unaffected by arousal changes, as folk and professional theories predict they should be. Notice, then, that the arousal results are not entirely specific, but the effects of arousal are exactly as specific as they "should" have been. That is, they match very nicely our understanding from other kinds of research about which particular emotions normally involve arousal.

In sum, in every study in which the conditions and measures were adequate to test the strongest version of sufficiency, it was supported. Many, many more studies only provide conclusive support for the weaker versions, because the manipulations and/or measures were not specific enough. Of course most of these could be, and probably are, reflecting more specific processes that were not measured with sufficient precision.

Why has so much of this research failed to test the strongest version of the self-perception hypothesis? I think the answer is clear: In the early stages of self-perception research, any demonstration of an impact of behavior on feelings had news value. Those of us who were doing the research in those days were, after all, just beginning to doubt the commonsense sequence. If we could demonstrate that one or two behaviors affected feelings, we felt we had made a step forward. It was only after the basic effect had been demonstrated a number of times that we moved on to more specific questions and more specific experimental designs.

EXPERIMENTER BIAS AND COMPLIANT PARTICIPANTS

The primary threat to the sufficiency conclusion is the potential that the self-perception effects might have been produced by experimenter bias (Capella, 1993; Fridlund, 1994). Two kinds of bias might have occurred. In one, the manipulations may have in some way revealed to the participants what was expected of them, and then they may have complied. For example, if people recognized that they were being asked to smile, this recognition clearly implies what feelings they should report. The second possibility is that the experimenters may have unconsciously affected the participants' feelings by other aspects of their behavior and manner. For example, perhaps while manipulating participants into smiles the experimenter was also acting more jovially than when manipulating frowns. Many self-perception studies are vulnerable to this possibility because the experimenters had to be aware of the participants' actions in order to produce proper expressions, postures, and so on.

All the experimenters have been highly aware of the first kind of danger and have tried hard to minimize its likelihood. Most of these studies have employed elaborate cover stories, such as Schachter's about the perceptual effects of Suproxin or the claim by Strack et al. (1988) that their study concerned the proper pen position for quadriplegics writing with their mouths. To test the effectiveness of the cover stories, participants almost always have been elaborately debriefed, both in writing and orally. If they could identify the experimenters' hypotheses, they were excluded from the analyses. In addition, in many of these studies participants encountered only one of the experimental conditions, making it much less likely that they could have discerned what was expected of them.

Some of these studies involved manipulations that were so well disguised that none of the participants revealed any awareness of the intended effects. Strack et al.'s (1988) use of the pen held in the mouth is one such example, as was their technique for manipulating posture by simple changes in the height of the work surface (Laird et al., in press; Stepper & Strack, 1993). Zajonc et al.'s (1989) vowel pronunciation task is another well-disguised task. Recall that the participants were simply making noises or reading stories aloud and, in the latter case, certainly did not realize that the purpose of the reading was to induce them to make the appropriate noises. In none of these manipulations did they recognize that the vowel sounds required them to adopt emotion-like expressions, and these expressions led to changed emotional feelings.

The deceptive cover stories, the inquiries into participants' awareness of the hypotheses, and the especially subtle manipulations of expressive behaviors all combine to make very remote the possibility that the participants were just being cooperative. One of the standard results in many of these studies strengthens that conclusion. In many of these studies the dependent variables included psychophysiological measures, such as increases in heart rate, skin conductance, or skin temperature (e.g., Lanzetta et al., 1976; Levenson, 1992). Since autonomic responses are ordinarily outside of conscious control, these results could not have been produced by participant cooperativeness.

These various procedures and results make it very unlikely that self-perception effects are attributable to conscious or nonconscious cooperation by the participants. However, they do not rule out another, subtler kind of bias that might have emerged from the experimenters' unconscious influence on the participants' feelings.

An early attempt to deal with this problem was to try to measure it. In my first expression manipulation study (Laird, 1974), I used a procedure that Fridlund (1994) has called the *pseudoexperimental control*. Two participants were run simultaneously and were treated identically, except that only one made the facial muscle contractions that produced the expressions. Since the unmanipulated participants were equally close to the experimenter (me) and could see and hear everything that I did, they should have been as affected by my behavior as the manipulated participants. However, the observer participants did not change their feelings to match the manipulated participants' expressions, so it seems unlikely that I had influenced the manipulated participants through some other aspect of my behavior. (Interestingly, I still remember that the knowledge that the unmanipulated participant was present provided a constant stimulus to keep my behavior as standard as possible between conditions.) This pseudoexperimental control procedure was replicated by Rutledge and Hupka (1985) with the same results: predicted changes in the manipulated participants, and no changes in the observers.

While the pseudoexperimental control reduces the likelihood of experimenter bias, such bias could still have occurred. It would have required an improbable (at least to me) degree of interpersonal sophistication to have induced one person to feel happier while leaving another person 6 inches away unaffected. But it could have happened.

What is needed is a true double-blind design in which neither the experimenter nor the participants are aware of which treatment the participants were receiving. Unfortunately, in almost all this research, the experimenter administers the treatment and has to know what it is supposed to be. However, many of the studies discussed already contain a different kind of "double blindness." In these studies, the expectation is that individual participants will differ in their response to the self-perception manipulations, and these differences will be predictable from some other measure. For example, in two studies people who were field dependent were not expected to respond to self-perception manipulations, whereas those who were field independent would (Edelman, 1984). In one of these, Joan Duncan (Duncan & Laird, 1977) manipulated facial expressions into smiles and frowns and might have influenced people to be happier in the smile and angrier in the frown. However, she also was expecting that only some of the participants would show this effect, those who were field independent. Since at the time of the expression manipulation procedure, she had not yet administered the Embedded Figures Test, she would have had no idea which participants she should "influence." Later, when she administered the Embedded Figures Test, she still had not looked at participants' emotion reports, much less performed the rather complicated scoring that determined whether or not the participants were considered to have responded to the expressions (personal cues).

The result is that although she was not blind to the main effect conditions of the expressions, she was blind to the interaction of expressions and field dependence. Similarly, the participants might have been willing to be cooperative and respond as Duncan wanted them to, but they would have had no way to know whether they were in the group that "should" have responded or in the other group. In effect this is a double-blind control, where both experimenter and participants are blind to the predicted interaction between two or more independent variables.

The double-blind interaction control was a feature of many of the experiments already discussed. Once the role of individual differences in response to personal cues had become apparent, we routinely predicted, and found, that self-perception procedures affect people who are responsive to personal cues differently from those who are unresponsive. Most frequently we assessed response to personal cues by the expression manipulation procedure in which people were induced to smile and frown and then after each expression were asked how they felt. Some people consistently feel angry when frowning and happy when smiling, whereas others are unaffected by the expressions. The first group, who were identified as responsive to personal cues, have also been found to feel more love when gazing into a stranger's eyes (Kellerman et al., 1989) and more guilt when avoiding a stranger's eyes (Schnall et al., 2000), to feel smarter if wearing glasses

(Kellerman et al., 1989), and to change their attitudes in the induced compliance paradigm (Duncan & Laird, 1977; Rhodewalt & Comer, 1979). In contrast, people who are unresponsive to personal cues in the expression manipulation paradigm feel more love for a stranger if they meet in a romantic setting (Kellerman et al., 1989), conform more (Comer & Rhodewalt, 1979), and are more influenced by the experimenter's suggestions about how they should feel (Kellerman & Laird, 1982).

In all these studies, the double-blind interaction condition was met. That is, at the time the experimenter was manipulating the crucial independent variable, he or she did not know what the participant's status was on the interacting variable.

In many of these studies, the basic prediction was that some people would respond to a manipulation, but others would not. However, in many, including the preceding examples, the much stronger interaction prediction was that one group would respond in one way and the other group would respond in essentially the opposite way. For example, Joan Duncan (Duncan & Laird, 1980) reasoned that the standard placebo response depended on an absence of disconfirming bodily information: If someone tells you a pill will make you calmer, but your body says it is aroused, then you probably will not feel calm. Thus, she predicted that only people who were unresponsive to personal cues would show the standard placebo effect. In contrast, people who were responsive to personal cues would be expected to experience the placebo instructions as a context in which to interpret their bodily sensations and might conclude they were especially aroused, and hence show a negative or reverse placebo effect. Their responses might be as if they had thought, "The pill should be making me feel calm, but I am as aroused as ever. So I must be especially afraid." (Once again, I need to add the caveat that this loose talk about interpreting and "concluding" is meant to be metaphoric. The process is entirely nonconscious, and the language of interpretation is meant only to capture the relationships between conditions and experiences. It is "as if" people were interpreting and concluding.)

To test these ideas, Duncan asked mildly snake-phobic participants to approach and, if they were willing, to touch a snake. Before approaching the snake, the participants were given a placebo pill that was supposed to either arouse or calm them.

The opposite kinds of placebo response were exactly what occurred: situational cue participants approached the snake more closely and reported less fear if told the pill would calm them, and they avoided the snake if told the pill would arouse them. In contrast, the personal cue participants avoided the snake if told the pill would calm them and approached the snake when told it would arouse them. Note that in this study, Duncan was unaware of the participants' response to personal cues when they were approaching or avoiding the snake and thus could not have known which participants to influence (intentionally or unconsciously) in which way.

Kathy Wilcox's study (Wilcox & Laird, 2000) of women's response to pictures of superslender and normal-weight models was similar, in that the predictions were for opposite effects on self-esteem, and the experimenter was blind to the group membership at the time the manipulations were administered and the measures taken. In response to pictures of the slender models, the self-esteem of women who were more responsive to personal cues declined, whereas the self-esteem of situational cue women went up.

In sum, numerous studies have demonstrated self-perception effects in "double-blind interaction" designs that could not be explained by any combination of participant compliance or subtle, unintentional experimenter influence. Even in the extremely unlikely event that the participants could have identified the experimental hypotheses, they could not have known which group they were in, and hence how they should have acted. Equally, the experimenter had no way to know group membership and the "desired" responses for the participants while they were participating.

ARE EMOTIONAL BEHAVIORS NECESSARY FOR EMOTIONAL EXPERIENCE?

Specific emotional behaviors seem to be sufficient to produce specific emotional feelings, and the results supporting this conclusion do not seem explainable by experimenter artifact. The next question is, Are emotional behaviors also necessary for emotional feelings?

Once again, there are relatively strong and weak versions of the necessity question. The strongest version would hold that some specific emotional behaviors are essential for particular emotional feelings. Perhaps the closest to that kind of view was Schachter's early version of his two-factor theory, which seemed to require that some level of arousal be present for any intense emotional experience. Tomkins's (1982) early assumption that facial expressions were essential was also of this strong type. These strong versions of necessity do not seem popular now. A weaker version of the necessity question is that no one kind of behavior is necessary, but some kinds of cues for emotional feeling must be present for the experience to occur. The strongest empirical test of this view would be to somehow prevent all possible cues, with the expectation of no feeling at all. Such a test is probably impossible, because the variety of kinds of cues is too great. It is difficult to imagine how one could prevent facial expressions, postures, arousal, gaze, tone of voice, and breathing patterns. Furthermore, everyone uses expectations about what they should be feeling, which we have been calling situational cues. When there is no conflict, even people who are most responsive to personal cues respond to situational cues as well.

The feasible empirical version of the necessity hypothesis is that removing or somehow disqualifying a source of cues will result in less intense feelings. The number of studies showing this kind of reduction in feelings is smaller than the "sufficiency" studies, but it is still substantial. The largest number of studies demonstrating a reduction in emotional experience were those in which autonomic arousal was prevented or misattributed. When people take beta-blockers (Ratey et al., 1992; Volavka, 1988) or suffer pure autonomic failure (Critchley, Mathias, & Dolan, 2002), they feel less intense anxiety and anger. Similarly, when they are led to think their emotional arousal is caused by a placebo pill, the loss or discounting of their arousal makes them report less intense fear and anger, and romantic love (Foster et al., 1998; Olson, 1988; Slivken & Buss, 1984).

A smaller number of studies show that inhibiting facial expressions also reduces the intensity of emotional experience (Gross & Levenson, 1993, 1997). When response to personal cues has been included in "necessity" studies, only participants who are responsive to personal cues also show diminished emotional feelings after expression inhibition (Duclos & Laird, 2001; Laird et al., 1994).

None of these kinds of behaviors seem to be direct causes of feeling, in the sense that they are either sufficient in themselves or absolutely necessary for emotional experience to occur. Instead, there are a multitude of kinds of cues that combine to constitute the emotional experience. The cues include those arising from facial expressions, postures, gaze, actions, autonomic arousal, and situational definitions of what is appropriate. All these may contribute, but none are absolutely necessary.

The parallel with complex object perceptions seems particularly apt here. In a complicated perceptual experience like that of depth, a multitude of cues contribute, including linear perspective, superposition, gradients of texture and color, binocular disparity, motion parallax, and so forth. A great many perceptual experiments have demonstrated that each of these may, in the absence of the others, create the experience of relative distance, or depth. None is absolutely necessary, all may contribute, and in everyday life, our experiences are an inseparable blend of all.

Similarly, our everyday experiences of emotion are undoubtedly a combination of cues from postures, expressions, arousal, actions, and situational norms. Usually most of these cues are consistent, working together to produce the final experience. But subtracting any of these cues tends to weaken the experience, just as the experience of depth in a Ponzo illusion is meager compared with in an Escher etching, which, impressive as it is, still falls far short of your experience if you raise your eyes and look across the room.

In sum, there is a very large amount of evidence that performing emotional behaviors is sufficient to produce emotional feelings, and that behaviors are necessary, in the weak sense that removal or prevention of behaviors reduces the strength of emotional feelings. These results are not explainable by experimenter bias or by overly cooperative participants.

Not all manipulations that reduce expressive behavior produce significant reductions in feelings. Gross and his colleagues (Gross, 1998; Gross & Levenson, 1993; Gross & Levenson, 1997; Richards & Gross, 2000) usually find no effect of suppressing expressive behavior on self-reports of feelings. However, in many of these studies, the measures of feelings were relatively simple and global and may not have captured changes in feelings. These studies also did not distinguish personal and situational cue responders, so that the lack of response by the situational group may have obscured effects in the personal cue group. Consistent with that idea, in most of these studies, some decline in feelings was observed, but it was too small to be significant. This explanation is, of course, entirely speculative at the moment, and so we are left with a substantial amount of research showing opposite effects. Resolving these differences will require some more research.

EXTERNAL VALIDITY: DOES SELF-PERCEPTION OCCUR OUTSIDE THE LABORATORY?

Granted that behaviors lead to feelings in experiments, is this direction of the relationship the norm in everyday life? The alternative is, of course, that this unexpected, backward sequence might occur only in the exotic, artificial conditions of the psychological laboratory. Like a number of other questions, we can frame a stronger answer about external validity after considering a wider range of phenomena in the next few chapters, but we can begin to answer it now.

First of all, a few studies have related the individual differences in response to personal cues to reports of everyday life experiences. Sarah Strout and Sarah Bush (Strout, Bush, & Laird, 2004) interviewed people about their everyday life experiences of emotion and then administered the expression manipulation procedure to determine response to personal cues. The interviews were scored for the degree to which the respondent spontaneously mentioned bodily reactions during emotional episodes. These "embodiment scores" were significantly higher among personal cue participants. Since the scorers of both measures were blind to the results of the other measures, these results seem likely to reflect real differences in everyday experience.

Sarah Strout (Strout, Sokol, Thompson, & Laird, 2004) also explored adult attachment style and cue response. She reasoned that one potential explanation for differences in response to personal versus situational cues might be whether one's own actions or the demands and expectations of other people were better predictors of one's own future actions. In a somewhat similar theoretical suggestion, Chisolm (1999) has proposed that humans have evolved to adopt one of three (more or less) attachment styles, and that the "toggle" that determines which is adopted is the reliability of information from the child's adult caretakers. These two lines of thinking combine to generate the prediction that people who respond more strongly to personal cues would show less secure attachment in adulthood. That prediction was confirmed. Obviously, both the measures of attachment and of cue response were obtained in the laboratory, but the attachment measures are directly connected to behaviors and relationships in the outside world.

A number of the studies I have discussed already connect laboratory results to events in the real world. For example, the studies of romantic love include some that were conducted outside the laboratory: In at least one study, the experimental manipulation was crossing a high, rickety bridge, and the dependent variable was a call to make a date (Dutton & Aron, 1974).

A number of others studied romantic attractions that, as far as the participants were concerned, were going to be acted on outside of the laboratory. Many of the studies of drug effects on arousal, such as those on beta-blockers and performance anxiety, also involved real-world experiences such as giving speeches and competing in sports (Mattes, 1985; Noyes, 1985; Slivken & Buss, 1984). Obviously, the experiences of people suffering from panic disorder take place outside the laboratory, in everyday life.

Among the studies of facial expressions, most were quite artificial, but a few do connect to events outside the laboratory. For example, two studies examined mimicry of movies (Laird et al., 1994). When people observe the facial expressions of others, they tend to mimic those expressions (Dimberg, Thunberg, & Elmehed, 2000), and this mimicry is thought to be a mechanism of emotional communication (Hatfield, Cacioppo, & Rapson, 1994). It seemed to us that mimicry would be far more likely if the person was responsive to personal cues, since it would provide useful information to the mimic. On the other hand, if subjects were unresponsive to personal cues from their facial expressions, they would gain no useful information from mimicry. In the first of two studies, we observed people watching a frightening movie sequence and found that people identified by the expression manipulation procedure as more responsive to personal cues did indeed mimic the expressive behavior of the movie character more. In a second study, we showed that preventing mimicry also reduced the emotional reaction to the film clips.

These studies took place in the laboratory, to be sure, but the subjects were doing something they do in everyday life, watching movies. And they were not instructed to watch in any particular way. While watching the movie clip, they were not doing something artificial or "experimental."

The participants in Joan Duncan's study of mild snake phobics (Duncan & Laird, 1980) also faced their fears in a laboratory, but the snake was completely real, serpentine, and (speaking as one who was not snake phobic before the study, but now . . .) also bad-tempered and creepy. Of course the snake was in a well-covered, glass box, but it was a genuine snake, and the principle difference between the participants' circumstances and "real life" is that they probably would not ever have gotten as close to a snake without the experimenter's urging.

Similarly, when pain is induced in the laboratory (Genov et al., 2000), there is no reason to think that it would be different if it occurred in the kitchen or garage. Certainly participants in an experiment who have been warned what to expect and who know that their well-being has been the concern of institutional review boards have no reason to fear that the pain signals serious bodily damage. But the pain sensations must surely be the same as those that we experience after banging our head on a low beam or ill-advisedly grasping a hot pan. Still, however, these are experiences in the laboratory, so some uncertainty must remain.

A little more distance outside the laboratory and into the outside world is provided by two recent studies of premenstrual tension. Simone Schnall

(Schnall et al., 2002) reasoned that the hormonal changes of the menstrual cycle may create the equivalent of a natural self-perception experiment. These hormonal changes would first affect the women's bodily sensations, producing the bodily personal cues of emotions. Then these bodily changes might be experienced as emotions.

The self-perception interpretation suggests that women who are responsive to personal cues would be more likely to experience effects of their menstrual cycle on mood. Women who were unresponsive to personal cues might have the same bodily changes but would be less likely to experience them as emotional.

This line of reasoning led to a preliminary study in which women were asked to describe their emotional feelings and bodily sensations every other day for 2 months. Mood changes associated with the stage of a woman's menstrual cycle that were consistent over the 2 months were the index of premenstrual tension. At the end of the 2 months, each woman went through a standard expression manipulation procedure to determine her response to personal cues.

Unfortunately, because the procedures were demanding, a great many subjects were lost before completion of the study. In the end, only 19 subjects were available for the final analyses. Of these, 9 were identified by the expression manipulation task as responsive to personal cues, and 10 were designated as the situational cue group.

For each woman, we calculated an analysis of variance of her moods comparing the 7 days prior to menstruation with the other days of the 2 months. The effect size produced by this ANOVA was then the dependent variable in a comparison between high and low responders to personal cues. The mean eta squared value for the personal cue group was approximately twice as large as for the situational cue group, a difference that was significant. Perhaps more important, the eta squared for this comparison, between personal and situational cue groups, was .37. Clearly, we were able to predict with very substantial power which women would experience mood changes related to their menstrual cycle.

A second study, with 146 participants, was cross-sectional rather than longitudinal and employed a misattribution methodology. If premenstrual mood changes are caused by misunderstanding hormone-induced bodily changes as emotional, then it should be possible to reduce these feelings by reminding women that they were premenstrual. The procedure in this study was simple: Women were given two questionnaires, one that asked them to describe their feelings at the moment, and another to tell us when their last period had occurred and when the next was due. (There were various distracter questions and a cover story to disguise the purposes of all this.) The experimental variable consisted simply of the order in which these two questionnaires were administered. If the menstrual cycle questions were first, then the women were considered to have been "reminded" while they filled out the subsequent mood questionnaire. A group variation of the expression manipulation procedure was also administered.

The results were clear: When they were not reminded, women who were both responsive to personal cues and in their premenstrual week reported more negative feelings than if they were not premenstrual. Stage of cycle made no difference to the situational women. When they were reminded that they were premenstrual, however, the moods of personal cue women were better than if they were not premenstrual. The situational women were unaffected by the reminder, as they had been by the fact of their menstrual cycle status. (There was even a nonsignificant suggestion that the situational women felt *more* premenstrual syndrome (PMS) when they were reminded.)

In sum, two studies have demonstrated that susceptibility to PMS is much greater among women who are responsive to personal cues. More concretely, only women who feel happy if induced to smile and angry if induced to frown also feel angry, anxious, or depressed during their premenstrual weeks. Of course, these differences do not mean that PMS is in fact a kind of self-perception-induced misunderstanding. Doubtless some other connection between response to expressions and personal cues could exist. However, the fact that self-perception theory predicted these effects, while no other theory seems even able to account for them in any direct way, must add some confidence to our self-perception account.

Another half step outside the laboratory is provided by studies relating body weight and responses to self-perception tasks. This line of research was originally inspired by a theory of the origins of obesity that is no longer popular. Stanley Schachter and others (Rodin, 1981; Schachter, 1968) proposed that people differed in whether they ate in response to internal or external cues. Internal cues were sensations from stomach contractions, blood sugar levels, or other physiological signals that the organism needed food. External cues arose in the situation and included the sight of food, its taste, and even knowledge that it was the right time of day to be eating. According to Schachter, people who ate in response to external cues were prone to becoming overweight because their eating was not connected to organismic needs, and because we live in a society filled with external food cues. (This research will be discussed more fully in a later chapter.)

Many studies did demonstrate that when external cues were present, overweight people ate more than normal-weight people. More recently, some uncertainty has arisen about the causal role of excessive response to external cues in obesity. Dieting or some other aspect of being obese may lead to greater response to external cues. However, whether being overweight is cause or effect, overweight people are more responsive to external cues (e.g., Rodin, 1981).

"Internal" and "external" cues seem very similar to "personal" and "situational" cues,[1] and that similarity suggested that overweight people would not respond to the expression manipulation procedure. That is exactly what has been observed a number of times (Comer & Rhodewalt, 1979; Edelman, 1984; MacArthur et al., 1980). In addition, overweight people do not respond to the self-perception effects involved in the foot-in-the-door manipulation, whereas their normal-weight peers do (Wagener & Laird, 1980a). In all these studies, one portion was still a laboratory manipulation, but the other half of the relationship certainly was not. Becoming overweight is something that people do on their own time, in everyday life.

The research enterprise has not yet stepped very far out of the laboratory. We have two or three examples of phenomena that had been brought into the laboratory from the cooler temperatures of real life: emotional response to films (but only film clips), pain produced by ice-water immersion, and fear of a snake. All seem robust enough to have survived the trip inside, but we cannot be sure. Two other bodies of research, on PMS and on eating/obesity, have gone further but still have made only half the trip. Both PMS and obesity occur only outside the laboratory, but both were brought in to the self-perception theoretical range by laboratory tasks involving manipulating expressions and measuring feelings. Phobic responses also seem to fit the self-perception model very nicely, but as yet this connection is only in theory. In sum, we do not have a great deal of evidence that emotional processes do occur in real life as self-perception theory predicts, but all the evidence we have supports that conclusion. We will see in subsequent chapters that the same general state of the evidence obtains in regard to other feelings—some evidence for self-perception in the real world, but as yet it is not conclusive.

THEORETICAL EXPLANATIONS OF THE EFFECTS OF BEHAVIORS ON FEELINGS

If emotional behaviors lead to emotional feelings, both in the laboratory and in everyday life, the next step certainly is to ask why. We need some sort of explanation for this phenomenon now that it seems to be real, substantial, and arguably characteristic of normal emotional processes. I have opted for the self-perception explanation, but a number of others have been proposed. Before we consider the various possible explanations, and why I think self-perception theory is the best choice, a review of the facts to be explained will be helpful.

1. *Expressions, actions, and autonomic responses all do lead to feeling.* This is what all these theories are trying to explain, although many of them are concerned only with a part of the findings, such as expressions alone or autonomic responses alone.
2. *Emotional behaviors do not lead to feeling for all people.* The amount of research that supports this conclusion is much less than for the first, but it is substantial. A large number of studies have shown individual differences in the impact of expressions on feelings. A smaller, but still substantial, number of studies show similar differences in the effects of gaze, action, appearance, and posture. Finally, a few studies have demonstrated individual differences in the impact of autonomic activity on feelings. Furthermore, the absence of more data on individual differences seems to reflect a fail-

ure to look for them, not any difficulty in observing them. As far as I can tell, whenever anyone looks, they find these differences.

3. *Individual differences in the effects of self-perception manipulations are consistent across a wide variety of manipulated behaviors and feelings.* Since many self-perception experiments share the same logical shape and produce logically identical results, we would naturally assume that similar processes were involved. The individual difference results strongly reinforce that assumption, because they establish empirical links among the effects of the different kinds of emotional behaviors. The same process seems to lead from mutual gaze to romantic love, from a smile to a feeling of happiness, from increases in arousal to feelings of anger or fear, and from changes in posture or appearance to feelings of confidence. Clearly, any theory about the effects of behavior on feelings needs to be able to account for these consistencies across kinds of feeling and kinds of behavior.

Single-Factor Theories

Among the theories proposed to explain the effects of behavior on feelings, some have been directed at only one kind of response system, such as facial expression (e.g., Tomkins, 1982; Zajonc, 1985) or arousal (Schachter & Singer, 1962). Although these theories were proposed for a single kind of response system, in principle they might be extended to account for other kinds of behavior-feeling relationships—after all, any theory must begin somewhere before it expands its scope. In fact, however, most of these theories are not easily extended to a wider range of phenomena. For example, Zajonc (1985) suggested that the effects of facial expressions on feelings might be explained by a mechanism first proposed by Waynbaum more than 100 years ago. Waynbaum imagined that changing configurations of facial muscle contractions would change the flow of blood to the brain, and that the patterns of cerebral blood flows caused the different feelings.

Zajonc recognized that Waynbaum's theory was not consistent with modern knowledge about blood flows or cerebral function, so he proposed a variant in which changing patterns of facial muscle contraction would produce changes in the blood temperature in the cavernous sinus. These changes in blood temperature would then affect the temperature of the brain areas to which the blood travels next. Zajonc's studies have shown the standard facial feedback effect. They also show, as Zajonc's theory predicts, that different facial expressions produce changes in temperature of the region of the face over the cavernous sinus, and that the temperature changes are correlated with the corresponding changes in feeling (e.g., McIntosh, 1996; Zajonc et al., 1989). Thus, his theory is initially plausible.

However, three features of the research on facial expressions and feelings are difficult for Zajonc's theory to explain. First of all, the theory assumes a mechanism that varies on only a single dimension, from warmer to cooler.

His dependent variables are unidimensional as well. Consequently, his theory would have difficulty with the fact that facial expressions produce effects that are far more specific and that cannot be fit to a single dimension (e.g., Duclos et al., 1989; Ekman, Davidson, & Friesen, 1990). By itself, this problem might not be insurmountable, because the emotion system might be like visual perception of color. All light lies on a single dimension—that of the wavelength of electromagnetic radiation—yet gives rise to distinctive, separate experiences of red, blue, yellow, and all the other specific colors. However, the remaining two problems are not so easily overcome.

The second problem for Zajonc's vascular theory is that it would not readily explain the individual differences in the effects of facial feedback. One would expect that the effects of facial muscles on blood flows and temperatures would be the same for everyone, and therefore the connection from blood temperature to feeling presumably would be invariant and probably innate. There seems to be no room to explain the individual difference results. At the least, Zajonc would seem to need to add some mechanism by which different people would react differently to the same expressions.

Finally, the third and perhaps most difficult kind of observation for the vascular theory to explain is the parallel between the effects of facial expressions and the effects of postures, gaze, and so forth. Postures and gaze and hand holding are unlikely to connect in any way to mechanisms involving blood temperature. Wearing eyeglasses seems even less likely to affect cerebral blood flows, even though the effects of expressions are correlated with the effects of eyeglasses.

In sum, Zajonc's version of Waynbaum's theory will not accommodate the bulk of the results I have reviewed here. No doubt changing facial muscle activity changes blood temperatures, and no doubt cool air is pleasanter to breathe ((McIntosh, 1996; Zajonc et al., 1989). Conceivably, the expression/blood temperature mechanism may mediate some aspects of felt pleasantness and unpleasantness. However, cerebral blood temperature does not seem likely to be the mechanism of action of most facial expressions and most feelings.

Tomkins's (1982) theory of emotional experience shares with Zajonc's an exclusive focus on facial expression. In Tomkins's early views, proprioceptive feedback from the facial muscles was the key element (Tomkins, 1962, 1963), but later he emphasized feedback from the skin. Tomkins's theory has fewer difficulties than Zajonc's, since it does not assume a single dimension of variation. However, Tomkins's theory has no obvious machinery to explain the individual differences in response to facial (and other) manipulations, and it does not explain why the same effects occur with manipulations of postures, tone of voice, gaze, and so on.

Some years ago Carroll Izard (1977) shared Tomkins's emphasis on the face; more recently Izard (1993) has expanded his theorizing so that it would accommodate the other effects that Tomkins could not. His theory is very elaborate and largely concerned with issues that are not relevant to self-perception, but he would seem to have become a "fellow traveler" with self-perception theory in that he identifies a role for other behaviors. Izard (1993) has argued strongly that feelings and behaviors are intrinsically connected from birth, a view that I think is dubious. I will discuss that issue in chapter 10, since I have yet to discuss some of the evidence most germane to this question. However, with the exception of this mild uncertainty, Izard's theory now seems essentially like self-perception theory.

Although their focus was on arousal rather than expression, Schachter and Singer (Schachter, 1964; Schachter & Singer, 1962) expound a theory that is similarly inadequate to deal with the range of self-perception phenomena. They proposed that arousal mediated the intensity of emotional experience, while the quality of emotional experience was determined by "cognitions" about the situation. However, a great deal of evidence has shown that the quality of emotional experience is determined by facial expressions, postures, gaze, action, and so on. The Schachter and Singer theory could easily accommodate these results by adding these factors to cognitions as determinants of the quality of experience, but then, of course, it would have become essentially identical to self-perception theory.

A second problem with the Schachter and Singer theory is their hypothesis that arousal mediated the intensity of all emotional experiences. Even their own data did not support the arousal-intensity hypothesis with respect to happy feelings, and considerable evidence indicates that arousal cannot be readily "misattributed" to all emotions. On the contrary, arousal itself seems to be relatively specific, with different patterns associated with different emotional states (Ekman, Levenson, & Friesen, 1983). In sum, only emotions that are ordinarily considered to be high-arousal emotions, such as fear, anger, and passion, seem to fit their theory.

With these restrictions in place, we can see that their theory has now become entirely consistent with self-perception theory. This is hardly a criticism, since another way of describing their theory is as one of the origins of self-perception thinking in psychology, especially as the source of misattribution research. Their initial assumptions seem to have been too narrow in regard to the determinants of the quality of feelings and too broad in the assumption that arousal was necessary for all emotions, but their general view of emotional feelings seems to have been correct.

In sum, no theory that focuses on a single component of the emotional process seems able to account adequately for the full array of data. Undoubtedly, all theories could be extended to accommodate all these results, but it seems likely that the result would be an increasing evolution toward self-perception theory.

Neural "Short-Circuit" Theories

A number of modern emotion theories explain the impact of behavior on feelings in ways that include or could include many sources of input, but these theories propose mechanisms relating behavior and feelings that are different from those proposed by self-perception theory. Probably the most common suggestion has been some variant of the idea that behaviors and feelings were intrinsically linked, as a function of the way that we human beings are built. In one view, some part of the brain might send impulses to the body to produce behaviors and at the same time send related impulses to another brain system that generates the feeling. This is a kind of "short-circuit" version of the Jamesian, self-perception idea, since it preserves the idea that the generation of the behavior is an essential accompaniment of the feeling. The difference lies only in whether the information arriving at the "feeling center" of the brain has come from the receptors in the skin and muscles or instead has come from the motor cortex or even from motor neuron collaterals (Buck, 1985; Ekman, 1992b, 1993; Izard, 1990). For convenience, in the next few paragraphs, I will refer to these theories as *short-circuit theories.*

This kind of theory can readily explain the effects of facial expression manipulations on feelings and could accommodate postures as well as some arousal effects. However, many of the observations described earlier would be very difficult to fit into a short-circuit theory.

A short-circuit theory would be especially hard-pressed to explain much of the evidence regarding arousal. One could imagine a short-circuit system of arousal effects in which the neurons leading to the adrenal medulla and other parts of the sympathetic nervous system would also provide the collaterals to the "feeling center." The difficulties arise from a second assumption made in most such short-circuit theories, more or less explicitly. Perhaps because their theoretical impulse is so close to the structure of the nervous system, these theories usually assume that the hypothetical neural connections are innate and thus imply that the mechanism itself would function invariantly. Of course, a great deal of the evidence I have discussed in the previous chapters is inconsistent with any invariant, hardwired model. For example, in some misattribution studies the arousal is produced by normal emotional processes but then is misattributed to a nonemotional source. Before and after misattribution, the motor-collateral activity would be the same, and presumably "emotional," but the effects on feeling are very different. In other misattribution studies, the arousal is produced by nonemotional means, such as exercise, and if the process is invariant, it should not include any collateral messages to the "feeling center." Of course, this arousal has the same effects on feelings as emotional arousal. In both kinds of research, the effects depend not on differences in the hypothetical motor-collateral activity but, rather, in the larger pattern in which that activity is understood, its meaning. This larger pattern is precisely what is not readily included in the motor-collateral theories.

Another difficulty for the motor-collateral, short-circuit theories is presented by the individual difference results. In study after study, people perform identical behaviors and presumably generate identical motor-collateral activity, yet only some of the people report corresponding feelings. Some explanation for these results is required, but is certainly not integral to the motor-collateral theories or consistent with their tacit assumptions of innate mechanisms.

So, in some experiments we see different individuals with the same arousal and, presumably, the same motor-collateral activity but with different feelings. In other experiments, one person has the same activity at different times yet reports different feelings. Obviously, no theory that assumes the connections between behavior and feelings are innate and invariant can account for these observations.

The motor-collateral theories could, perhaps, be adapted to account for these phenomena by inserting a more interpretative step between the behavior and feeling. At that point they would be very similar to self-perception theory, except for the "shortcut" through motor collaterals. That is, information about behaviors would have to be combined in a constructive, perceptual way. A part of that process would also have to include situational cues.

However, there is quite a bit of evidence that no motor-collateral theory seems able to accommodate. For example, in the gaze studies, attraction was increased only when people shared their gaze with their partner. Since the motor messages would presumably have to be the same, whatever one's partner was doing, a motor-neuron-collaterals theory could not readily explain these effects. It is even more difficult to imagine how such a theory could explain the effects of hand holding, essay writing, self-disclosure, or wearing glasses. Finally, in many of the arousal studies, the arousal was produced by injections of exogenous epinephrine or other chemicals. In this case, there would have been no motor-neuron-collateral activity, but the effects of arousal on feeling occurred nonetheless.

In sum, the motor-collateral theories do not seem adequate to handle a substantial part of the emotion data. As we will see in succeeding chapters, there are a number of other phenomena that are linked by the individual difference consistencies that would be even more problematic.

Howard Leventhal (1980) proposed an interesting, if quite complex, theory that handles many of these phenomena, although it seems to me to require perhaps more complexity than necessary. His theory is basically like self-perception theory—compared with all the types I have discussed—in presuming that emotional experiences arise from emotional actions. He also emphasizes the constructive, perceptual nature of the process. However, in contrast to self-perception theory, Leventhal assumes that the emotional experience arises from a comparison of the peripheral feedback with information from a feed-forward mechanism arising from the systems that generate emotional behaviors. If the feedback matches automatic motor "scripts," then the comparator generates an emotional experience; if the match is with a voluntary motor pattern, there is no feeling. This comparison function is clearly useful in explaining many kinds of misattribution phenomena, since it provides some theoretical room for the behaviors to be "disqualified" if they are too deliberate and conscious. However, self-perception theory seems to do that job equally well. Leventhal's model also would have the same difficulties as other motor-collateral theories with phenomena such as the effects of gaze, or speeches, or wearing of eyeglasses—all of which are linked empirically to the effects of expressions.

NEUROPHYSIOLOGICAL MODELS

Many theories of emotional processes have focused on the parts of the brain that generate emotional responses. Two recent, particularly well-known examples are the following: the work of LeDoux (1996) identifying the amygdala's role in emotional activity, especially during fear, and Damasio's (1994) exploration of the role of the medial prefrontal cortex in emotional processes and judgment. As a good, card-carrying antidualist (but not a materialist—see chapter 11), I assume that everything that people do involves some area of the brain. I also assume that eventually our knowledge of brain circuitry will help us understand the functional processes, just as a better understanding of functions will help to guide the search for brain circuits. However, these theories all seem to operate at a different level of organization than the functional level that is the home ground of self-perception theory. Putting it crudely—undoubtedly too crudely—the brain location theories tell us where certain processes occur, but the functional theories tell us what processes must be located somewhere. For that reason, brain theories of emotion seem interesting in their own right but are not directly relevant to self-perception theory.

Damasio's theorizing is a notable exception, since he includes an explicit endorsement of what is essentially self-perception theory. His theory of brain organization includes the role of bodily feedback in generating feelings, which in turn guide decisions and judgments. His theory seems, then, to be Jamesian or self-perception theory, with the addition of some very specific, intricate psychophysiological specifications.

Classically Conditioned or Other Network
Connections Among Responses

One potential explanation for the various self-perception effects is that in ordinary circumstances, all the components of the emotional response occur together, none leading to any of the others. However, when only a part of that pattern is created, as in a self-perception experiment, it would evoke the remainder of the pattern. The capacity for one part of the pattern to evoke the others might come about because the response systems exist in a "network of connections" (Berkowitz, 1994). These connections might have been established because the constant association of each response type with each of the others leads to classical conditioning (or something like that) of each to the others. The result would be that any one might become capable of generating the others, in a laboratory or in real life.

Some features of the research support this classical conditioning—network hypothesis. For example, a number of studies that we have discussed already do show that behaviors do not just lead to feelings. The behaviors also often lead to other kinds of behaviors as well. A very large number of experiments have demonstrated that changing facial expressions produces corresponding changes in autonomic responses (e.g., Kleck et al., 1976; Kraut, 1982; Lanzetta et al., 1976). Furthermore, different facial expressions produce different patterns of autonomic response (Ekman et al., 1983; Levenson, 1992). The converse also occurs. Beginning with Schachter and Singer (1962), studies of the effects of arousal have found changes in expressive behavior as well (Olson & Ross, 1988).

Arousal manipulations often affect action as well, and indeed actions are often the dependent variables in studies of the effects of misattributions (e.g., Duncan & Laird, 1980; Dutton & Aron, 1974; Nisbett & Schachter, 1966) and transfer of excitation (Zillmann, 1996). Thus, all three of the primary behavioral components of emotion—expressive behavior, autonomic responses, and action—have been shown to affect each other.

Strikingly, often they actually seem to affect each other more than they affect feelings. In a number of studies, manipulations of expressions affected autonomic responses without producing significant differences in feelings (e.g., Colby, Lanzetta, & Kleck, 1977; Ekman et al., 1983; Vaughan & Lanzetta, 1981). Similarly, in misattribution studies, measures of action often change without any demonstrable change in feeling. For example, in two excellent misattribution studies of speech anxiety, the effects on how smoothly and easily people could talk were much greater than the effects of the misattribution on reports of feelings (Olson, 1988; Olson & Ross, 1988).

Two conclusions about the effects of these behaviors on each other seem reasonable. The first is very clear: that manipulating one of the three types of emotional behavior produces changes in the other two, as well as in feelings. The second is less certain but still probable: that these effects on behaviors can occur without any corresponding effects on feelings. Bem (1972) discussed a number of other examples, especially in the domain of attitudes.

At first glance, the observation that behaviors affect other behaviors more reliably than they affect feelings may seem somewhat embarrassing for self-perception theory. After all, the theory seems to require that if anything is affected, it would be feelings. However, the embarrassment is, in fact, on the cheeks of conventional, commonsense theories. Self-perception theory only predicts that *if* one feels an emotion, this feeling is derived from the behavior and its context. But there is no requirement that one must feel the emotion. Quite the contrary, it is obvious that we often perform emotional actions without the corresponding feeling. Sometimes we are simply too busy doing something else to notice that we are acting angrily or joyfully. People also seem to differ chronically in how readily they recognize their own emotional behavior. For example, individuals with type A personalities are relatively unaware of how often they react with anger or irritation to others around them. For self-perception theory, these failures to feel are not at all surprising.

On the other hand, the commonsense theory that feelings cause actions is seriously challenged by these observations. If the feeling of anxiety is the cause of speech "disfluencies" (Olson, 1988), then in order for any treatment of speech disfluencies to work, it must first change the experience of anxiety. But if we can influence the action without changing the feeling, then rather clearly, the feeling cannot be the cause of the behavior.

What is going on here? To make sense of these results we need to consider some additional facts about emotions. None of these is entirely without its skeptics, but most people seem to agree they are true.

1. Emotional expressions are substantially similar in all the cultures in which they have been studied (Izard, 1977). Repeatedly, investigators have found that pictures of expressions in one culture are readily recognized by members of very different cultures. Certainly cultures do impose "display rules" (Ekman, 1993) about when and how one can display certain emotions, but the raw materials on which these display rules work seem to be universal. Furthermore, even in cultures in which people appear to display very differently, they readily recognize each other's expressions.

2. Autonomic reactions are also the same among all cultures. Apparently, little research has examined the possibility of cultural differences in autonomic response, no doubt reflecting the plausible assumption that expressive behavior, action, and feeling are more amenable to cultural work than are autonomic responses. However, at least one study demonstrated cross-cultural similarities in autonomic responses to different emotions, including the specific patterning of responses for specific emotional feelings (Levenson et al., 1992).

3. Emotional action patterns have an equal consistency across human cultural groups, and many are shared by both humans and other complex animal species. The basic patterns of fleeing dangers, attacking rivals, pursuing mating partners, and grieving for lost loved ones can be seen everywhere in humans, and often in animals (e.g., Plutchik, 1980).

These three features of emotional reactions have led observers since Darwin (1872) to propose that emotional action patterns are first of all adaptive—they are useful in ensuring that the species will endure (e.g., Buck, 1985; Ekman, 1993; James, 1884; Plutchik, 1980). It appears that we humans, and many other species, come with some preprogrammed patterns of action that have adaptive utility. Some of these patterns may call for violent effort, and a part of these patterns is an autonomic response that, as Cannon (1936) long ago pointed out, mobilizes the organism for more effective "flight or fight." Because we are a social species, we have acquired a signaling system to ensure that our conspecifics know what we are doing. Finally, the kinds of situations that call out these patterns seem equally consistent across cultures (Mauro, Sato, & Tucker, 1992).

Actions, arousal, and expression are all parts of a coherent system of integrated responses to broad classes of events that are common in everyone's life. Since each pattern is a coherent, integrated whole, it is not surprising that inducing one part of the pattern could tend to call forth the other parts of the pattern. The evolutionary logic requires that the patterns have evolved together in order to work together as an integrated system. Thus, the fact that parts of the pattern evoke the other parts is not at all surprising.

If feelings were equivalent parts of these patterns, then we should expect that feelings would be generated at least as often as any other part of the system. But that is what the data suggest does not happen. The connections between the other components seem to be much more consistent and invariant than those between any of the behaviors and the feeling.

This pattern suggests that feelings are not just another one of the components of the emotional episode, but have a different status. Of course, self-perception theory makes precisely that assumption—that feelings are information about the behaviors that are going on, in relation to the context in which the person is acting.

In sum, the data on the relationship between behaviors and emotional feelings are inconsistent with common sense and strongly supportive of Jamesian/self-perception theory. Feelings have been demonstrated over and over to be the consequences of behaviors, not the causes. What we need is a theory that accounts for the effects of all emotional behaviors on emotional feelings that can accommodate the extensive individual difference results and that does not include implausible neurological links. The only remaining candidate seems to be self-perception theory. As we will see in the next few chapters, this is only the beginning of the reasons we should adopt self-perception theory. Self-perception theory seems to do the best job on the emotion literature, but it is virtually the only candidate for many of the other kinds of findings in other areas. In addition, self-perception theory certainly is the only candidate that can accommodate the empirical and theoretical links among all these areas.

SELF-PERCEPTION THEORY AND INDIVIDUAL DIFFERENCES

By now, individual differences in the effects of behavior on feelings have been described in exhaustive detail. At first glance, these differences seem to impose a serious limit on Jamesian/self-perception theories of emotion, which now seem to describe the behavior of only a part of the population. Indeed, these individual differences do constitute a major qualification of James's theory, which he assumed applied to everyone.

However, the individual differences that have been observed are completely consistent with the essential point of self-perception theory. At least with Ryle (1949) and Wittgenstein (1953), self-perception theory does not begin with assumptions about the relationship between behavior and feeling. Instead, self-perception theory begins with skepticism about purely "mental" origins of feelings, and the commonsense assumption that we know our feelings by introspection of some inner, private domain. The central premise of self-perception theory is that when we feel something we come by that feeling from logically public sources (Ryle, 1949). This means that we know ourselves from essentially the same sources as we know other people: I know that I am happy or sad in the same way that you know I am happy or sad.

The most unusual of the potential sources of self-awareness is perception of one's own behavior, and the bulk of the research has therefore concentrated on that possibility. This is the research that produces the most dramatic and intriguing results. However, situational cues are equally "public" kinds of information from which people might understand their own emotional state. Indeed, situational cues are probably at least as useful to us in understanding others as are the behaviors of others. Although I might be a bit uncertain of the meaning of your scowl, the insult you just received may be less ambiguous. Given the importance of situational cues in the perception of others, it would actually have been a serious challenge to self-perception theory if people did not respond to situational as well as personal cues in determining their own feelings.

Thus, far from being a problem for self-perception theory, the role of situational cues is actually completely consistent with the theoretical premises of that model. Our feelings arise from the same data that another person could use to identify our feelings: our actions and the circumstances in which we are acting.

SELF-PERCEPTION, CONSCIOUS, AND UNCONSCIOUS

In chapter 1 I asserted strongly that self-perception processes, and ordinarily the cues they work on, were not available to conscious awareness and self-report. Virtually everyone who has taken a self-perception-like position, from James onward, has at least implied that the processes were not conscious (Bem, 1972; James, 1884; Laird, 1974, 1984; Laird & Bresler, 1992). The reason is, of course, that no one ever reports experiencing self-perception processes occurring in their everyday experience.

Nonetheless, many observers have misunderstood the self-perception position to hold that these processes are conscious (e.g., Adelman & Zajonc, 1989; Capella, 1993; Fridlund, 1994; Stepper & Strack, 1993; Strack et al., 1988). There are probably two reasons for this confusion and misunderstanding, one deriving from some unfortunate rhetorical practices of self-perception authors, including myself, and the other from some easily misinterpreted empirical observations.

The rhetorical source for believing self-perception theorists were talking about conscious cues and processes is that often their (our) examples have suggested consciousness. The clearest instance of a misleading example is Bem's famous summary of how self-perception processes work. He suggested the parallel with how he would answer the question "Do you like brown bread?" to which he would respond to himself, "I must, because I eat it all the time." By putting this example in the form of a dialogue, he encouraged people to imagine similar internal dialogues that would probably be conscious. The advantage of such examples is that they capture clearly the kind of process one imagines is occurring, but the cost is the risk of implying the wrong view of the conscious status of the process. You are no doubt thinking at this moment of a number of places in earlier chapters in which I have done exactly the same thing, although in each case I tried to remember to follow my dialogue example with an explicit disclaimer. I have also done my bit in the past to confuse the issue by speaking of self-attribution rather then self-perception (e.g., Laird, 1974). Attribution processes are almost certainly no more conscious (Bargh, 1997) than I am asserting self-perception processes are, but many people have assumed a more conscious status for attribution.

Compounding the problem, however, is that many experimental operations confuse this issue, too. I have discussed a great many studies, especially in the many forms of misattribution, in which the key experimental manipulation consists of an explicit verbal statement by the experimenter about the sources of arousal or behavior. Clearly, in order to work at all, misattribution manipulations must be fully conscious at the time that they are delivered.

If one part of the information that generates a feeling is conscious, then it seems reasonable to expect that all the information, and perhaps the process by which the information is combined, is equally conscious. After all, we have many examples of processes in which everything seems to take place either outside or inside of consciousness. For example, when we look at a picture, we know that a multitude of hierarchically organized processes occur, beginning at the ganglion cells of the retina, which reach consciousness only with the final perception of the object. On the other hand, making a reasoned decision seems to consist entirely of conscious, deliberate consideration of all the options and their values. Thus, it seems reasonable to assume that there are only two kinds of process, one conscious and one unconscious, and that membership in these categories is all or nothing. In particular, if part of the process is conscious, then all of it must be.

The problem with this sort of plausible division of the psychological world is that very few psychological processes actually lie solely on one or the other side of the boundary. Certainly neither of my examples does. In the case of conscious decision making, a great deal of research reveals that we are not as rational, and certainly not as conscious of how we do it, as we like to think (Janis & Mann, 1977; Kahneman & Tversky, 1972; Nisbett & Wilson, 1977).

More relevant to the self-perception case is the hierarchical processing of visual stimuli, which is equally not neatly outside of consciousness. If we think of the process in a bottom-up way, it seems that a great many complex events go on without any input from "consciousness" before we reach the end. However, the processes are not solely bottom-up, nonconscious constructions. In addition, there are many "top-down" factors involved, in which conscious knowledge affects how the lower level, nonconscious processes work. As one example, consider Figure 5.1.

The visual processing of this figure is initially difficult for most people and comes to a halt at the level of knowing that it is a pattern of black

Figure 5.1. What is this a picture of? It is also an example of top-down processing.

spots on the page. But once one has the additional information that in the middle foreground is a spotted dog, with his head down and tail up, walking on a speckled leaf-strewn field, the picture gets processed quite easily. The information that this is a picture of a spotted dog is conscious, but we have no sense of how that information combines with the nonconscious information from visual processes to make the final experience. Note that after the dog is seen, we still have no more experience of how the dog percept is built from the scattered patches of dark and light. But we do know it is a dog.

This is, I think, an excellent analogue for the way in which misattribution information enters the self-perception process and interacts with the other, nonconscious information to produce a different kind of experience. Being told that the picture topic is a spotted dog and that one's arousal symptoms are due to a pill are both conscious, and both combine with nonconscious information about spots and body sensations to produce distinctive combinations of the conscious and nonconscious information: the percept of the dog, or the feeling of calmness.

The analogy between object perception and self-perception in misattribution contexts would be more satisfying if we knew more about either. That is, we really do not have a very clear understanding of the role of consciousness in object perception. Consequently, the analogy with the self-perception case is more interesting than illuminating. Thus, we are left with a new and genuine puzzle. How does material that is conscious combine (if indeed that is the proper metaphor) with material that is not conscious to produce some new conscious experience or action?

This is only one of the many puzzles that surround consciousness (Davies & Humphreys, 1993; Dennett, 1991; Searle, 1992). I will struggle a little more with these problems at the end of the book, when we have more pieces of the puzzle put in place, but this particular puzzle will not be solved, if indeed any are.

SUMMARY

Despite the many unanswered questions, we do have a reasonably clear conception of the emotion part of the picture. Emotional processes are innate, adaptive, complex integrations of action, autonomic preparation for action, and expressive signaling of the impending action sequence. Feelings are the recognition of these complex patterns. An emotional feeling is information about what actions are going on and plays the same role in subsequent activity as any other kind of information. That is, it provides guidance and defines the context of subsequent actions. Feelings do not, however, play the compelling, driving role that common sense assumes. In the last two chapters I will expand on the apparent role of feelings in action and on the model of human beings that it implies. In the next few chapters, I will examine some other kinds of feelings and the evidence that they, too, arise from self-perception processes.

NOTE

1. Actually, the latter terms were coined after *internal* and *external*, and they were designed to avoid the implication that the essential difference was inside or outside the skin.

6

Nonemotional Feelings: Confidence, Pride, and Self-Esteem

Early in my career, Ron Comer and I each happened to have similar, disturbing experiences. Ron had been working in a hospital emergency room, providing psychological support for people in distress. A young husband had rushed his wife to the hospital with a sudden illness. Ron was present when the doctor told the husband the totally unexpected news that his wife had died. The husband's first reaction was to ask something like, "What did we do to deserve this?" My experience was less direct, but of exactly the same form. A young friend was dying of terminal cancer and one day raised the same question with a friend, "I wonder what I ever did to deserve this."

Ron and I were struck with the injustice of the feelings that lay behind these Jobian questions. Bad enough that these terrible things had befallen these people, but to feel that they deserved it as well seemed a cruel twist of the human mind. Obviously these catastrophes happened purely by chance, and no one was to blame, least of all the victims. We decided to try to investigate this self-blaming in some way.

Starting from our somber beginnings, we finally hit on an experimental model that instead usually evokes some amusement when I have described it, either to classes or to groups of professionals. I am sure Ron has had the same reactions. We were seeking an experimental procedure in which people could be unexpectedly, and purely by chance, faced with enduring an unpleasant experience. Then we needed to be able to measure how they came to understand this experience, to see if a random bad event could change their view of themselves and perhaps make them believe they deserved their suffering. Since it was only an experiment, the event and suffering could not be very bad, of course.

In the final design (Comer & Laird, 1975), the participants were recruited for a study of psychophysiological reactions to various tasks. A few weeks before their actual participation, they responded to some questionnaires, including a self-esteem measure. When they arrived for the experiment, they were first reminded forcefully that they were of course free to terminate their participation at any time, for any reason. Then it was explained that we had a variety of tasks and that they would be randomly assigned to one. They would perform it, and then we would go into the adjacent room to obtain psychophysiological recordings of heart rate, skin conductance, and so on. Was that OK? Everyone said yes, of course.

Then we explained the two tasks and showed them the table at which they would sit to perform them. One was a simple weight discrimination task. A group of small weights were clustered on the table, and the participants' job would be to compare pairs of them to see which was heavier.

The other task was to eat a worm.

On the side of the table opposite the weights was a plate with a large night crawler on it, with a knife, fork, napkin, and glass of water. Then we explained that the task assignment would be determined by the flip of a coin, which genuinely was how they were assigned. Was this OK with the participant? It was.

Then the coin was flipped, and the participants were seated in front of their assigned task, either comparing little weights or eating a worm. They were asked to wait while the equipment in the next room was prepared, and they sat and contemplated the task for about 8 minutes. Then they were asked to fill out some questionnaires.

After about 10 minutes, the experimenter returned and, shamefaced, explained that he had made a mistake: The participants should not have been assigned to their task by a coin flip but rather should have been allowed to choose. So which task would they like to do? Not surprisingly, none of those assigned the weights chose to eat the worm. But very surprisingly, only about 20% of the participants assigned to the worm took the opportunity to escape their mini-fate. Eighty percent chose to eat the worm. As the title of the article says, they were choosing to suffer as a consequence of expecting to suffer.

What was going on here? We had expected that anticipating a negative experience, and moreover one that they had freely chosen to expose themselves to, would lead them to try to "make sense" of their fate. Three potential ways to make sense of the worm eating seemed possible. One would be the kind of thinking that inspired our research—they might decide that they were bad people who deserved to suffer. A second, almost reverse, was that they were heroes who were suffering for science. The third was that they might decide that worms were really not so disgusting after all. The questionnaires that they had filled out 2 weeks previously and after the 8-minute waiting period were actually measures of these three kinds of thinking so that we could detect changes.

As it turned out, somewhat fewer than a third of the participants changed in each of these ways, and if they changed in one way, they did not change in either of the others. Furthermore, it was clear that it was these changes that led to the choice of worm eating, since the 20% of the participants who did not change in any of the three ways were the 20% who also did not choose to eat the worm when offered the choice.

An additional set of conditions provided a further test of the role played by these changes in thinking about one's self and worms. The beginning of the experiment was the same, with participants randomly assigned to the worm, contemplating it, and responding to the questionnaires. The change was when the experimenter returned and confessed his "error," at which point he said that the participants should have been in one of the other two conditions, the weights or the self-administered shock condition. In that condition, he explained, they would give themselves a series of painful shocks using the shock generator that sat on a table in the experimental room.

If they had made sense of their impending worm eating by deciding that they were heroes for science, or that they were bad people who deserved to suffer, then the shock choice would be appropriate. However, if they had decided that worms were not so bad to eat, they would have no reason to choose the shocks. Again, somewhat fewer than a third of the participants showed each kind of change, and the outcome was precisely as expected—only those who had decided they were heroes for science or bad people chose the shocks. Those who had not changed in any of these ways did not choose shocks. Most important, those who had come to see the worms as not so bad also did not choose the shocks.

Clearly, most of the participants were changing their views of themselves, or of worms, in response to finding themselves facing a disgusting task. It was absolutely clear that they were assigned to the worm by chance, since they watched the coin flip. That is, the assignment was random and senseless, but nonetheless they tried to make sense of it by changing their views of themselves or the worms. Only about a third changed in the way that we originally imagined, lowering their view of themselves and thus viewing themselves as deserving of suffering, but still, most changed in some way.

Many people react to descriptions of this study with assertions that they would never have agreed to participate in such a study. Perhaps. However, our experience was that refusals were remarkably rare. Sixty-two people began to participate, and only two refused, one before the task assignment and one who was assigned to the worm refused after the waiting period but before the worm choice was offered.

Perhaps the participants did not really believe they would have to eat the worm? Of course that cannot be entirely ruled out, especially because we did not in fact let them eat the worm. After they had made the final choice to eat the worm, or experience the shocks, we ended the experiment and debriefed the participants. However, one participant revealed how seriously he took the task by cutting the worm into bite-sized pieces during the waiting period. (We have never been sure whether or not he took a bite while he was waiting.) During debriefing, none of the participants revealed any doubts that they would be expected to eat the worm. In a somewhat similar study (Foxman & Radtke, 1970), participants were told they would eat a large caterpillar. These caterpillars are a genuine delicacy in some parts of the world and had been prepared for human consumption, but they looked quite disgusting to Americans. All these participants were allowed to eat the caterpillar and did.

Two of the three ways in which people made sense of the worm eating were to change directly their self-concepts and self-esteem. Some people thought of themselves as making sacrifices for science, and they endorsed items that described themselves in more positive terms after the worm experience. In the opposite direction, the people who had devalued themselves changed on explicitly self-evaluative items. They became more negative about their own attributes.

How does self-perception theory explain these changes? At first blush, the manipulations would seem to involve situational cues, since the situation changed to become one of unpleasantness and at least mild suffering. However, two features of the procedure make it seem more likely that the cues people responded to were personal. First of all, the procedure included repeated reminders that the participants could leave the experiment if they chose and frequent queries about whether the participant was willing to continue. As a result, the participants probably perceived themselves, at least tacitly, as having acted to put themselves into the position where they might face the worm-eating outcome. In addition, their assignment to the worm-eating condition was a property of them. That is, it was a personal cue in the same way that, for example, wearing eyeglasses or being assigned to make a particular speech was a property of the participants in those studies.

Of course, we could have been more certain of this interpretation if we had measured responses to personal cues in this experiment. Unfortunately, at the time it was run, we were just beginning to recognize the importance of these individual differences and so did not include that measure. In a much more recent study that also involved changes in self-esteem, we remedied this oversight.

Before we leave the worm-eating study, I would like to return to the far more serious phenomena that originally inspired our research. Many commentators have observed that people often blame themselves for chance disasters that befall them. Women who have been raped often reproach themselves for not having acted in some way to avoid the rape (Janoff-Bulman, 1992). Similarly, people who are suffering from terminal illnesses often wonder why they have deserved their fate. These phenomena and our worm-eating study suggest that at some basic, unrecognized level people do not genuinely accept the possibility of pure chance. We seem to need to believe that nothing happens for no reason at all, that everything makes sense, and that the balance is such that bad things only happen to bad people.

Mel Lerner (Montada & Lerner, 1998) has studied this phenomenon extensively, as it applies to our evaluation of others and our understanding of the misfortunes of others. He has demonstrated a widespread human tendency to blame victims for their own misfortunes, a behavior he attributes to our need to believe in a just world. A just world is one in which bad things do not randomly fall on good people. Thus, just world thinking is reassuring because if the world is just, then we need not fear the disasters that befall others. We can avoid disaster by behaving well, so that we will not deserve suffering.

The defensive aspect of just world thinking does not make much sense when we turn to our understanding of ourselves. After all, if we have already suffered a misfortune, believing that we deserve it will not necessarily make us less susceptible to that or another disaster. Instead, I suspect that the mechanism is more basic still, a powerful tendency that all of us have to perceive good things as "naturally" belonging with other good things. As a result, we tend to remember other people as "consistent" packages of attributes that are all good or all bad (Crockett, 1974). This tendency is so strong that we often are unable to recall reliable information about another person if that information is inconsistent with our initial impression. This same process seems to apply to our impressions of ourselves. If we automatically assume that good "goes with" good, and bad "goes with" bad, then if a bad thing happens to us, we must be bad.

Whether it was Just World thinking or evaluative consistency (or whether in fact these two are not really different), the clear demonstration here is that our actions and their consequences are experienced as evidence of our natures. At least some aspects of our self-concepts seem to arise from the consequences of our actions, even if the consequences were unforeseeable or the result of pure chance.

SELF-ESTEEM, SOCIAL COMPARISON, AND RESPONSE TO PERSONAL CUES

A very different kind of impact of our activities on our self-concepts was discovered by Kathy Wilcox, who noticed an interesting experience she frequently had while looking through one of the conventional women's magazines. Initially, she was interested in the advertising pictures that make up the bulk of the content. After a few minutes, however, she found that she was feeling uncomfortable and would stop looking at the magazine. She realized her reaction was to the pictures of superslender models in the photographs. As a number of previous studies have demonstrated, women are made uncomfortable by the standards embodied literally, if not very substantially, in the models who appear in the media (Crouch & Degelman, 1998; Pinhas, Toner, Ali, Garfinkel, & Stuckless, 1999; Posavac, Posavac, & Posavac, 1998). However, this observation contains an apparent paradox: Why would these magazines still exist if all women reacted with discomfort? One possibility is that the effects occur only among some women, not all.

The models depicted in advertising can serve two potential functions for an observer, as identification objects and as standards in social comparison processes. If someone identifies with the models, then she should feel relatively good for the moment because she can, in effect, imagine herself as like the model. On the other hand, if the models function as social comparison standards, then the vast majority of women will find the comparison disturbing.

Social comparison and identification certainly differ in a number of ways, but one of the most obvious is in how aware one is of one's own body. In social comparison, one needs to be simultaneously aware of one's self and the standard, whereas in identification, one need only be aware of the standard. Indeed, awareness of one's self should interfere with identification. This difference would imply that women who were more responsive to personal cues, and hence more aware of their own bodies and their personal attributes, would be more likely to engage in social comparison, whereas those who were less responsive to personal cues would be more likely to identify.

To test these hypotheses, Kathy Wilcox (Wilcox & Laird, 2000) asked women to inspect one or the other of two sets of pictures of women. One set was taken from women's magazines and consisted of the usual superslender models. The other set was taken from catalogs for clothing for women with "fuller" figures. The women in these pictures were actually of about normal weight and certainly did not look overweight.

After viewing their assigned picture set, the women responded to a self-esteem scale and a body satisfaction measure and provided an open-ended description of their feelings while viewing the pictures. Finally, they responded to a paper-and-pencil version of the expression manipulation procedure to determine the level of their response to personal cues.

The women who were less responsive to personal cues apparently identified with the women in the pictures. When the women who were less responsive to personal cues viewed the superslender models, they reported higher self-esteem, higher body satisfaction, and more positive emotional reactions than did those who viewed the normal-weight women. The exact opposite occurred among the women who were more responsive to personal cues. They reported significantly lower self-esteem, lower body satisfaction, and more negative emotions if they viewed the pictures of superslender models.

In sum, two studies have demonstrated changes in self-esteem and self-regard as a consequence of self-perception kinds of manipulations. One of these also explicitly links the self-esteem changes to the network of findings on individual differences in cues employed in self-perception.

CONFIDENCE AND APPEARANCE STEREOTYPES

Confidence is a close family relation of self-esteem, although perhaps it is a bit more temporary and hence an even more likely candidate for self-perception processes. One lever into the self-perception of confidence is through stereotypes. Self-perception theory asserts that we know our own attributes in the same way that we know about the attributes of others. If that is the case, then stereotypes about appearance that affect our judgments of others should affect our judgments of ourselves as well. Certainly stereotypes are powerful determinants of our judgments of others. For example, more attractive people are routinely judged to be smarter and more humorous and to have performed better at a variety of tasks (Dion, Berscheid, & Walster, 1972). Tall people are more likely to be seen as leaders; conversely, people who have achieved leadership positions are judged to be taller than they actually are (Jackson & Ervin, 1992; Montepare, 1995; Wilson, 1968). Unfortunately for experimental design purposes, most stereotypical aspects of appearance, such as attractiveness or height, are not easily manipulated. Fortunately, one is. This is the stereotype that people who wear glasses are more intelligent. To demonstrate this stereotype, a number of studies have employed the same basic methodology: Photographs are taken of the same person with and without glasses, and then judges rate the person's intelligence. Routinely, the person is judged to be more intelligent when wearing glasses (Harris, 1991).

Joan Kellerman (Kellerman & Laird, 1982) asked whether this stereotype would apply in self-perception as well. The experiment was a self-perception equivalent of the photograph study described in the previous paragraph. Subjects were recruited for a study of the effects of a new lens material developed by a well-known optical company in a neighboring town. The subjects were told that there was some concern that the new plastic might interfere with perceptual performance. The subjects were asked to solve embedded figures problems and respond to half of the Binet vocabulary test, with half of subjects wearing nonprescription glasses and the other half not wearing glasses. (No subjects ordinarily used eyeglasses. If we had removed the glasses of someone who needed them, we would not have been surprised if they felt they were less successful at a perceptual task.) A mirror was present in the room, although while the subjects worked on the tests, they were not looking into the mirror. After each part of the testing, the subjects rated how well they thought they had done.

Wearing glasses did not affect the subjects' actual performances on either vocabulary or embedded figures. However, consistent with the stereotypes, when subjects were wearing the glasses, they judged their performance to have been significantly better and felt much more confident. People were "stereotyping" themselves on the basis of their own appearance.

One's appearance is only arguably an action. On one side, we do not really do anything to be attractive, or to wear glasses, and certainly we do not do anything to be tall (except perhaps to eat our vegetables when we are young). In another sense, however, we do have to work a bit at being attractive, or as attractive as most of us can manage, we do put on our glasses, and so forth.

But whether or not appearance is properly called an action, it is definitely an example of a personal cue as defined here. That is, appearance is like a smile or a slouched posture in being something that we would know about another person only if we observed him. We could not know how a person looked without observing him, just as we could not know what he was doing.

If appearance is a source of personal cues, then we would expect that only subjects who were responsive to personal cues would be affected by their appearance. That was exactly what happened in this study. Response to personal cues was determined in a separate procedure in which subjects' expressions were manipulated and their emotional feelings assessed. Wearing glasses increased feelings of confidence and judgments of better performance only among those subjects who were more responsive to personal cues.

All subjects were told initially that the glasses might interfere with their performance. Thus, the subjects who were more responsive to personal cues, and who felt they were performing better with the glasses on, were responding in a way opposite to their expectations. These expectations constitute a clear example of a situational cue about how people would be expected to feel about their performance. Consistent with this analysis, the subjects who were identified as *less* responsive to personal cues, and hence presumably more easily influenced by situational cues, did in fact rate themselves as significantly less effective with the glasses on. Those who did not respond to personal cues did respond to the situational cues.

In sum, our appearance affects how we feel about ourselves, in the same way that how we act affects our feelings. In both cases, we know ourselves in the same way that others would know us.

CONFIDENCE AND BEHAVIOR

Twenty years ago, Jim Hamilton (Hamilton & Laird, 1981) ran a study that produced results that probably would not be too surprising to athletes in these days of trash talking. He reasoned that self-perception theory would predict that boasting would make one more confident. His study was simplicity itself: People were given somewhat unusual tasks to perform, ones with which they were unlikely to have any experience or any grounds for evaluating their performance. Then they were induced either to brag or to behave modestly in describing their performance to another person. Finally, they were asked to judge how well they had actually performed. Bragging increased their ratings of their own performance.

A similar effect was observed in a study of self-presentation (Baumeister, Hutton, & Tice, 1989) in which one member of an interaction pair was asked to "brag" or to present him- or herself very modestly. This behavior in turn affected how the naive partners in each pair behaved, making them act less or more modestly to match. The interesting self-perception result was that this shift in self-presentation by the naive participants also changed their reports of their self-esteem. Nonconsciously adopting the bragging or modest style of their interaction partners led them to feel correspondingly better, or worse, about themselves.

Another study of confidence and self-perception might have been designed by my grandmother. Indeed, both my grandmother and the military seem to have had some intuitive appreciation of self-perception theory. My grandmother often urged me to "stand up straight, don't slump." And in my brief encounter with the military, it *required* that I stand straighter. Both my grandmother and the U.S. Navy probably simply wanted me to look more confident and competent (Mehrabian, 1968, 1969), but both also seem to have had some sense that if I acted more confidently and competently, I would also feel more confident. In a direct test of the hypothesis shared by my grandmother and the military, Kate Kuvalanka and others (Laird et al., in press) asked participants to stand normally, especially erect, or in a slumped posture with curved shoulders and head dropped to their chest. While in these postures, participants made speeches that they believed would be videotaped and shown to others, supposedly as a test of the effect of a speaker's posture on the effectiveness of a persuasive speech. After making the speech, they were asked how confident they felt about their ability to persuade others. The normal and erect postures did not differ significantly, perhaps because the majority of our participants had better normal posture than I do. But the slumped posture significantly reduced their confidence in their performance.

In a second study reported in that paper (Laird et al., in press), Kuvalanka adopted a posture manipulation that was invented by Stepper and Strack (1993). In this procedure the manipulation is very subtle, and none of their participants or ours recognized its purpose. The procedure consists of asking participants to perform a writing task (in our study it was solving anagrams) on one of two work surfaces. The ostensible purpose was to explore "ergonomic working conditions." One of these work surfaces was a normal height for a seated worker; the other was very low, below the level of the chair on which the participant sat. The result was that in the low-surface condition, the participants had to bend over into a curled-up posture, with their hands between their knees. After completing the anagram task, they were asked to rate their confidence in their performance. When working in the curled-up posture, they were significantly less confident, although in fact their anagram performance was the same in the two conditions.

In both of the posture and confidence studies, we also measured response to personal cues by a variant of the expression manipulation procedure. In the first study, we employed a highly schematic, undisguised expression manipulation procedure that we had never previously used, and there were no differences between those who were identified as more or less responsive to personal cues. However, the problem seems likely to have been with the expression manipulation procedure, and therefore we changed to a more elaborate expression manipulation procedure in Study 2. With this procedure, the usual and expected effect occurred: Postures affected confidence only among people who were more responsive to personal cues.

In sum, in five studies confidence was affected by standing or sitting positions, by boasting, and by appearance. In the two studies with the best procedures, we also found that the effects on confidence were related to effects of expressions on emotional feelings. Thus, once again the same process seems likely to have been involved in both the emotional and the confidence self-perception processes.

In a closely related study, Michael Fishbein (Fishbein & Laird, 1979) examined the effects of a very different kind of behavior on evaluation of one's performance. He began with the observation (no doubt in response to some unfolding political scandal of the day) that a particularly dramatic piece of information about others was the recognition that they were trying to hide something. If we know someone does not want us to know something about them, then we already know it must be bad. He then applied the usual self-perception premise, which is that the way we know ourselves is like the way that we know others. The result was the hypothesis that if we hide something about ourselves from other people, we will come to think the hidden information is somehow less positive.

In order to provide his participants with some ambiguous information, Michael gave them a series of complicated perceptual and intellectual tasks, chosen because pretesting had indicated people could not evaluate their performance on them. The test battery was described as evaluating intellectual ability and creativity. After a brief delay, ostensibly for scoring the tests, he returned and told each person that his or her score was some arbitrary number, such as 114, chosen because pretesting had also indicated that people were uncertain whether this was a good or bad score. Without leaving time for any questions about what the score meant, he then explained, "The experiment was actually on the effects of expectation on performance, and you were in the no-expectation control group. Usually we have a confederate administer the expectation, but our confederate has the flu today. Would you be willing to administer the expectation to the next subject, who has to be told what to expect?" (This was an adaptation of the original 1959 Festinger and Carlsmith dissonance experiment instructions.) Then each participant was assigned to either the reveal or the hide condition. Those in the reveal condition were asked to have a brief conversation with the other participant in which they should casually slip in the information about their score. Those in the hide condition were told to talk about the experiment but to be very careful not to reveal their score, even if asked directly. The other "subject" was actually a confederate, blind to the participants' assigned condition, who asked a standardized series of questions, adapted to follow naturally the course of the conversation. The discussion/questioning culminated in a direct question about the real participant's score, if it had not already been revealed.

Finally, the confederate and participant were separated, and as part of a postexperiment questionnaire, the real participants were asked how well they thought they had done on the tests. The results were exactly as self-perception theory predicted: People who hid their score judged their performance to have been relatively mediocre, whereas those who "bragged" about their score thought they had done quite well.

Once again, it would have been nice to have examined separately the responses of people who were more or less responsive to personal cues, but this experiment, too, was run before the importance of cue response had become clear to us.

POSTURE AND PRIDE

Sabine Stepper and Fritz Strack (1993) originally developed their posture manipulation for a study of pride. Pride differs from confidence primarily in its temporal orientation. Confidence looks forward, to future performance, or at least to future judgments about performance. Pride looks backward, to performances that are already completed and evaluated. As a consequence, Stepper and Strack's procedure was a bit complicated, because the participants had to be provided with a performance about which they could feel pride. The important part of their procedure was that these performances were carried out either on the low work surface or on a normal-height work surface. And the result was as we would expect: Participants who worked on the low surface reported significantly less pride than participants who worked at a normal height.

SUMMARY

In this chapter I have examined a group of studies on the self-perception processes that seem to lead to various self-evaluative feelings of confidence, self-esteem, and pride. In every case, we have seen that acting as if one is confident and proud makes people feel confident and proud. In addition, if one is by chance required to face an unpleasant experience, or to compare one's self unfavorably, then one's self-esteem falls. Or, at least, these conclusions are true of the people who are more responsive to personal cues. Whenever we have tested for the impact of personal cues, we have found that the effects are predictable from cue response. These connections with cue response suggest strongly that the same kinds of processes are at work in generating emotional experiences from emotional behaviors, and in *generating* feelings of self-esteem and confidence from confident behaviors.

Confidence, self-esteem, and pride are feelings, and they are close to emotions, but most emotions theorists would not include them among the prototypical emotions. Consequently, self-perception theory has been extended a little away from one of its home domains, emotions. In the next few chapters we will get even further away, to include eventually most kinds of feelings.

7

Motivation and Hunger

Almost all the research I have discussed thus far was directed at emotions, or inspired by work on emotions. In pleasant contrast, two bodies of research in the general area of motivation are direct applications of self-perception principles, with little influence from emotions research. The two topics of self-perception research on motives are on the overjustification effect and on hunger, eating, and dieting.

OVERJUSTIFICATION AND MOTIVES TO ACT

The overjustification research is based on a principle we have already seen applied numerous times to produce misattributions. The principle is that behavior produced naturally as part of an emotional or other feeling episode may be "disqualified" as a source of feelings if it is attributed to some other source. For example, Nisbett and Schachter (1966) gave people a placebo pill that was supposed to produce increased arousal and then asked them to endure painful electric shocks. The result was an increase in pain tolerance, presumably because participants had attributed the arousal produced as part of the pain experience to the pill, rather than the pain.

Note that this research highlights one of the features of self-perception theory that perhaps has not been emphasized sufficiently in the earlier chapters: Feelings are not derived solely from behaviors. Rather, the feelings represent a kind of "interpretation" of both the behavior and the context in which it occurs. Or, more directly, the content of feelings, what the feeling is "about," is the relationship between action and context. Smiling when uncoerced may be happiness, but the same smile in response to a photographer's request is not happy. Gazing into another's eyes with no

125

other aim is experienced as passionate love, but gazing in response to the experimenter's request to count eyeblinks has no implications for affection. And arousal occurring automatically is part of the pattern of anger or fear, but arousal that is experienced as due to a placebo pill has no effect on our feelings. Thus, we can manipulate feelings either by inducing people to perform feeling-relevant actions or by changing the context in which they interpret their actions.

Deci (1971) seems to have been the first to apply this idea to motivation. He began by asking participants to play an interesting game. In a second segment they played it again, with half the participants being paid a substantial amount of money for doing so. Finally, in a third segment, they all played it again without pay. Those who were paid to play in the middle segment showed a much larger drop-off in performance. Presumably, all the participants initially played because of feelings of intrinsic interest, but the payment had led them to "conclude" (usual disclaimer: not consciously) that their behavior did not represent their actual interest or motivation—hence less play in the final, test phase.

This effect was labeled "overjustification" by Lepper, Greene, and Nisbett (1973), who added an important qualification to the basic effect. In their study, nursery school children drew pictures with a magic marker, a presumably intrinsically interesting activity, under one of three reward conditions. In the first condition the children expected to receive a reward (a fancy "good player" award) for drawing, in the second they received the reward unexpectedly, and children in a third group received no reward. Only the expected reward produced a decrement in performance, during a later "free play" period, as compared with the other two groups. The overjustification effect seemed to be due not to the reward itself but to the implication that the reward was the reason for the behavior. Only if the participants knew a reward was coming when they performed the behavior would it undermine their intrinsic interest in the task.

As a further demonstration that the way the reward was understood was critical, Michael Ross (1975) demonstrated that even an anticipated reward would have no impact on task enjoyment if the reward was not salient, or if the child was distracted from thinking about the reward even when it was salient. In order to undermine motivation for a task, the child had to be able to notice the reward and able to think (at least nonconsciously) about the contingency of reward on performance.

Rewards affect the quality of the activity as well as its persistence. Amabile and her colleagues (Amabile, 1979, 1983; Amabile, Hennessey, & Grossman, 1986) demonstrated that reward reduced the creativity of the productions of children and adults. Creativity has been notoriously difficult to measure, or even define, and clearly most standard creativity tests at best capture only some small component of what we usually mean by creativity. Amabile's solution cleverly circumvents this problem by avoiding definition. She enlists experts in whatever the appropriate field—artists, if the productions are artistic, for example—and asks them to judge the quality of the productions. Although no explicit definition of quality is provided, these judges agree far above chance, indicating that they are employing some consensual, if implicit, standard. Using this kind of criterion, Amabile and her associates have demonstrated repeatedly that creativity declines when performance is extrinsically motivated by reward.

As one might expect, the impact of these studies was substantial, especially in quarters where extrinsic rewards and punishments for performance are common, such as business and education. These results seem to suggest that paying people for their work or giving students grades might undermine the intrinsic interest that workers and students are presumed to bring to their tasks. Within the psychological research community, overjustification was equally controversial, since it seemed to contradict a cardinal principle of behaviorism: that rewarding an activity should increase its frequency, not reduce it.[1] As a result, a multitude of studies have explored other aspects of overjustification, with all the controversy one might have anticipated.

A number of qualifications of the basic reward-behavior link have been identified. For example, the overjustification effect occurs only when the initial level of interest is high (Loveland & Olley, 1979; McLoyd, 1979). This conclusion hardly seems controversial, since it would be particularly difficult to undermine an already low level of motivation, but lots of good ideas look obvious after someone else has proposed them. Similarly, rewards only undermine motivation when they are experienced as the reason to perform at all, and motivation is unaffected if the reward is experienced as information about one's performance (Deci & Ryan, 1985). In fact a reward that is experienced as information that one has performed well will often increase the duration and intensity of activity. People can even be trained to avoid the impact of reward on their intrinsic motivation (Hennessey, Amabile, & Martinage, 1989).

Enough research on overjustification has accumulated so that two substantial meta-analyses were conducted not too long ago (Cameron & Pierce, 1994; Eisenberger & Cameron, 1996; Tang & Hall, 1995b). Perhaps not surprisingly, they reached somewhat different conclusions, although the differences seem to reflect theoretical perspectives rather than substantial differences in findings. The most important question about overjustification is whether it is a real effect. In both reviews, the classic conditions for producing an overjustification effect produced the expected performance decrements. These were the studies in which three conditions were met: (a) the participants were led to expect rewards before performing the behavior, (b) the rewards were tangible, not just verbal praise, and (c) the rewards were independent of the participants' level of performance. These are, of course, the exact set of conditions originally designed by Lepper et al. (1973) and duplicated in a large number of subsequent studies.

Both reviews also demonstrated that verbal feedback, which usually takes the form of praise, increases time and quality of later performance.

This latter effect probably reflects that verbal praise is usually experienced as information about one's performance, not an inducement for performing.

Following these agreements, the two reviews seem to have taken slightly different directions and reveal something of the complexities of meta-analysis. Eisenberger and Cameron emphasized the different patterns of results that appear for measures of subjective task evaluation, or "liking," as opposed to duration of actual task performance. Measures of subjective task evaluation generally were unaffected by tangible, expected rewards. The only two factors that affect reported liking for the task are verbal rewards and quality-dependent tangible rewards, both of which increased liking. This is hardly surprising, since we have already seen in my brief review of the early research that anything that tells someone they have done a good job increases their attraction to the activity. The meta-analytic results include, of course, these studies, among many others like them.

Tang and Hall (1995a) began in a different place, with level of initial interest in the task as the first cut, and found, as noted earlier, that only when initial interest is high does one get a decrement due to overjustification. After that, they explored other variables, arriving at the conclusions noted previously. Tang and Hall did not, apparently, separate studies according to whether the dependent variable was task performance or subjective liking.

The differences in the two meta-analyses may say more about the uncertainties of performing meta-analyses than about overjustification. Because Eisenberger and Cameron (1998) did not analyze for level of initial task interest, the remainder of their findings are potentially confounded with or moderated by interest level. Similarly, because Tang and Hall did not distinguish types of dependent variables, their results are subject to the corresponding uncertainties. Apparently, nothing is quite so important in conducting meta-analyses as a good theory to guide the choice and order of consideration of the variables.

Eisenberger and Cameron (1996) were eager to defend reinforcement techniques for behavior change. Perhaps for that reason, they argue that the "detrimental effects of reward occur under highly restricted, easily avoidable conditions" (p. 1153). They find that reward reduces interest or performance when the rewards are tangible, expected, and independent of performance. As noted earlier, these are of course exactly the conditions that Deci, Lepper, Greene and Nisbett, and many others, first defined. So, despite their commitment to reinforcement theory, Eisenberger and Cameron are in agreement with their critics about the reality of the overjustification effect and the conditions under which overjustification is most likely to occur.

The remaining disagreement hinges on how common these conditions may be in schools and workplaces and how easily the conditions can be avoided. Fortunately for our purposes, we do not have to solve that problem. It is enough to recognize that a nice, clear self-perception effect has been demonstrated in the motivation literature.

One feature of these results deserves highlighting: Overjustification more powerfully and consistently affects behavior than it does self-reports of feelings. We already have seen this in a number of places, and as I noted earlier, this is a particularly embarrassing pattern for the commonsense conceptions of the feeling-behavior link. If the feelings play some role in instigating the behavior, then behavior change should occur only when the feelings have previously changed. On the other hand, self-perception theory (as well as reinforcement theory) assumes that the feelings are the result of the behavior and its context, and that often people may be distracted or occupied with other thoughts and not "recognize" and experience their behavior/context pattern.

HUNGER AND EATING

Two or three times a day, most of us have an experience that seems to contradict the essential core of self-perception theory. We get hungry and then eat until our hunger is assuaged. These daily experiences seem to provide constant proofs that our feelings are the causes, and not the results, of our behavior.

The fact that hunger seems so clearly to affect behavior is not inconsistent with self-perception theory, however. The essential point of self-perception theory is that feelings of any sort, including hunger, do not arise from some purely "mental" source but rather from some logically public kind of information. The principle advantage of self-perception theory is that it locates feelings firmly in the natural world, as an integral part of the same fabric as bodies, and without any dramatic separation from the physical world. In this kind of naturalistic view of feelings, we would certainly expect feelings to have some utility, some impact on subsequent behavior. As I said in chapter 1, self-perception theory definitely does *not* view feelings as epiphenomena. I will take up this issue at length in chapters 10 and 11.

In this section I will review a great deal of research that identifies the variety of cues that produce feelings of hunger. All the cues for hunger are public in the philosopher's sense. This does not mean, of course, that they are easily observed or recognized in other people. However, they are in principle observable and are difficult to observe only because they occur within the body, or involve the movements of chemicals through the body. But as we will see, the mechanisms that produce feelings of hunger fit very smoothly into a self-perception perspective.

INTERNAL AND EXTERNAL CAUSES OF EATING

Much of the interest in the mechanisms of eating arises from attempts to understand eating disorders. Twenty-five years ago, Stanley Schachter moved on from emotions to propose an explanation of obesity that stimulated a great deal of research. His theory eventually began to seem too simple and is no longer seen as an adequate explanation of obesity or other eating disorders (Lowe, 1992; Rodin, 1981). However, some of the main implications of his theory seem as reasonable today as they did then, so a brief review of the history of this theory and the research it inspired seems worthwhile.

Schachter observed that there seemed to be two kinds of reasons that people ate. One was "internal": the state of their organism—how long since they had eaten and thus how empty their stomachs were, and/or the level of their blood sugar, or, we now know, the levels of various chemical "messengers" (Woods, Schwartz, Baskin, & Seeley, 2000). The other kind of reason for eating was a wide collection of external stimuli, such as the sight, smell, or taste of attractive foods and the knowledge that it was time to eat. Schachter (Nisbett, 1968a, 1968b; Schachter, 1968; Schachter, Goldman, & Gordon, 1968; Schachter & Gross, 1968) and Rodin (Schachter & Rodin, 1974) proposed that people varied in how strongly they responded to internal and external cues for eating. In our society, people who were most responsive to external cues were at risk for becoming obese because they lived in a world filled with external cues for eating. At least in cities, the streets are filled with restaurants and stores trying to attract eaters, and the media are filled with ads for foods. Even at home we are not safe from the allure of external cues, since most homes in the West have plentiful supplies of food waiting just around the corner in the kitchen.

Schachter's theory predicted that manipulations of external and internal cues should have very different effects on people who were of normal weight or overweight. Schachter, Nisbett, and Rodin, and their colleagues, conducted a long series of clever, intriguing studies that demonstrated such differences.

For example, in one study (Schachter & Gross, 1968) both normal-weight and overweight subjects were recruited for an experiment involving "taste tests" of a purportedly new kind of cracker. In fact, the taste test was a subterfuge to make available an unlimited supply of food—the crackers—and the amount eaten was the dependent variable. The independent variable was the time that appeared on a clock on the wall of the room in which the subjects were doing their tasting. In fact, the clock was rigged so that it would run faster or slower than normal. The subjects were given a series of other tasks to fill up enough time so that the clock could plausibly be manipulated so it could be half an hour fast or slow relative to the real time. And the real time was arranged to be either before or after the subjects' normal meal time. Thus, there were two independent variables—the apparent time on the clock and the real time perceived by the subjects' stomachs.

As was expected, the normal-weight subjects ate primarily in response to stomach time. After their usual eating time, they ate more than the group whose members were eating before their usual time, regardless of the time on the clock. For the overweight subjects, the result was the reverse: They ate in response to the clock. If the clock said it was dinnertime, they ate more, whatever their real state of deprivation, but if the clock said the time was before dinner, they ate less, even if they were in fact late for dinner. In other words, their eating was under the control of their beliefs about whether or not it was dinnertime.

A clever parallel example in real life was also observed. Schachter and his colleagues (Schachter et al., 1968) asked Air France pilots to report on the effects of transatlantic travel on their eating patterns. The normal-weight pilots reported they experienced considerable difficulty, because they were often arriving in New York or Paris when they felt hungry and wanted to eat, but it was not mealtime locally, or they arrived when every-one else was eating, but they had no interest. The overweight pilots re-ported much less difficulty. Caricaturing the results, we could say that they ate whatever everyone else was eating, wherever they were. If they had just had dinner on the plane, but it was dinnertime again, they would eat another dinner. But if they had not eaten for a long time, and it was past dinnertime locally, they could cheerfully go without eating.

Notice that in both of these studies, the overweight people did not nec-essarily eat more than the normal-weight people. When external cues in-dicated that it was not time to eat, they ate less. This result was consistent with Schachter's argument that becoming overweight was a result of the interaction between the properties of the person and the nature of the sit-uations in which we find ourselves in our society. Someone who ate in re-sponse to external cues such as the time of day would become overweight only in an environment in which external cues were plentiful.

Another kind of external cue is the appearance of food. As French chefs have known for a long time, the appearance or "presentation" of a meal contributes to the diner's enthusiasm. Nisbett (1968b) examined the ef-fects of the sight of food on overweight and normal-weight subjects by ma-nipulating how much food was in view. The subjects were told that as part of a study of metabolism they would be "preloaded" with food and were asked to eat as many roast beef sandwiches as they liked. They were told that an adjacent refrigerator contained dozens of sandwiches and that if they finished those on the plate before them, they could get more.

There were two experimental manipulations. The first was the amount of time since the subjects had last eaten—for some it was only a little while, but other subjects had not eaten since the previous day. The second ma-nipulation consisted of varying the number of sandwiches on the plate—either two or four.

The normal-weight subjects ate primarily as a consequence of the time since they had last eaten. The subjects who had eaten recently ate a sandwich or two, no matter how many were on the plate. The normal-weight subjects who had not eaten since the previous day ate more than two sandwiches; if there were only two on the plate, they went to the refrigerator to get more.

In contrast, the overweight subjects tended to "clean their plates," but no more. When there were four sandwiches on the plate, they ate four, even if they had recently had lunch. If there were only two, they ate the two sandwiches, but did not go to the refrigerator for more, even if it was

18 hours since they last ate. Nisbett suggested that in this last case, eating the sandwiches also meant consuming the cues that were instigating the eating for the overweights: the sight of the food. Once the food was eaten, there were no more cues for eating.

A charming real-life study of the impact of the sight of food was conducted in a "moderately expensive French restaurant" (Herman, Olmsted, & Polivy, 1983). Diners in the restaurant were assigned to two categories of weight, either "chubby" or heavier, or normal weight or slimmer. The dependent variable was dessert choice. For half the subjects, the experimental manipulation of visual cues consisted of having a dessert available for inspection in the waitress's hand at the time the subjects made their dessert selections. Overall, overweight subjects were not more likely than normal-weight subjects to eat dessert. But those who were shown a dessert were significantly more likely to choose the dessert they saw, whereas the normal-weight subjects' choices were unaffected by the showing.

A third frequently studied external determinant of eating is the taste of food. A number of studies have shown that both normal-weight and overweight people eat more when food is particularly tasty, but the impact of taste on amount eaten is greater for overweight people. Overweight people are particularly responsive to sweet tastes (Cabanac, Duclaux, & Spector, 1971). Overweight people also continue to prefer sweet tastes even after being given a "preload" that is sweet tasting, whereas normal-weight subjects seem to find the sweet taste cloying and stop preferring it (Esses & Herman, 1984).

These studies, and many others like them, demonstrated that overweight people responded more strongly to external cues. Other studies showed that overweight people were less responsive to internal cues, at least as produced by "preloads" of food in their stomachs. A standard manipulation consists of asking subjects to first consume a high-calorie milk shake, followed by an opportunity to eat freely as much as they wanted. Normal-weight subjects usually eat less after being preloaded, whereas among the overweight, the reduction in eating caused by the preload is characteristically less or none (e.g., Pliner, 1973).

The studies described so far and many others like them confirm the first, most basic point of Schachter's theory of obesity. Overweight and normal-weight people do differ in their responses to external and internal food- and eating-related cues. However, all these studies examine the person's current behavior and do not demonstrate that externality *causes* obesity.

THE CAUSAL ROLE OF EXTERNALITY

Charming and elegantly simple as the externality theory of obesity was, it appears to have been wrong. A number of strands of evidence all suggest that, although overweight people are often more responsive to external cues, many normal-weight people are also more responsive to external cues. Furthermore, normal-weight people are not reliably more responsive to internal cues than are overweight people (Rodin, 1981). Of course, one potential reason is relatively obvious: Many people diet to control their body weight, so that perhaps many people whose weight is normal would be overweight without the dieting.

Indeed, one contributor to the confusion in this literature may simply be the transition from one cultural epoch to another. When Jay Wagener and I first used body weight as an experimental variable in the late 1970s (Wagener & Laird, 1980a), we could recruit a group of overweight college students relatively easily. Within 5 years, very few college students qualified as overweight, and they had become so self-conscious about their weight that we felt it was impossible to raise issues of body weight explicitly. For example, we did not feel comfortable telling participants in research that they had been chosen because they were overweight. The newspapers and media have made much of the "fattening" of America recently, but, at least at Clark University, anyone who might have been overweight in previous eras is now firmly dieting. (Indeed, it appears that just as the nation moves toward greater and greater disparities in income between those at the top and those at the bottom, it is simultaneously moving toward greater differences in body weight as well.)

An alternative view of the externality and body weight linkage was proposed by Herman and Polivy (1975), who suggested that it was the dieting itself, the exercise of restraint, that produced the excessive response to external cues. They demonstrated that most of the characteristics previously identified in the obese were actually better predicted by restraint. Restrained eaters also showed a particularly distinctive pattern of behavior: If they were given a high-calorie "preload" of a milk shake or a piece of cake, they then ate much more than non-preloaded restrained eaters. Nonrestrained eaters, in contrast, ate less in response to the preload (Polivy, 1998). This pattern seems to demonstrate two phenomena. First, the restrained eaters seem to be insensitive to the internal cues that their stomachs were full of high-calorie food. Second, once their restraint had been broken by the preload, they seem to have "decided" they might as well eat a lot. Consistent with this cognitive interpretation of the impact of preloads, there need not be many calories in the preload. As long as the restrained eaters believe there are lots of calories, they feel free to eat unrestrainedly (e.g., Knight & Boland, 1989). They may even be released from their restraint by the belief, produced by a false-reading scale, that their dieting has not been successful (McFarlane, Polivy, & Herman, 1998). In this study, the participants were told they weighed more or less than they really did, and then they were given an opportunity to eat all they wanted. The restrained eaters who were told they were heavier ate significantly more, although since their moods were also undermined by this manipulation, we cannot be sure it was a simple effect of release from restraint. Perhaps they were eating as consolation for their failure to diet successfully.

Presumably individuals who are restraining their eating become hypervigilant about eating threats, especially external cues. Although they may be able to maintain their restraint, they do so at the cost of thinking about food and eating (Polivy, 1998). Lowe (1992) suggests that repeated attempts at restraint may actually cause a reduction of response to internal cues, although a single loss of weight does not increase externality (Rodin, Slochower, & Fleming, 1977). Lowe argues that during dieting the person "practices" ignoring the internal cues for eating and then, when the diet fails, as almost all do, practices ignoring internal cues for satiety as well. The final outcome may be unresponsiveness to internal cues, and hence an overresponse to external cues.

I have just skimmed the surface of a very large literature on eating and weight control, but fortunately for our purposes, this is another area in which we do not need to resolve the complexities of large research literatures. The reason is that whatever the causal role of externality in obesity may turn out to be, there seems to be little disagreement that people who are restrained eaters (which of course includes many overweight people) are definitely more responsive to external cues. And these differences in response to external and internal cues are similar in their impact to the differences I have discussed at length already between people who are more responsive to personal or to situational cues. These parallels support a self-perception view of hunger and eating and also suggest a simple empirical prediction.

Externality in Eating and Response to Other External Cues

The parallel between "externality" in the eating literature and cue response in self-perception research is most directly tested by studies in which people's response to other self-perception tasks is related to body weight, dietary restraint, or some other measure of externality in eating. The first study to compare the effects of a self-perception manipulation on overweight and normal-weight people was performed by Leslie Zebrowitz (MacArthur et al., 1980). She and her colleagues manipulated facial expressions of emotions and found that overweight participants were unaffected by the expression manipulations, whereas normal-weight people reported the usual result, feelings that were consistent with their expressions.

Another study showed the same effect (Comer & Rhodewalt, 1979): Overweight participants were unaffected by their expressive behavior. Comer and Rhodewalt also found that the overweight participants did not change their attitudes in the induced compliance paradigm. In contrast, normal-weight participants changed in both of those procedures. Here we see three distinct classes of personal cues, facial expressions, counterattitudinal speeches, and internal bodily cues for eating related in one study.

A third example of this sort was the study mentioned previously, in which Jay Wagener (Wagener & Laird, 1980a) looked at the effects of body weight on response to a foot-in-the-door manipulation. Overweight and normal-weight participants were asked to volunteer for a lengthy, boring-sounding experiment. Before this request, half of each group had been asked to fill out a brief questionnaire for the same experimenter. This early request led to higher levels of agreement, but only by the normal-weight group. Presumably, the overweight participants were insensitive to the cues from their initial volunteering behavior and so did not show the usual foot-in-the-door effects.

Barbara Edelman (1984) applied this kind of thinking directly to issues of body weight and eating. She predicted that three quite different factors would contribute independently to determining body weight. Two of these were concerned with the probability that a person would ingest too many calories. She reasoned that, following Schachter's theory, perhaps one might eat too much because one ate for external reasons. A second factor leading to excess consumption would be eating as a solace for emotional discomfort. Finally, a third factor that would determine body weight would be the amount of calories a person expended in exercise.

Edelman measured energy expenditure in two ways, by a pedometer and by an exercise diary. She measured "emotional" eating by a questionnaire she developed that assessed the likelihood a person would eat for any one of a number of emotional reasons, such as anxiety, boredom, depression, and so forth. Finally, she measured response to personal cues in two ways, by the usual expression manipulation procedure and also by the Rod and Frame Test for field dependence.

She found that all three of these factors contributed to predicting body weights. The less people exercised, the more they ate for emotional reasons, and the less they responded to the expression manipulation procedure, the more likely they were to be overweight.

For our immediate purposes, the most important of these results was the relationship between body weight and response to the personal cues of the expression manipulation procedure. This was the fourth example of a study showing that people who were overweight were less responsive to personal cues in self-perception manipulations.

In chapter 3, I described a study of placebo responses of people who were more or less responsive to personal cues. People were asked to approach a snake after taking a placebo pill described as increasing or decreasing arousal symptoms. People who were unresponsive to personal cues showed conventional placebo effects, whereas those who were more responsive to personal cues had a reverse placebo effect: They reported less fear and approached the snake more closely when told the pill would arouse them (Duncan & Laird, 1980). Two nearly parallel studies demonstrated similar effects of placebo messages on hunger in restrained and unrestrained eaters (Heatherton, Polivy, & Herman, 1989). Participants were given a pill that ostensibly would make them feel full or hungry, and then were given an opportunity to eat ice cream. Restrained eaters who were presumably most responsive to situational cues showed the usual placebo response: If told the pill would make them feel hungry, they ate more, and if told it would make them feel full, they ate less. Unrestrained eaters showed exactly the reverse pattern, eating less when told they should be feeling full.

In chapter 3, I also described a number of studies that demonstrated that increases in arousal produced increases in the intensity of emotional responses. Some other studies, including Joan Duncan's study cited in the previous paragraph, showed that people who are unresponsive to personal cues from their expressions are also relatively unaffected by arousal changes. If overweight and/or restrained eaters are unresponsive to personal cues from arousal, we would expect them to be unaffected by arousal manipulations. That is exactly what was observed in a study by Polivy, Herman, and Warsh (1978) in which restrained and unrestrained eaters were given either caffeine, which increases arousal, or a placebo and then described their emotional reactions to positive and negative slides. The unrestrained eaters responded to the emotional slides with stronger emotions if they had received caffeine, whereas the restrained eaters actually responded with less intense emotions. Clearly, the arousal produced by the caffeine was not mediating the emotional feelings of the restrained eaters.

Overweight people also seem to be more responsive to situational cues that are not directly related to eating or hunger. For example, in a study that showed the usual overresponsiveness of the overweight to the sight of food cues (Herman et al., 1983), overweight people were also more responsive to social influence (see also Rodin & Slochower, 1974).

In sum, at least nine studies have identified empirical links between people's response to personal cues in self-perception manipulations and their body weight or restrained eating status. People who are overweight, or of normal weight because of restraint, are more responsive to cues from their situations about how they should be feeling and unresponsive to personal, emotional cues. The feeling of hunger clearly seems to emerge from the same sorts of self-perception processes that also generate feelings of emotions and attitudes.

Many of the studies discussed in this section were inspired by the observation that the internal-external distinction in the eating and body weight literature seemed to be identical with the personal-situational distinction in self-perception research. In fact, when we first observed the differences between personal and situational cues, we toyed with using the internal-external labels, but they seemed too casual and imprecise. The problem lies in defining the boundary between inside and outside. For example, taste is an external cue, presumably because it is a property of the food. However, food is tasted only after it is inside the mouth. The simple geographic distinction implied by the external-internal labels seems inadequate.

SUMMARY

In this chapter I have discussed two substantial bodies of literature on motivational feelings. The research on overjustification derives explicitly from self-perception theory and continues to support that theory. The research on hunger, eating, obesity, and restraint has its own, somewhat different, historical origins but winds up equally supportive of self-perception theory. Of course, a multitude of specific motives have been studied in detail, but in ways that are orthogonal to the concerns of self-perception theory.

NOTE

1. Self-perception theory grew directly out of Skinnerian behaviorism (Bem, 1965) and directly gave birth to the overjustification effect, so it is particularly ironic that overjustification should be seen ultimately as somehow in opposition to reinforcement theory (Eisenberger & Cameron, 1996).

8

Cognitive Feelings of Knowing, Familiarity, and Tip of the Tongue

What was the name of your third-grade teacher?
Who was Franklin Roosevelt's vice president?
What is the name for "A navigational instrument used in measuring angular distances, especially the altitude of sun, moon and stars at sea"?

Brown & McNeill, 1966

Perhaps the answers to all these questions were clear, and even before the answers came to mind you were sure that you knew them perfectly. Instead, perhaps you knew immediately that you did not know the answers to some of these questions, and no amount of thought would yield an answer. But perhaps for a moment or two at least you could not answer one or more of them, but you were sure that with a little more struggle you could. As we say when this kind of thing happens to us in everyday life, the answer is "on the tip of my tongue." Feelings like these are the focus of this chapter. They are feelings rather than judgments, in the sense that they come to us immediately, without conscious awareness of any supporting evidence. We just know that we know something, or we do not. Or, we know something but cannot think of it now. And we also do not know how we know that we know these things. These feelings are different from those discussed in previous chapters in that they are about our cognitive operations, our memories and knowledge, rather than about our emotional or motivated behavior. But as we will see, these feelings, too, fit the broad self-perception paradigm.

Four distinct phenomena can be identified among these cognitive feelings.

1. *Feelings of knowing.* A group of interrelated research programs have examined the "meta-memory" feelings that we know or should know something. In all these the target of remembering is factual, declarative knowledge about the world—"facts." The meta-memory question is, "Do I know this or that fact?" In the case of tip of the tongue (TOT) feelings, the question we are implicitly asking ourselves is usually, "Will I come up with the answer eventually?" In

formal research, the most common way of measuring "feeling of knowing" is to ask people whether they think they would recognize the correct answer in a list of choices.

2. *Feelings of familiarity.* The second group of research programs focuses on a different kind of memory content, about our own lives and experiences. An extensive program of research has looked at how we come to feel that we have encountered some objects previously, or if instead they are new in our experience. Another body of research looks at how we know where and when we learned something. Did we hear it from a reliable source? Did we experience it ourselves? Was it something we actually heard or did, or was it something we imagined, dreamed, or heard someone else describe?

3. *Heuristics.* The third body of research involves a different approach but reveals some of the same phenomena. This research examines the feelings arising from some nonconscious processes that help us "arrive" at decisions and judgments. The largest body of work in this area goes under the rubric of "heuristics," which are automatic processes that generate estimates about probabilities, estimates that are experienced as feelings.

4. Finally, we will look briefly at research on feelings of boredom. Boredom is a feeling we all know well, but what is less obvious is that feelings of boredom seem to reflect problems with attention. Although this research fits only loosely with the other topics in this chapter, it does not really seem to fit better anywhere else, and I include it because some is work carried out by one of my friends and me.

FEELINGS OF KNOWING

A cautionary and/or apologetic note: The field of meta-memory is extremely active these days, and the literature is correspondingly large and growing. I have not attempted to deal with the breadth of the literature, much less the technical complexities of an extremely technical and complex field of research. Instead, I have just described enough of the research to make clear how it fits with the general self-perception view of feelings, a view that is common among meta-memory researchers (e.g., Johnson, Hashtroudi, & Lindsay, 1993; Kelley & Jacoby, 1998; Metcalfe, 1998).

Tip of the Tongue

William James has been the star of this book, so we should not be surprised that he discussed the tip of the tongue phenomenon in his usual insightful way (James, 1890). He captured the two essential features of the experience, beyond its compelling feeling that we *will* remember, any minute now. The first is that TOT feelings have a great deal of content—we know that the navigational instrument is not a compass, that our third-grade teacher had beautiful red hair, that Roosevelt's vice president became president and decided to drop the atomic bomb (or at least one of his vice presidents did that). The second and undoubtedly more important observation about the tip of the tongue is that all these related memories, hints, and impressions are likely to be true. (*My* third grade teacher really did have red hair, and I thought she was beautiful, although I still cannot quite remember her name.)

Brown and McNeill (1966) developed a clever technique to make this unpredictable experience accessible to systematic observation. They gave people lists of word definitions, including the definition of *sextant* in the first paragraph (you were wondering, weren't you?), and asked them to produce the word. With 49 such definitions, all but 9 of 56 participants reported at least one instance of TOT. Brown and McNeill asked a series of questions about these experiences, such as the number of syllables in the word and the letter the word began with,. They found that the participants' guesses about these matters were not always correct but were accurate far more than one could reasonably expect from chance. For example, they guessed the initial letter correctly 57% of the time.

That leads us to the question of why we can access partial but correct information, and how our memories work in order to make that possible. Before presenting the currently most reasonable explanation, I want to begin by clearing away two alternative models that seem at first glance to be attractive but that are contradicted by a great deal of data.

Our commonsense theory of memory suggests that the answer or name we seek is stored somewhere in our minds, along with various associated bits and pieces of information. If so, it is not surprising that we can retrieve some accurate pieces. Perhaps our attempts to come up with the target word have scraped up some portions of the word, including literally the first letter. According to the model implicit here, eventually we will manage to catch enough pieces so the whole word can be produced.

A more contemporary model suggests that our memories are organized like libraries or computer memories, with two separate kinds of information (Hart, 1967). One kind of information is the actual material; to find that material, one first consults a list of the material available, like a library catalog or computer directory. Following this model or analogy, feeling of knowing might be produced by consulting the directory without accessing the files described there (Koriat, 1995). In the tip of the tongue situation, in which the "directory" seems to be telling us we have this information in storage, something else may be, for the moment, preventing us from accessing the file, and since the directory and files are separate systems, we could have a directory entry that pointed to an inaccurate, or even empty, file. (Notice that this model fails to account for the accuracy of the parts that are retrieved. This problem can be ignored, because the model faces much more difficult challenges.)

Unfortunately, these simple explanations of tip of the tongue feelings as partial access to the target information in memory will not do. The most obvious demonstration of why is a series of studies by Schwartz (B. L. Schwartz, 1998; B. L. Schwartz, Travis, Castro, & Smith, 2000), which demonstrated that tip of the tongue feelings can be generated by questions that do not have any answer. For example, Schwartz asked people, "What was the last name of the only woman to sign the Declaration of Independence?" and "What is the name of the only living reptile that flies?" (To avoid potential embarrassment to readers, I hasten to add that no women signed the Declaration of Independence, nor are there any reptiles that fly. Fortunately, as author, I have no obligation to reveal my own feelings when I first encountered those questions.) These and questions like them often produced tip of the tongue feelings, but clearly these feelings must have been based on something other than partial retrieval of the correct answer or its directory entry.

We are left with an apparent contradiction now: TOT feelings sometimes are entirely illusory, suggesting that they arise from a process that has little to do with actual remembering. However, the associated, partial information that we retrieve is usually somewhat accurate, suggesting that TOT feelings are related to accurate recall. Resolving that contradiction requires a substantial revision of the commonsense view of remembering.

Note that both the partial retrieval and the directory ideas share the assumption that somewhere, at least most of the time, there is a genuine memory store, filed away and awaiting access. This kind of memory store is assumed to contain all the information, organized as it will be reexperienced during recall. Remembering consists of some kind of privileged access to these memory traces. Such access is described as "privileged" in that it is unavailable to anyone else. The privilege is that of the owner only.

The commonsense theory of emotional experience is a similar example of this kind of privileged access model. In contrast, self-perception theory does not assume privileged access to some inner mental state and has generated all the evidence discussed thus far. The evidence locates the source of feelings in public cues and therefore raised major doubts about privileged access. The same kind of skepticism arose concerning the feelings of knowing.

Feeling of Knowing

The most obvious way to demonstrate that feeling of knowing was not a direct reflection of the stored memory was to identify operations that affected one without affecting the other. But first we need to imagine some factors that might play a role in feeling of knowing that were not something like a directory of memory contents. The obvious answer was something to do with the act of remembering itself.

We have already seen one of the most obvious potential candidates, the kinds of partial information that emerge in tip of the tongue experiences and that are more or less accurate. Perhaps the more information that comes to mind as one tries to recall, the stronger the feeling of knowing— even if the amount of information is not enough to generate the actual answer or if the information is not actually accurate.

Asher Koriat (1993, 1995) has demonstrated that indeed the more information that comes to mind, the greater the feeling of knowing. A typical study to test this idea begins with a collection of questions such as, "What is the name of the jazz player known as 'Bird'?" and "Who composed the *Unfinished Symphony?*" These questions differ in how likely they are to generate an attempted answer and in how likely the answer is to be correct. After participants had answered or not, they were asked to estimate the probability that they would recognize the correct answer in a later multiple-choice repetition of the same questions. This estimate of future recognition was the feeling-of-knowing measure.

Koriat reasoned that the questions that generated more answers were probably also producing more partial cues, and hence should produce stronger feelings of knowing. Of course, if the participant also gave the answer correctly, then the result would be ambiguous. Yet if the participants reported stronger feelings of knowing to these questions even when they got the answer wrong, then it would be clear that the feeling of knowing was not a reflection of actual correct knowledge. That was the case. For example, very few people offered an answer to the "Bird" question, but 83% of those who tried an answer were correct ("Charlie Parker"). In contrast, 94% tried an answer to the *Unfinished Symphony* question, but only 9% got it right ("Schubert"). Nonetheless, the feeling of knowing was much higher for questions like the "Schubert" question. Apparently if something—even something incorrect—comes to mind, you feel a strong feeling of knowing, even though in fact you *do not* know.

Parallel with the kind of results that Brown and McNeill found in their tip of the tongue study, Koriat also found that guesses about initial letters, number of syllables, and other features of the answer were above chance in their accuracy and, more important, were associated with greater feeling of knowing. The more partial cues that were generated, the more participants felt they knew when they were unable to come up with any answer. And their feelings of knowing increased even when the partial cues they generated were in fact wrong—the first letter of *sextant* is not a *b*, but thinking it is gives you a stronger feeling of knowing.

The partial information that leads to feelings of knowing need not be concrete properties of words, like the initial letter or number of syllables. In another study, Koriat (1993) asked participants to learn supposed Somali translations of words with positive and negative connotations. Later, participants were asked to remember the meaning of these Somali words and, if they failed, to judge whether it was good, bad, or no response. Following the guess about the evaluative content, the participants gave a feeling-of-knowing judgment. First of all, when they made a guess about whether the word was good or bad, they were correct more than chance. Their feeling of knowing was higher when they made correct judgments than when they made none at all, but it was also higher when they made incorrect judgments. In short, anything that people remember makes them feel that they know the answer, even a vague sense that the answer is positive or negative, and even when that sense is wrong.

Another property of the retrieval process that might affect feeling of knowing is the speed and ease with which information comes to mind. Koriat (1993, Study 2) found that, indeed, faster retrievals, even of inaccurate information, led to stronger feeling-of-knowing judgments. Apparently, when trying to remember feels easy and quick, we tend to feel we must know whatever it is we are trying to remember.

Which of these two factors, the amount of information retrieved or the ease of retrieval, is most important? In many designs the two are confounded, so that it is impossible to say which one is the active ingredient in feelings of knowing. Traci Higgins (1999) found a way to put the two in opposition by adapting a technique used in studies of self-concepts (Schwarz et al., 1991). Her participants were asked to list items relevant to a question that shortly would be the basis for feeling-of-knowing judgments. For example, the question might be, "What is the small animal that catches and eats snakes?" Before seeing this question, the participant had to name a number of small mammals. Sometimes the requested number would be large, and sometimes it was small. When the number was large, the participant would have retrieved a great deal of information potentially relevant to the question. However, it would have been relatively difficult to come up with enough examples, so the participant would have lots of information but a strong feeling of effort. In the small-number condition the person would have retrieved little information, but it would have felt easy. When experienced ease and amount of information were put in opposition in this way, the results were complex, but both contributed to the feeling of knowing. In general, ease was more important than amount of information. If we can think of something relevant easily, or we can think of lots of relevant information, we think we know, even if in fact we do not.

Another component of the retrieval process is an obvious candidate for the same kind of influence on the feeling of knowing: the question that starts the process off. The more difficult to comprehend the question is, the less likely we are to know the answer. How that might work is clear enough if we think of a question so complex and obscure that we do not understand the words in the question. We would be quite sure that if we cannot understand the question, we certainly will not know the answer. Thus, our feeling-of-knowing judgments would be very low.

Of course, we cannot simply ask painfully difficult questions. Not only will the question be difficult to process, but also the answer will be equally complicated, and differences might reflect answer properties rather than question processing. The solution is to manipulate the ease of processing of the question in a way that is unrelated to the knowledge of the target information. The easiest way to do that is by priming. In priming manipulations, a participant is given some sort of reminder of something that will shortly be useful to know. This kind of preliminary encounter will increase ease of processing. For example, it is quite well established that if individuals read a list of names of cities, including *Washington* and later are asked to name the person who built the house called *Mount Vernon,* they will answer more easily. Or, if they read *cat* and shortly are asked to fill in the a blank before the letters *ouse*, they are more likely to say *mouse* than *house*.

To make the interpretation of the effects of these reminders clearer, the priming is often done in a way that leaves the participant unaware of having been reminded. For example, in some studies the prime is presented before the actual stimulus, but so rapidly that the person is unable to detect it. In others the priming is accomplished by including a reminder stimulus among a variety of apparently irrelevant similar items.

In the preceding examples, the answer to a question (or at least the general domain of the answer) was primed. Alternatively, we could prime the question in a way that makes the question easier to understand but does not help with the answer. For example, we might use the same prime as before—a list of U.S. cities. But now the question would be something like, "What is the population of Washington?" Notice that the prime would make the question easier to read, but it does not add any useful information for answering the question.

When features of the memory question are primed, the question is read and understood more easily and quickly, and this increase in ease of processing has the effect of increasing feelings of knowing. However, since the prime is of the question, not the answer, neither the accuracy nor the accessibility of the answers is increased. It is as if we operated on the assumption that if the question feels easy, then we must know the answer (Metcalfe, 1996). On the other hand, priming the target, like the earlier examples, increases the likelihood that the answer will be retrieved immediately but does not affect how easily we process the question. Hence, it does not increase feelings of knowing, even though we actually do know more.

Another, similar source of feelings of knowing is tied to the cue rather than the target. Often the cue defines a general area of knowledge; for example, the question about Washington's house has something to do with American history. A history buff is likely to experience stronger feeling of knowing for questions in her area of expertise, such as the question about Washington, than for questions in some other area (Connor, Balota, & Neely, 1992).

In sum, much research has shown that our feelings about our own ability to recall facts are not a direct reflection of whether we will actually recall those facts—now, in the future, or ever. Instead, these feelings of knowing, including tip of the tongue feelings, arise from events during the process of trying to remember. If we remember some plausibly relevant part-facts about the target, then our feeling of knowing will be strong. The more part-facts remembered, the stronger the feeling of knowing. If the facts come easily and quickly, and also if our comprehension of the question itself is easy and quick, then our feeling of knowing will be stronger. And if the domain of knowledge is familiar, or we know many related facts, then our feeling of knowing will be stronger. All of these are quite independent of whether the part-facts we recall are accurate, or whether in actuality we ever will recall the target.

The overall pattern suggests an "accessibility heuristic" (Koriat, 1995) that automatically and unconsciously follows something like an inferential process. To repeat the hazardous practice of modeling nonconscious processes with explicit language, it is as if we said to ourselves, "If I can understand the question so easily, remember this much that seems relevant this fast and easily, then I must be able to remember that target later." (Repeat of the usual disclaimer: No one does or should believe that this kind of internal monologue actually takes place.) That is, what we are seeing here is a self-perception process in which the person perceives the fluency of his partial memory. This perception of fluency is experienced as a feeling. The person's feeling in this case is an estimate of what his future memory attainments will be.

Earlier I mentioned an apparent contradiction that needs clarification: Feelings of knowing are not reflections of what we actually do know, but they are still accurate. Feelings of knowing are accurate in two senses. First, they are reasonably good predictors of later actual memory performance; second, when partial information is retrieved, it is usually reasonably accurate. The answer to the apparent contradiction seems to be that the information that feeds into the accessibility heuristic is usually associated with accurate recall in everyday life (Koriat, 1995). Questions that induce illusory tip of the tongue feelings or that have been primed are relatively rare except in psychological experiments. In ordinary life, easier understanding of the question, quicker access to some hints of an answer, and some beginnings of a response are all reflections of earlier interaction with the information, and hence are likely to be associated with memories that we will be able to recapture. That is, our feelings of knowing are predictive of later actual knowing because the feelings are based on phenomena that happen to be related to knowledge, but the feelings are not incomplete access to that knowledge.

Finally, before leaving this topic, I want to emphasize that the reason for discussing this research in a book on self-perception is because the evidence is clear that feelings of knowing are often "perceptions" of parts of the process of remembering that are diagnostic of but quite independent of actually knowing.

Judgments of Learning

Sometimes people are asked about their feelings of knowing at the time that they are learning new material, not at some later time. The form of these judgments may be identical, but the early queries are usually called *judgments of learning*. Note that judgments of learning have considerable practical importance, since in many everyday life circumstances the person may (or even must) decide how much to study. As we might expect, judgments of learning, like feelings of knowing, are subject to various influences that are unrelated to actual learning or later performance. For example, in one study (Dunlosky & Nelson, 1992), participants learned to associate random pairs of words. They were told that later they would be given the first part of the pair as a cue and asked to report the second, or target, word. After studying the list, they were asked how well they had learned each pairing. In one case they made this judgment while looking at both the cue word and the answer, and in the other they saw only the cue word. Immediately after the learning, these two conditions produced equally strong judgments of learning, which in fact were not very accurate at all. Apparently, because participants had just finished studying the pairs, they still remembered the two words and could not estimate how much their performance would decline with time. After a delay, they again made judgments with either just the cue word or both cue word and answer in view. With both in view, even after a delay, their judgments of learning were high and highly inaccurate. With the delay and with only the cue word to look at, however, they were probably quite aware of how much they had already forgotten, and now their judgments of learning were more realistic and accurate predictors of actual later performance. The point of this study was that people were unable to recognize that the reason the cue and target association seemed so easy was because the pair was sitting on the screen in front of them. More generally, judgments of learning were based on the illusory ease with which the participants "examined" their knowledge of the pairing.

A similar effect was observed by Jacoby and Kelley (1987), who provided one group of participants with a list of anagram problems and their solutions, while another group just saw the problems. The second group recognized that the problems were quite difficult, no doubt because they were experiencing their own struggles and frequent failures. The first group, on the other hand, believed the problems were easy, and that they would have been able to solve them readily. Presumably, they underestimated dramatically the impact of seeing the solutions on their apparent ability to come up with the solutions on their own.

In sum, the research on feeling of knowing, judgment of learning, and tip of the tongue shows a consistent theme: What we believe about our memories is not a reflection of what we might actually remember. Instead, we infer (unconsciously) the state of our memory from the characteristics of our remembering activities. Feelings about knowing are, like other feelings, perceptions of our ongoing activities.

FAMILIARITY AND OTHER EPISODIC MEMORIES

A useful, if somewhat controversial, distinction among memory systems is between semantic and episodic memory (Tulving, 1985). Semantic memories are for facts, such as the definitions of words and answers to questions that were the focus of the feeling-of-knowing research discussed in the previous section. Episodic memories are for events in our lives. So, when you recall that one of Roosevelt's vice presidents was Harry Truman, that is a semantic memory, whereas your recollection that you encountered that example earlier is an episodic memory. We could talk about knowing that this example was used earlier and then could talk about feelings of knowing about that knowledge, but instead the meta-memory of episodes is usually discussed under the rubric of "familiarity."

One might naturally suppose that when individuals are asked to judge whether they had encountered some object previously, they might recall their previous interactions with the object and that this recollection would guide their judgments about previous acquaintance. By now we have reviewed enough research on cognitive feelings so that any reader will suspect that such a direct-access process is unlikely. In fact, the familiarity literature contains the same pattern that we have seen in the feeling-of-knowing studies: Judgments of familiarity are not always based on actual episodic memories of earlier encounters with the stimulus object. Instead, feelings of familiarity often reflect the ease of processing of the cue or question.

A particularly clever study demonstrated this effect (Jacoby et al., 1989). The participants read on a computer screen a list of names that included both ordinary, nonfamous people and some minor celebrities. The participants' task was to judge which names were famous and which were not. Before each name appeared on the screen, there was a brief flash that was too rapid for the participants to be able to identify its contents. Part of the time, this flash was the name that would shortly appear on the screen for judgment. This kind of early flash of a subsequent stimulus is called a *self-prime* because the prime and the target are identical. This kind of priming has the effect of making reading of the subsequent word proceed more rapidly, even when the prime is too fast to be identifiable. The result of this manipulation was that primed, nonfamous names were likely to be judged as famous, apparently because the prime-induced ease of processing was mistakenly attributed to prior acquaintance with the name. As a further test of this attributional, self-perception-like explanation, Jacoby et al. lengthened the duration of the priming stimulus until it was recognizable. Now the effect was the reverse: Famous names were judged to be nonfamous, apparently because the participants attributed their ease of processing to the prime rather than to actual fame.

As a further test of the role of fluency in judgments of fame, Jacoby and his colleagues (Jacoby, Woloshyn, & Kelley, 1989) influenced ease of processing and the participants' understanding of its sources in a different way. Participants read a list of names, none of which were famous. Some read this list by itself, while the others had to perform the additional simultaneous task of monitoring a stream of numbers to identify a particular pattern. The result of the second task was that participants were not able to pay full attention to the list of names. Or, in the jargon of the trade, their consciousness of the list-reading task was divided. Later they read a new list of people, some of whom had appeared on the earlier list and others that had not, some of whom were famous and others that were not. When they had read the first list under divided attention, they were likely to select those names as famous, even when they were explicitly told that every name on that first list was nonfamous. Presumably, the earlier reading of the names led to faster, easier processing when reading the new list. If participants had been able to devote full attention to the first reading, they also might have recognized the first reading as the source of their greater fluency. But when they were distracted by the parallel task, the fluency remained without the recognition of its source. The "accessibility heuristic" would have concluded that these names had been encountered often in real life, and hence were famous.

Fluency has been varied in other ways, with identical results. For example, in a study by Jacoby and Whitehouse (1989), words that had been previously read were presented in a list with new words, and the participants' task was to identify the old words. The words were presented with a dot mask covering them so that they were slightly hazy looking and more difficult to see. The result was that words presented in a hazy way were more likely to be judged as new, whereas words presented more clearly were likely to be judged as old. Participants seem to have misattributed the decreased fluency produced by the haziness of the word presentation to novelty. Neatly, the converse also occurred. When participants' task was to identify how clearly the stimuli had been presented, previously read (and therefore primed) words were judged to be more clearly presented. The accessibility heuristic seems to be relatively promiscuous, simply assuming that any aspect of the situation that is serving as a target must be appropriate to the values of the other aspects.

Fluency need not be manipulated at the perceptual level. Whittlesea (1993) had participants read the usual list of words that later would be distinguished from new words. At the later, identification stage, both old and new words were presented as the last word in sentences. Some of these sentences provided a context in which the final word had been prepared, in the same way that encountering the word *cat* primes the word *mouse*. In other sentences the final word could have been almost anything. For example, if the target word was *boat*, one sentence was "The stormy seas tossed the *boat*." The mention of stormy seas provided a context in which *boat* was a probable word. In contrast, the comparison was "He saved up his money and bought a *boat*." Here, of course, the last word could have been anything at all. In the first kind of sentence, new target words were judged to be old ones from the earlier list, apparently because the word was more easily processed when the sentence had set the conceptual stage and the participants misattributed that ease of processing to familiarity.

The fluency studies show that greater or lesser effort leads to judgments of familiarity and fame. Apparently a symptom of effort is sufficient to produce these sorts of effects. In a procedure that connects directly with the self-perception work described in chapters 2 and 3, Strack and Neumann (2000) induced people to furrow their brows in order to create a facial expression of effort, the "deep thought" expression. When frowning this way, the participants judged celebrities as less famous, apparently because they interpreted the need for effortful thought as an indication that the person was not well known.

In sum, a number of converging techniques for manipulating speed and ease of processing have all demonstrated that increased fluency leads to the experience of familiarity.

Recently Whittlesea and Williams (1998, 2001) have pointed out an important qualification of this principle. To use their example, no feeling of familiarity occurs when one encounters one's spouse in the kitchen at home, despite the fact that this must be one of the best-practiced and most "fluent" experiences. They propose that the experience of familiarity arises only when the processing is more fluent than one would expect. Only if you encountered your spouse in a completely unexpected setting would this experience of familiarity occur.

To test this notion Whittlesea and Williams conducted a variety of studies in which participants saw materials that were cleverly contrived to be "more fluent than one would expect." One kind were non-English words that were nonetheless easily pronounced and sounded like English words, like *phrawg* and *bautel*. The participants read these words, nonwords, and real words. Then they were asked to pronounce the word, identify the word if its oral form was a word, and state whether they had read the word or its English homophone on an earlier list. The procedure produces a kind of surprise that the initially strange-looking homophones actually are English words when pronounced. Thus, the word/nonword judgment becomes easier than expected, and so the homophones are assumed to be old and previously experienced.

The converse was also observed. Whittlesea and Williams presented nonwords that were easy to read because they followed English conventions about form and pronunciation, like *hension*. The ease of pronunciation then set up an expectation that the next task, making a word/nonword decision, would be automatic and easy. In fact, it became difficult; the result was that the participants attributed the ease of pronunciation processing to having previously read the items.

In a variant of this procedure, Whittlesea and Williams (2001) presented participants with three kinds of musical tunes. One kind were familiar, well-known melodies. The second were new but musically typical and well organized, and the third were "musically unstructured" combinations of notes that did not make up melodies. Later they played the same tunes again, as well as a set of new versions of each type. As usual, participants were asked to identify which stimuli had appeared in the first list. The unexpected ease of processing of the new but musically correct melodies led to their misidentification as old more frequently than either real tunes or unstructured notes.

In this last set of results we see the usual result that identifying material as having been previously encountered does not depend on the actual recall of that encounter. It depends instead on the ease and speed of processing with which items come to mind. We also see that fluency does not lead automatically to the experience of familiarity. Instead, the experience of familiarity arises from the relationship between fluency and its context.

Fluency that is unexpected is experienced as familiarity, whereas fluency that is less than expected is experienced as novelty.

The parallel with many misattribution phenomena in the emotion area is striking. In the emotion literature, too, the effects of cues depend on their context. For example, in Joan Duncan's placebo study (Duncan & Laird, 1980), people's naturally produced arousal led to greater feelings of fear if they believed their arousal was greater than appropriate to the context provided by the pill. Likewise, they felt less fear if their arousal was below expectation. The myriad of misattribution studies show essentially this same kind of result.

REALITY AND SOURCE MONITORING

If you know (or think) that you have had a thought or feeling or experience before, your next question is, where and when? Did your best friend tell you, or was it a chance acquaintance, or did you imagine it? These are the issues of source monitoring: determining the source of experiences. Memories for sources represent a further addition to the content of our episodic memories, since the issue is not just whether we have encountered a target before, but where and how.

Johnson et al. (1993) identify three questions or issues that are contained in the broader source-monitoring question: external, internal, and reality monitoring. External monitoring concerns identifying which external source produced the experience. External monitoring is perhaps the least novel, since we all know the problem of trying to recall whether something was said by one person or by another. Less obvious is internal source monitoring: Did I say that or just think it? Did I imagine it or dream it, or really experience it? Finally, reality monitoring concerns the tension across the external and internal domains—did I see that happen, or just imagine it? Did she tell me, or did I think she might say it?

To anticipate what we will find about these questions, of course people are reasonably good at all of these, but none of us is perfect. The reasons, once again, are that we know the answers to these questions only by inferences, from cues and data that are only contingently related to the reality.

Probably the best known examples of failures of external source monitoring are the studies by Loftus and her colleagues on eyewitness testimony (Loftus, 1979). She has shown repeatedly that memories about a witnessed event can be added to or altered after the fact by new information. For example, she and her associates (Loftus, Miller, & Burns, 1973) showed a group of participants a series of slides depicting a traffic accident. Later the participants responded to a questionnaire about what they saw; one of the questions asked if another car had passed while the target car was stopped at a "yield/stop" traffic sign. For half the participants the sign was a yield sign, and for the other half it was a stop sign. For half the participants the sign mentioned in the question was different from the one they saw (for instance, they saw a yield sign but were asked about a stop sign). Later they were shown pairs of slides that were identical, except that one showed a stop sign and the other a yield sign, and were asked which they had seen before. When given correct information in the question, 75% accurately selected the slide they actually had seen. However, of those given inaccurate information, only 41% were accurate. Many of the participants appear to have mistaken the source of the sign information and believed they saw what they had actually only read in the question.

Consistent with this interpretation, Lindsay (1990) tested the intrusions of erroneous details under two conditions. In both conditions the test occurred 2 days after the participants viewed the event. The difference was that in one condition they received the misleading suggestion just after they viewed the event and 2 days before recall, whereas in the other they were misled 2 days after viewing the event and just before taking the memory test. In the latter condition, where the two sources were maximally different, no confusions occurred. The condition in which both sources were 2 days old maximized the chances for confusion, and many participants reported seeing the details that had been suggested to them, even when they were warned that all the details in the written material were false.

In general, confusions between external sources seem to be easier the more similar the sources are in form (both viewed or both read), the more time has passed, the less importance the participants attributed to the details at the time they encountered them, and the more the participants are distracted or stressed (Johnson et al., 1993). All these are consistent with the source-monitoring view that distinguishing sources is a kind of nonconscious interpretation of various kinds of cues. Anything that interferes with the accurate interpretation of these cues will reduce accuracy.

Just what are these cues? Johnson et al. (1993) suggest that the most important cues are greater "sensory detail; embeddedness in spatial and temporal context; embeddedness in supporting memories, knowledge and beliefs; affect; and the relative absence of consciousness of the cognitive operations producing the event or belief" (p. 14). In one example of studies demonstrating the importance of these factors in reality monitoring (Johnson, Foley, & Leach, 1988), participants heard another person speak and in a separate procedure also imagined themselves speaking. Participants had a relatively easy time distinguishing the other's speech from their imaginings, except if they had been asked to imagine hearing the words in the other person's voice. Then, with greater sensory similarity, they experienced significantly greater difficulty distinguishing imagined from real.

In sum, the reality-monitoring/source-monitoring literature demonstrates once again that our feelings about our memories are inferences from a variety of cues that reflect only indirectly the events that are being remembered. When distinguishing what has really happened to us from imaginings, dreams, or delusions, we are using some rough-and-ready rules of thumb. Lily Tomlin says in her one-woman show *Search for Intelligent Life in the Universe,* that reality is all right in small doses. She goes on to say she is not that concerned about reality because, after all, "What is reality, but a collective hunch?" If not a collective hunch, our perception of reality does seem to be at most a reasonably well-founded guess, based on cues that are usually, but by no means always, associated with the real.

HEURISTICS

Which is more dangerous, traveling by airplane or by car? Which kill more people each year, honeybees or poisonous snakes? Which is the more dangerous profession, policing or commercial fishing? The answers to questions like these require information that most of us do not have about numbers of deaths in these cases, and yet we have opinions and answers. Somehow, we just "know" what the answer seems to be. That is, we have a "feeling." We do not know how this feeling arises or whether it is accurate. In fact, these examples were chosen because our feelings or "intuitions" tend to be wrong. Far more people are killed in cars, both absolutely and per mile traveled, and by allergic reactions to honeybee stings, and while fishing. We are in familiar territory here, since clearly we are encountering a process that generates "cognitive" feelings about the world that are not direct reflections of what is either true or known. And, once again, we have no idea how we come by these feelings.

Kahneman and Tversky (Kahneman, Slovic, & Tversky, 1982; Tversky & Kahneman, 1974) proposed an explanation of our errors and, more important, the much more frequent times that we are correct. They identified a group of habits of thought that they called *heuristics*. They observed that human beings often need to make estimates of the probability or importance of events, and that we are usually in a poor position to collect systematic data to support our judgments. In these circumstances we use other kinds of inference procedures. For example, a very common heuristic is one they called "availability." When we have no other grounds for estimating which of two or more events is more important or probable, we may simply assume that the event that is most "available" in memory is the most important or likely.

Thus, Kahneman and Tversky explain that we perceive that policing is more dangerous than commercial fishing because the relatively rare killings of policemen (at least prior to September 11, 2001) are well publicized, are the subject of many fictional accounts, and seem particularly heinous because they are so often deliberate. In contrast, the regular disappearance of commercial fishermen over the sides of their boat rarely rates any attention in the media. Similarly, an airline crash anywhere in the world is reported and catches our attention, whereas we all treat automobile wrecks as routine. The principle of availability is that whatever comes to mind first must be more important. Notice, too, that although availability leads to errors in some cases, it probably is correct far more often. For example, if we used availability to answer which is more dangerous, airplanes or trains, we would probably choose airplanes and be correct.

In these cases, the media play some role in creating availability, but their role is not at all necessary. For example, Tversky and Kahneman

(1973) asked people how many words in English begin with the letter *r* and how many have an *r* in the third position. The first number was overestimated, whereas the second was underestimated. The researchers argued that this was because words beginning with a particular letter are readily available in memory, but words with a letter in the third (or presumably any later) position are hard to recall.

Another famous example of a source of cognitive feelings, also identified by Kahneman and Tversky, is the "representativeness" heuristic. In some circumstances we make judgments about the likelihood that people possess some attribute on the basis of how "representative" the person is of those who do possess the property. So in their most famous demonstration, a woman named Linda was described as "single, outspoken, and very bright. As a student she majored in philosophy and was deeply concerned with issues of discrimination and social justice" (Kahneman & Tversky, 1996, p. 587). After hearing this description, people were asked to choose whether it is more likely that Linda is a feminist, a bank teller, or a bank teller who is a feminist. The point of this example is, of course, that the description of Linda is very "representative" of many people's image of a woman who is a feminist. Consequently, people who hear this description are drawn to describe Linda as a feminist. (Note that representativeness could also be described as stereotyping worked backward from a social category to an individual rather than the usual reverse.) The more striking finding is the second choice that people make: They judge that Linda is more likely to be a feminist bank teller than that she is a bank teller alone.

The choices that the participants are offered in the Linda example are not a part of the representativeness heuristic but rather are meant to demonstrate the power representativeness can exert. That is because to choose the "bank teller *and* feminist" option is to commit a relatively obvious logical error, that the conjunction of two less-than-perfectly-probable events has to be less than the probability of either alone. Since Linda is described as a bank teller in both alternatives, if there is a tiny chance that she is not a feminist, then the combination has to be less likely than the bank teller alone. Thus, the use of the conjunction technique is essentially a rhetorical device to persuade us of the power of representativeness.

Notice that the participants in these studies were almost certainly entirely unaware that they were using "availability" or "representativeness," and that they had committed logical or empirical errors. From the individual participant's perspective, they are asked a question that they must make some uncertain judgment about, and they "go with their feelings." The heuristics are descriptions of the cognitive operations that lead to these feelings. And like the other cognitive feelings, their most striking property is that they have no necessary relation to any objective facts in the world, or objectively accurate memories or thoughts. Instead, these heuristics are based on simple rules of thumb: If it comes to mind first it is most important, and if she seems like that kind of person, she probably is.

Recently Gigerenzer (Gigerenzer & Goldstein, 1996; Gigerenzer & Todd, 1999) has proposed a different set of heuristics that are extremely simple but, he believes, far broader in their application. Gigerenzer also argues that these simple heuristics are what we usually use to make decisions, and that they are in fact more efficient than more sophisticated alternatives. For example, he argues that we often use a heuristic he calls "take the best." If we need to decide between two alternatives that have many properties, some shared and some not, we could try to do some exhaustive evaluation of their differences, and the probable values of each of their pros and cons. Gigerenzer suggests that instead we may just scan the two alternatives until we come upon some property that gives an advantage to one or the other, and then simply choose the one that came out best. This sounds remarkably simpleminded, since the next feature we come across might reverse our choice. However, Gigerenzer demonstrates that the "take the best" heuristic actually functions remarkably well, operating far faster than more sophisticated techniques and making decisions that are on average just as accurate.

Again, the important point for our purposes is that Gigerenzer's heuristics are entirely unavailable to our conscious experience. Our subjective experience is simply of contemplating two choices, followed relatively rapidly by a sense that one is preferred. To put it in the quasi-inferential language of self-perception, it is as if people are saying to themselves, "If it seems better at first glance, it probably is." (One more time: This is an example, and no one believes that people really say such things to themselves during these decision processes.)

In sum, the literature on heuristics shows another group of "cognitive feelings" about which things are important, frequent, or preferred. These feelings are produced by underlying processes that are not at all conscious. The parallel with other self-perception processes is clearest in regard to the availability heuristic, in which we might produce one of those hazardous sentences about inferences that are actually not conscious. Here it would be, "If that came to mind so easily and quickly, it must be more important (or more frequent, etc.)." In the case of representativeness, the inferential sentence would be something like, "If he quacks like a duck, walks like a duck, then he is a duck."

BOREDOM

Feeling bored is different from feeling that you will remember something, or that you have studied enough, or that a remembered event really did happen, but it obeys the same kinds of principles. In particular, like those other "cognitive" feelings, boredom arises at least in part from the monitoring of other mental activities.

To test a self-perception analysis, one begins with the usual self-perception premise that any feeling is a perception of some activity of the person. The way to demonstrate the self-perception of boredom would be to identify a behavior that leads us to attribute boredom to others, and then to see if that behavior produces boredom in the actor as well. Unfortunately, boredom seems to have no obvious, overt action associated with it. Yawning and falling asleep are certainly related, but obviously are more directly related to feelings of sleepiness than boredom.

London and Monello (1974) explored one side effect experience of boredom from a self-perception perspective. They observed that a prominent feature of the boredom experience was that time seemed to pass very slowly. They arranged their experiment so that time did indeed pass slowly for some participants. All participants in their study actually spent 20 minutes on the experimental task. On the wall of the room was a clock that had been altered so that for some of the participants 30 minutes seemed to have passed, and for others only 10 minutes appeared to have elapsed. At the conclusion of the task, the participants who thought that only 10 minutes had passed reported much higher levels of boredom than did the "30-minute" group. Time had literally dragged for them.

This result is certainly consistent with self-perception theory and with many of the other studies described in this chapter, since it shows that feelings do depend on interpreting a "mental" experience in its context. In this case the experience must have been some vague sense of how fast time seemed to be moving, and the context was provided by the clock that seemed to define how rapidly time really was moving. When time feels slower than expected, we know we are bored.

Robin Damrad-Frye (Damrad-Frye & Laird, 1989) focused on a different, and arguably more central, feature of the boredom experience. A number of earlier theorists had proposed that the central behavioral problem of boredom was keeping attention focused (e.g., Berlyne, 1960; Geiwitz, 1966). Of course, it is not easy to manipulate attention in a way that would not be noticeable by the participants. Damrad-Frye's solution was to adapt the procedure developed by Zillmann (1983), described in some detail in chapter 4.

Zillman wanted to "transfer" arousal produced by exercise to an emotional context. He reasoned that immediately after exercising, participants would be physically aroused but would also be explicitly aware that the source of their arousal was the exercise. After some delay they might not have recalled the effect of the exercise but would also no longer be aroused. At some intermediate time, however, the participants would be aroused but no longer so aware of the exercise as its cause. At this middle time, the arousal might be, and indeed was, transferable to other feeling states. Zillmann showed that people would not be more angered if insulted right after exercise, or after a long delay, but at an intermediate delay they would transfer their arousal and be more angry.

The essential feature of Zillmann's technique is not the timing but that the two processes at work in his experimental situation, the arousal and the understanding of its origins, might not be perfectly associated. If the likelihood of recognizing the source of the arousal declined more rapidly than the arousal itself, then at some intermediate point the arousal would remain without any recognition of its source. More generally, we might expect that at high levels of any treatment, the effects and the role of the treatment in producing them both would be salient. At some low level of the treatment, there would be no effects, but also no awareness that the treatment might cause these effects. Finally, at an intermediate level of the treatment, the effects might still occur, without the participants' recognition of their source.

Damrad-Frye applied this reasoning to the use of distraction to interfere with attention. Her participants were asked to listen to a tape recording of someone reading a moderately interesting article. While the participants listened, they heard from an adjacent room the apparently completely unrelated sound track of a soap opera. The soap opera was played at one of three levels of loudness. At the quietest, no sound was noticeable, and at the loudest the words were clearly distinguishable. At the intermediate level, the distraction was noticeable if one paid attention but was not usually commented on by naive listeners. At the end of the experiment all participants were asked if anything had distracted them during the experiment, and none of the low-noise people and few of the moderate-noise people reported any distraction. However, the majority of the high-noise group said they were distracted, and it was by the sound from the adjacent room.

When asked if their minds wandered, the majority of the low-noise group said no, the majority of the high-noise group said the noise next door made their minds wander, and the majority of the medium-noise group reported that their minds did wander, but as Damrad-Frye had predicted, they said their attention wandered because the tape they were listening to was boring. The middle group also rated the tape as less enjoyable and its content as less valuable and interesting. (These last three effects occurred only among extroverts, who are notoriously more distractible than introverts.)

The effect of the middle level of distraction was to draw the participants' attention away from their task, but it was sufficiently subtle that they were unaware of the impact of the distraction. Consequently, they attributed their inability to keep their attention "where it belonged" to the fact that the material they were supposed to be listening to was boring.

In sum, it appears that boredom is, like the other "cognitive feelings" discussed in this chapter, a result of monitoring our cognitive operations. In the case of boredom, the cognitive operation monitored is focus of attention, or the apparent speed with which time passes, rather than the by-products of the remembering process. In both cases, however, the feelings are interpretations of the activities.

SUMMARY

All the cognitive feelings discussed in this chapter share the basic property that we have found in earlier chapters to be common to other feelings: They are derived from actions and the context in which the person acts.

There is no evidence of privileged access to intrinsically private mental contents. Instead, people monitor, unconsciously, their own activities, and the experience of properties of those activities is the feeling.

Of course, there are some very important differences between the processes that generate cognitive feelings versus the processes that generate emotions and attitudes. The first and most important is that the actions that constitute cognitive feelings are not overt. They are various kinds of mental action. In most cases, these mental actions and their role in cognitive feelings can only be inferred, because the actors themselves are unaware of the occurrence of these actions and their properties. Speed and ease of processing, for example, are inferred from reaction times, numbers of questions answered, the nature of the answers, or the effects of priming stimuli.

The issues that have directed the research on cognitive feelings are also somewhat different from those that we found in earlier chapters. For example, no one seems to have been concerned with the issue of necessity as well as sufficiency. Necessity has simply been taken for granted. Fortunately, however, many studies in fact demonstrate that unless suitable kinds of information are available, feelings of knowing, familiarity, and so forth will not occur.

In the cognitive feelings research, little attention has been paid to demand characteristics and other potential sources of experimenter bias for at least two reasons. One is simply that the processes that are being studied are often so covert that it is difficult to imagine how experimenters or participants could influence them. The second is that typical methods in this research involve presenting stimuli by computer, with little interaction between experimenters and participants—and hence little opportunity for bias.

Finally, little attention has been paid to individual differences in the processes that lead to cognitive feelings. Considering that possibility seems likely to pay off.

In sum, the various cognitive feelings discussed in this chapter all arise from the perception of cues derived from underlying cognitive processes.

All of self-perception research threatens to upend our model of how human beings operate, what we are, and what our experiences mean. The view of human beings that emerges in the cognitive feelings research is disquieting in a somewhat different way. We believe that we can trust our memories about what events have happened and to whom they happened, but we have seen here that our memories are rather easily altered and falsified. If the conditions are right, we may mistake the source of our knowledge, make bad judgments about whether we have encountered an object or person before, misjudge the importance of events around us, and feel completely unjustified confidence in our mental processes. Of course, although all our cognitive feeling processes are subject to errors, they are also all that we have. And in real life, they are certainly adequate to guide our everyday behavior. But clearly, we could also do better, if we were more aware of the potential for error in our most direct and immediate experiences of knowing about the world.

9

Attitudes and Cognitive Dissonance

A character in one of E. M. Forster's novels remarks, "How do I know what I think until I hear what I say?" Self-perception theory assumes that we are all like Forster's character, and that for all of us, attitudes and beliefs are the interpretations of our actions.[1]

As we have seen repeatedly in previous chapters, a basic test of self-perception theory is to induce someone to act as if he felt something and then to ask how he does in fact feel. If the person reports feelings consistent with his actions, then we can infer that the feelings are in some way derived from the actions. The largest body of research showing these effects was inspired by cognitive dissonance theory (Festinger, 1957). In just under 20 years after Festinger proposed his theory, Wicklund and Brehm (1976) identified more than a thousand studies inspired by cognitive dissonance theory, most of which demonstrated the prototypical self-perception relationship between behavior and attitudes. Cognitive dissonance research drifted out of fashion for much of the later 1970s and 1980s. Since the 1990s, however, it has certainly returned to favor and interest (e.g., Aronson, 1992), and the number of studies has continued to grow. In experiment after experiment, people have been induced to act as if they liked or disliked some object, and then were asked how they actually felt. Over and over, the participants (almost certainly more than 50,000 of them by now) reported feeling as their actions implied. Since in most cases these reported feelings were different from attitudes measured a few minutes or days earlier, the conclusion was inescapable that the participants had changed their attitudes to match their actions.

The vast majority of this research was not inspired by self-perception theory. Instead, these studies were all derived from cognitive dissonance theory (Festinger, 1957). In fact, self-perception theory arrived on the scene just as social psychology's love affair with dissonance theory was waning (Aronson, 1992). It was intended as a substitute. Shortly I will discuss the conflict between self-perception and dissonance interpretations, and some potential resolutions to the conflict. A fairly leisurely consideration of the self-perception versus dissonance controversy is warranted because, first of all, one of the origins of self-perception theory was in this controversy. The second reason is that the number of dissonance-inspired studies is truly vast, and if even a portion of these actually reflect self-perception processes, we will have found substantial additional support for self-perception theory. However, before confronting the theoretical disagreement between dissonance and self-perception theories, a brief reminder of the kinds of experiments we are talking about seems useful.

STUDIES OF HOW BEHAVING LEADS TO LIKING

The original, classic dissonance experiment was performed by Festinger and Carlsmith (1959). Their participants first spent an hour doing very boring and obviously senseless tasks, such as putting wooden pegs into a board, then removing them and putting them back again . . . and again, and again, and again. At the end of the hour, they were told that the experiment was on the effects of expectations on performance, and that they had received no information about the task because they were in the "no-expectation" control group. In contrast, the experimental group would be told that the task was enjoyable. The experimenter then went on to explain that this "expectation message" was ordinarily delivered by a confederate who appeared to be a participant just leaving the experiment. Unfortunately, this confederate was unavailable for the next participant who was arriving in a few moments, so the experimenter asked the real participants if they would be willing to serve as the expectation-inducing confederate for the participant who would soon arrive. Actually there was no other condition, and the "participant" who was due to arrive was the real confederate of the experimenter. (Talk about levels and layers of duplicity! The participant believed he or she was a confederate talking to a real participant, who was actually a confederate.) The effect of this elaborate manipulation was to induce the real participants to first endure a boring hour-long task and then to describe this task as enjoyable to an apparently innocent stranger.

When the participants had delivered their cheerful message to the next "participant," they left the experimental room. Then, in the corridor outside, they were accosted by someone who claimed to be doing a survey for the psychology department on how participants felt about research participation. The participants' responses to a question about how much they enjoyed the experiment were the critical dependent variable. (Yet more deception within deceptions!)[2]

Festinger and Carlsmith reasoned that the participants in this procedure would be faced with a conflict, or "dissonance," between their knowledge that the task they had performed was boring and their knowledge that they had told another person that it was fun. The essence of Festinger's theory of cognitive dissonance was that such a conflict would be uncomfortable and that people would try to resolve it. In this case, their options for resolution were limited. They could not change their behavior, which was already completed, and so they could only change their attitudes toward the task to fit their actions.

This was exactly what was observed: Participants who had told another person that the experiment was enjoyable then reported they had in fact enjoyed the experiment. In contrast, participants who had only done the boring task described it accurately as boring.

A particularly important feature of this experiment was the variation in the inducement the participants received to perform the counterattitudinal action. Some participants were paid $1 to tell the other person the task was fun, and others were paid $20. One might expect that being paid $20 would make the task seem especially enjoyable, but in fact the results were exactly the opposite. Participants who were paid $20 did not report the task was really fun. Only those who were paid $1 showed the dissonance effect. Festinger and Carlsmith's explanation was that knowing they had received $20 was a consonant cognition that prevented the dissonance—$20 was more than enough explanation for their action. So, the action was not dissonant, and they had no need to change their attitude.

Another classic experiment of that era manipulated a very different kind of behavior, but once again a behavior that implied a strong opinion about something in the world. In this study, Aronson and Mills (1959) varied the degree of embarrassment that students had to endure in order to obtain membership in a group. After an "initiation" that was either uncomfortably embarrassing or bland, all participants heard the same, rather boring tape of a discussion by the group they would be joining. Those who had endured the more severe initiation found the group more attractive. For them, recognizing the boring reality of the group would have been dissonant with their acceptance of an uncomfortable initiation. They needed to believe that the group was "worth" the discomfort they had endured.

Perhaps the most common of the dissonance-inspired procedures was the "induced-compliance" or "forced-compliance" paradigm, which was a variation of the procedure employed by Festinger in the first dissonance experiment (Festinger & Carlsmith, 1959). In the induced-compliance procedure, participants were induced to make speeches or write essays that were contrary to their initial attitudes on issues such as tuition increases or dormitory policies. (Most participants were, of course, college students.) Characteristically, some participants made the speeches under conditions in which their freedom to refuse was emphasized (although in fact few, if any, participants ever refused), and others were explicitly required to do as they were told. The reason for varying the participants' experienced freedom was that, like the $20 payment in the Festinger and Carlsmith study, an explicit requirement that participants make a counterattitudinal speech or essay would be explanation enough of their actions, and no dissonance would result. When participants felt they had made a counterattitudinal speech freely, they changed their attitudes to match the speech. Changes were especially likely if participants were strongly committed to their action, and the issue involved their self-concept in some way (for reviews of this research, see Eagly & Chaiken, 1993; Harmon-Jones & Mills, 1999).

In time, the use of a "low-choice" comparison condition became quite standard as a check that dissonance was responsible for any changes that were observed. Note that in fact the choice manipulation was entirely directed at participants' experiences, not at their actual degree of choice. Participants in the "high-choice" conditions in these studies rarely refused to do whatever the experimenter asked, even while the experimenter was emphasizing that the participants were "completely free" to comply or not. Indeed, one of the hallmarks of this kind of procedure has been the arrangement of conditions and the experimenter's behavior so that participants do exactly as asked, without recognizing the degree of social influence that has in fact guided their behavior, hence the origin of the label for this procedure, *induced compliance.*

In the era of dissonance theory's flowering, psychologists manipulated a great many behaviors and produced corresponding changes in attitudes. People were induced to avoid an attractive object and later reported that it was less attractive (Aronson & Carlsmith, 1963). People reported greater liking after being induced to eat disliked vegetables (Brehm, 1960), or even grasshoppers (Zimbardo, Weisenberg, Firestone, & Levy, 1965), or, as we saw in an earlier chapter, earthworms (Comer & Laird, 1975). More recently, inducing attitude-relevant behavior has been used to produce safer attitudes toward sexual behavior (Aronson, Fried, & Stone, 1991) and to increase use of condoms (Stone, Aronson, Crain, & Winslow, 1994), to increase water conservation (Dickerson, Thoidbodeau, Aronson, & Miller, 1992), and to reduce phobic anxiety (Axsom, 1989; Cooper, 1980). Clearly, engaging in behavior that is discrepant with one's feelings does induce changes in those feelings.

COGNITIVE DISSONANCE VERSUS SELF-PERCEPTION EXPLANATIONS

In experiments like these, cognitive dissonance theory proposes that the sequence of events in the participants' minds is something like the following:

- The participants act.
- Then the attitude implied by the act is recognized: "If I said that, then I must believe . . ."
- Either before or after this interpretation, the participants recall their original attitude: "But I really believe the opposite."
- Next is the recognition of the inconsistency or dissonance between their original attitude and the implications of their action.

- Some psychologists (e.g., Cooper & Fazio, 1984) identify as the next step an increase in autonomic arousal, which accentuates the experience of discomfort and uneasiness. Others do not emphasize an intervening role of arousal.
- The next step is to experience dissonance, which feels something like discomfort or uneasiness (Elliot & Devine, 1994).
- To reduce this dissonance feeling, the participants adopt the attitude implied by their behavior.
- The last step is only one of many ways in which dissonance might be reduced, but most experiments are designed so that attitude change is the only, or at least most available, option.

Daryl Bem (1967, 1972) proposed that sometimes this procedure was short-circuited, so that the participants went directly from step 2 to step 7. That is, they recognized the attitude implied by their actions and simply adopted this attitude. This was, of course, self-perception theory.

Bem (1972) summarized his version of self-perception theory thus:

> Individuals come to "know" their own attitudes, emotions, and other internal states partially by inferring them from observations of their own overt behavior and/or the circumstances in which this behavior occurs. Thus, to the extent that internal cues are weak, ambiguous, or uninterpretable, the individual is functionally in the same position as an outside observer, an observer who must necessarily rely upon those same external cues to infer the individual's inner states. (p. 2)

Presumably, what Bem meant by "internal cues" included at least recall of earlier attitude-relevant behaviors and evaluations of the attitude object, and perhaps also feelings such as dissonance. If you do not know what you think about some object, what better clue than your behavior?

Bem's self-perception interpretation of the Festinger and Carlsmith (1959) study was that when the participants were asked at the conclusion of the study how much they enjoyed it, they simply might have remembered their enthusiastic statements of a few moments earlier and concluded that if they said they enjoyed the experiment, they must have done so. The difference between the $1 and $20 conditions would be explained as affecting how reliable the participants judged their own previous statements to be. If a person heard that someone else had been paid $20 to deliver a brief message, they would be unlikely to assume the message reflected the speaker's true feelings. Presumably the same logic applied to the participants' perceptions of their own behavior as fully bought and paid for.

To demonstrate that induced-compliance results might be produced by self-perception, Bem conducted a series of "interpersonal simulations." He argued that if participants were relying on observation of their public behavior, then observers who knew only about the experimental participants' behavior should interpret it in the same way as self-perception theory assumes that the actor does. In the simulation studies, "observer" participants were told the details of various dissonance-inspired experiments and then asked to predict how an individual participant would have reported his or her attitudes. These observer participants reproduced the results of the classic dissonance experiments very closely.

As Bem acknowledged (Bem & McConnell, 1970), these simulations do not *prove* that self-perception processes did indeed produce the induced-compliance effects, but the simulations do demonstrate that the possibility is real: Participants in the classic dissonance theory experiments *could* have produced all the usual results if in fact they were inferring their attitudes directly from their behavior, as self-perception theory proposed.

Following Bem's presentation of self-perception theory, an enthusiastic controversy developed, with many attempts to decide whether dissonance or self-perception was the better explanation of the effects of induced compliance. This dispute was contested around two major issues. The first concerned what participants were aware of during an induced-compliance experiment, and what difference their awareness made. The second concerned the physiological effects of dissonance arousal.

THE SALIENCE OF ORIGINAL ATTITUDES

A variety of criticisms of the interpersonal simulation studies appeared. One involved the participants' awareness of their original attitude. In his simulations, Bem had not informed his observer participants what the real participants' original, pre-behavior attitude had been. Dissonance enthusiasts argued that in real induced-compliance experiments, participants did know what their original attitudes were. A number of studies demonstrated that successful interpersonal simulations depended on not telling the observer participants what the participants' initial attitude had been (e.g., Jones, Linder, Kiesler, Zanna, & Brehm, 1968). When observer participants were told about the real participants' initial attitude, the usual dissonance results were not replicated.

This apparent weakness in the self-perception explanation turned out to be a strength. Obviously, if self-perception theory was correct, participants in real induced-compliance experiments should not be able to recall their initial attitudes. Bem and McConnell (1970) tested this implication directly by inducing participants to write counterattitudinal essays and then asking them to report what their original, pre-essay, attitudes had been. The attitudes they reported were in fact brand new and induced by their essay writing. The participants seemed to have adopted the attitude implied by their behavior and to have no knowledge that they had ever endorsed a different position. Self-perception predictions had been confirmed.

However, this result was not unambiguous either. Dissonance theorists countered that forgetting one's initial attitude was an essential part of the dissonance process, since otherwise one would face a new kind of dissonance: If I know I have changed my previously well-thought-out attitudes to match my recent, discrepant behavior, the conflict between my current attitude and my old one would be just as dissonant as knowing that I believed one thing and did another. In short, unless one had very good reason, any recognition of a change in attitude would seem likely to arouse dissonance or some other sort of discomfort. This analysis suggests that people should rarely recognize changes in their attitudes, whatever the reason. Consistent with that argument, when participants changed their attitudes in response to an explicit persuasive communication, they seemed to "forget" their original attitude and believed that they had always agreed with their persuader (Goethals & Reckman, 1973; see also Ross, 1989).

Note, too, that dissonance theory almost requires that this kind of forgetting process take place, because few if any of us can recall many instances in which we felt dissonance and then changed our attitudes. Either it is extremely rare for people (except perhaps social psychologists) to act in ways that are inconsistent with their attitudes and beliefs or the process of dissonance reduction must somehow include a final wiping from memory of the whole episode. Like good spies, we must destroy our instructions after we have acted on them.

These arguments suggested that measuring recall of initial attitudes would not help distinguish dissonance and self-perception explanations. The obvious alternative was to directly manipulate participants' awareness of their original attitudes by reminding them. Since dissonance theory assumes that people in an induced-compliance experiment remember their original attitudes, at least until the dissonance has been resolved and forgotten, it would predict that a reminder would not affect attitude change. At most, perhaps a reminder would increase dissonance and change. Self-perception theory, on the other hand, would assume that knowledge of one's original attitude would prevent one from adopting the position implied by a counterattitudinal act.

A number of studies pursued this approach. In one of these (Snyder & Ebbesen, 1972), participants changed their attitudes less when reminded of their initial attitudes, just as self-perception theory would have predicted.[3] In the tradition of complicated and conflicting results that characterized this controversy, a second reminder study (Ross & Shulman, 1973) produced the opposite effect. Participants reminded of their original attitudes changed as readily as unreminded participants. Steve Berglas and I (Berglas & Laird, 1972) did another such study that added to our confusion because we obtained results precisely opposite to those of Ross and Shulman (1973) and quite like those of Snyder and Ebbesen (1972).

Dennis Wixon and I (Wixon & Laird, 1976) noticed that the key difference between the Ross and Shulman and both the Snyder and Ebbesen and the Berglas studies was the time at which the reminder of the original attitude was delivered. In the Ross and Shulman study, the reminder came late enough in the process so that the participants probably had already formed an attitude based on their counterattitudinal behavior. If that was the case, then self-perception theory would have predicted that they would report a changed attitude, as well as some discomfort about the newly discovered conflict between their current and previous attitudes. The Snyder and Ebbesen and the Berglas reminders, on the other hand, came early enough that the participants had not yet formed an attitude based on their behavior and so were free to reject the implications of their actions.

To test this interpretation, Wixon asked participants to make videotaped counterattitudinal speeches, and he then systematically manipulated the time at which participants were reminded of their previous attitudes. We found both the Ross and Shulman and the Snyder and Ebbesen results, depending on the timing of the reminder. Up to the moment at which participants were induced to form an attitude, a reminder would prevent them from using their behavior to reach a new, "changed" attitude. However, once they had been directly or indirectly asked for their opinion about the attitude issue, and hence induced to form a new attitude, the reminder had no effect, and they reported new attitudes. Many of the participants were also remarkably persuasive during debriefing in denying that they had ever held attitudes different from the one they now endorsed. One participant who had been claiming stoutly to have "always" held his new attitude finally was confronted with his own copy of the questionnaire we had used to obtain a pre-measure a few weeks earlier. After looking at his mark on the relevant rating scale for a minute, he finally muttered adamantly, "I must have misunderstood the question the first time."

We also tried to measure the participants' experience of dissonance. They were asked how much "discomfort or conflict they felt about making the speech." Our reasoning was that the participants would feel discomfort only if they remembered their original attitude. Remembering their original attitude would, according to self-perception theory, reduce the likelihood of attitude change, so we would expect a negative relationship between change and discomfort. That was exactly what we observed: The more discomfort the participants reported, the less they changed.

We believed that the negative correlation between discomfort and change supported a self-perception rather than a dissonance interpretation of change effects. However, the timing of the conflict measurement is as important as the timing of reminders. We measured discomfort just after the participants had reported their new, "changed" attitude. According to dissonance theory, the discomfort should have been dissipated by the change and already been forgotten. Hence, only people who had not changed would still be experiencing dissonance. The net result is that dissonance theory might have predicted exactly the same negative relationship between change and discomfort as did self-perception theory. More recently, precisely this negative correlation between change and discomfort has been observed by experimenters who were operating from an explicitly dissonance perspective (Elliot & Devine, 1994).

In sum, the research on the salience of different aspects of the induced-compliance paradigm did not resolve the controversy between self-perception and dissonance explanations, although it did begin to hint that both processes might be at work in different conditions. Indeed, Bem (1972) and others (e.g., Greenwald, 1975) concluded that the dissonance/self-perception difference might be empirically unresolvable. However, research directed at the autonomic arousal components of dissonance seems to have moved us toward a resolution.

DISSONANCE AROUSAL AND PHYSIOLOGICAL RESPONSE

Dissonance is a temporary, unpleasant motivational state, so we might reasonably expect that it would be similar to other temporary unpleasant states, such as fear or anger. Since these and many other unpleasant states are accompanied by increases in physiological arousal, it seemed reasonable to expect that dissonance would be, too. In contrast, self-perception should involve no discomfort and should generate no autonomic responses.

The most direct test of this notion is to measure autonomic activity during an induced-compliance procedure. Some studies have found that electrodermal activity, one measure of sympathetic activation, was elevated following induced compliance, but only in the high-choice condition that would be expected to produce the most dissonance (Croyle & Cooper, 1983; Elkin & Leippe, 1986; Harmon-Jones, Brehm, Greenberg, Simon, & Nelson, 1996; Losch & Cacioppo, 1990). (Just what it might mean is unclear, but measures of heart rate have not discriminated high- and low-dissonance conditions in these studies.)

Although these direct measurements of physiological activity are consistent with dissonance theory, the most persuasive support for the role of dissonance arousal has come from a slightly different kind of experiment. In this second kind of study, the role of arousal has been demonstrated indirectly by showing that its effects can be "explained away" in a misattribution paradigm. Some of this research was described briefly in chapter 4 in the discussion of misattribution of arousal.

In these misattribution studies, participants who have been put through an induced-compliance procedure and who might be assumed to be autonomically aroused are then encouraged to attribute their arousal to some other, nonemotional source. For example, in the first of these studies (Zanna & Cooper, 1974), participants made counterattitudinal speeches and were given pills that they were told would make them feel either tense or relaxed. Compared with participants who were told nothing about the pill's effects, the participants who were told the pill would relax them changed their attitudes more, whereas those who were told the pill would make them tense changed less. Apparently, the last group attributed their dissonance feelings to the pill and felt no impetus to change their attitudes. In contrast, the participants who were told the pill would relax them presumably interpreted their dissonance-produced arousal as especially intense, since it overcame the calming effects of the pill.

Similar effects of misattribution on dissonance change have been observed in a number of other studies (Fazio, Zanna, & Cooper, 1977; Losch & Cacioppo, 1990; Pittman, 1975; Zanna & Cooper, 1974). A drug that prevented arousal from occurring also prevented induced-compliance attitude change (Cooper et al., 1978). Note that these studies have the interesting effect of supporting both dissonance and self-perception-like theories. The logic of misattribution is, as discussed extensively in earlier chapters, the logic of self-perception theory: that feelings, including dissonance, are based on some prior changes in bodily state, changes that can be misattributed. The short description of the misattribution of dissonance studies is first dissonance that produces arousal and then self-perception in the misattribution of that arousal.

It seems particularly appropriate, then, that the upshot of the research around the arousal effects of dissonance was the conclusion that both self-perception and dissonance effects occur, but in different circumstances. Fazio et al. (1977) were partly inspired by a number of studies which had shown that pro-attitudinal speeches that were more extreme than the participants' own attitudes would change their attitudes toward this more extreme position (e.g., Kiesler, Nisbett, & Zanna, 1969). These genuine changes seemed difficult to explain by dissonance theory, because the conflict between speeches and attitudes was relatively small. Fazio et al. (1977) proposed that self-perception effects occurred when the inconsistency between attitudes and behaviors was small, as it would be when the behavior was broadly consistent with the participants' attitudes, but more extreme. In contrast, they suggested that dissonance occurred when the inconsistency was greater, and especially when the behavior was on the opposite side of neutral, as when one argues in favor of something one is against. To test this interpretation, they conducted an elegant study in which they first measured the participant's initial attitude and then established "latitudes of acceptance" and "latitudes of rejection." Their procedure was to give each participant nine statements describing degrees of political liberalism or conservatism, and the participant was to choose his or her preferred statement and to indicate any others that were acceptable (the latitude of acceptance). Statements that were not acceptable were identified as in the latitude of rejection.

Immediately after this procedure, the participants were asked to write essays that were inside or outside their latitude of acceptance, although always on the same side of the issue. For example, a student might have selected "slight liberal" as his preferred position and would accept "moderate liberalism" as the limit of his latitude of acceptance. He then might be asked to write in favor of "moderate liberalism" or, in his latitude of rejection, on "extreme liberalism." As a misattribution stimulus, some participants were told that the booths in which they were about to write the essays might cause them to feel "tense or uncomfortable," and they rated their reactions "to the booths." These questions made salient the purported arousing effects of the booths. The usual low-choice comparison conditions were also run.

All participants were initially at least slightly liberal, and those who were assigned essays within their latitude of acceptance became somewhat more liberal. More importantly, the misattribution manipulation had no impact on their change. The participants assigned an essay position outside their latitude of acceptance also became more liberal, but only if they had not received the misattribution information. Thus, apparently they had experienced dissonance and, if they had no other explanation for their feelings, changed their attitudes. If they could attribute their bad feelings to the booth, they did not change. In short, both self-perception and dissonance were observed in the same study.

Subsequently, Fazio (1987) proposed a more general definition of the occasions in which self-perception might occur. In essence, he took seriously the part of Bem's earlier statement of self-perception theory that said, "when internal cues are weak, ambiguous or uninterpretable." He proposed that at least one kind of internal cue was an attitude and that self-perception occurred when these attitude cues were inaccessible.

Fazio (2000) defines an attitude as an object-evaluation association. He assumes a continuum, defined at one end by well-rehearsed, rapidly accessed attitudes in which the mere mention of the object immediately calls up the evaluation. At the other end of the continuum are nonattitudes. If asked for an evaluation of a nonattitude object, the person would have to create an evaluation on the spot. This rationale suggests that a good measurement of accessibility would be response latency when people are asked for their evaluation of an object. The quicker one can give an opinion, the more accessible that attitude must be.

Consistent with this expectation, Fazio (1995) presented participants with object-evaluation associations, and their task was to say as rapidly as they could whether they agreed or disagreed. In a number of studies, Fazio and his associates found that participants' access time was a good predictor of many other attitude effects. One such effect is how well the attitude predicts actual behavior. For example, consumer attitudes toward products were better predictors of actual choices if the attitudes were accessed more rapidly (Fazio, Powell, & Williams, 1989), and political attitudes that were accessed more rapidly were more predictive of actual voting behavior than were attitudes expressed more slowly (DeBono & Snyder, 1995). Making preference decisions is more stressful, as indexed by increased blood pressure, if the necessary attitudes are not as accessible (Fazio, 2000). Entering college students who have rapidly accessed attitudes toward the usual array of features of college life are less susceptible to stress and stress-related illnesses (Fazio & Powell, 1997), presumably because they are able to make many everyday life decisions more automatically and easily. Attitude accessibility can also be manipulated by giving people practice in accessing the attitudes. Practicing attitudes leads to quicker access and to more efficient processing of attitude-relevant information (Fabrigar, Priester, Petty, & Wegener, 1998; Schuette & Fazio, 1995).

Fazio (1987) reviewed a number of studies that showed that self-perception-like effects did not occur when original attitudes were made more accessible. His new conclusion was, therefore, that self-perception occurs when attitudes are relatively inaccessible. As a consequence, he suggested that "self-perception theory may be more relevant to the issue of attitude *formation* than attitude *change*" (p. 144, emphasis in original). To return to the induced-compliance ground on which the earlier battles were fought, the new resolution would be that dissonance occurs when attitudes are strong, well-developed, and, in Fazio's terms, prone to automatic activation of the evaluative component as the object was encountered. Self-perception would occur closer to the nonattitude end of the spectrum.

This final partition of the induced-compliance territory seems to have been more successful than many attempts to give warring opponents their own domains, since the disputes seem to have ended. After this the dissonance people continued to do their thing, albeit at a slower pace for some years. Unfortunately, like many victims of uneven partitions, the self-perception people seem not to have thrived. Little, if any, unabashedly self-perception-inspired research on the induced-compliance paradigm has since been conducted. In fact, with the exception of Fazio's very interesting research on attitude accessibility, self-perception theory seems to have left little mark on research on attitudes.

Fazio's (1987) partition was apparently uneven, since it allocated to self-perception theory only those occasions when people's behavior and their attitudes were almost consistent or their attitudes nonexistent. Such minimal discrepancies might be common but almost by definition seemed relatively unimportant. Dissonance theory got the far more interesting occasions when behavior and attitudes were dramatically in conflict and big changes might be required to bring things into balance.

EXTENDING THE ACCESSIBILITY IDEA TO OTHER COMPONENTS OF COUNTERATTITUDINAL RESEARCH

An alternative, more homey characterization of Fazio's accessibility idea is that the important variable is whether you remember or are reminded of your initial attitude before you perform the counterattitudinal behavior. If you are not aware, then self-perception will take place. If you are, it will be cognitive dissonance.

Fazio has shown that we are more likely to be aware if the attitude object or issue is important to us and we are well acquainted with it. We are also more likely to be aware if the circumstances in some way remind us of our initial attitudes. These two principles let us make some educated guesses about which kind of process is most likely to have occurred.

For example, consider Fazio et al.'s (1977) study intended to resolve the dissonance/self-perception controversy. When the study participants arrived at the experimental session, their first task was to identify their preferred position on the attitude issue and also to judge eight other potential positions along a continuum as to whether they were acceptable or unacceptable. Immediately after completing this task, the experimenter introduced the counterattitudinal essay task and assigned each participant to his or her specific essay position. It is hard to imagine any procedure that could have been better designed than the latitudes questions to ensure that the participants were acutely aware of their own position on the issue as well as of the conflict between their beliefs and the assigned essay. If the participants ever were to experience dissonance, this task should have ensured it for participants who were assigned to the highly discrepant latitude of rejection condition. It is hardly surprising, then, that they should experience dissonance and that the dissonance-produced arousal could be misattributed away.

In contrast, consider the procedure in Elliot and Devine (1994), who obtained the pre-measure of their participants' attitudes 4 to 10 weeks before the actual experiment. These measures were embedded in a larger questionnaire to disguise their later relevance, and every effort was made to prevent the participants from recognizing any connection between the two parts of the experiment. Many of the induced-compliance studies performed by self-perception advocates (which Elliot and Devine are not) followed this kind of procedure, precisely because often the question was whether or not participants would recall their original attitudes. Elliot and Devine's study maximized the probability that self-perception was occurring, whereas Fazio et al.'s maximized the probability of dissonance. If, indeed, Elliot and Devine had produced change through self-perception, it is not at all surprising that dissonance experience and change were negatively related.

AWARENESS OF THE ELEMENTS OF THE COUNTERATTITUDINAL BEHAVIOR/ATTITUDE CHANGE

The advantage of focusing on awareness is that awareness, unlike accessibility, applies equally to other components of the counterattitudinal situations. If self-perception occurs when people are unaware of their original attitudes and cognitive dissonance when they are aware, then we can predict different associations between the other variables in the induced-compliance attitude change procedure. When awareness of original attitude is low or unlikely, then we would expect that there would be no awareness of conflict and little arousal or experience of dissonance, and to the extent that these occurred, they would be negatively related to attitude change. On the other hand, if people were aware of their original attitude, then we would expect arousal and its potential misattribution, and dissonance feelings would occur. Anything emphasizing the conflict between original attitude and action would increase change, if dissonance is at work.

Unfortunately, experimental manipulations of awareness of original attitude have been rare, so most of our evidence will be somewhat indirect. That is, we can infer from the descriptions of the methodology whether the participants were likely to be aware or not, but that obviously is not as good as formal experimental manipulations. Furthermore, a complete review of the thousands of induced-compliance studies is well beyond the scope of this book, so what I have considered is a small, accidental sample of studies. With these qualifications, the evidence does seem consistent with the role of awareness of original attitudes that we have outlined.

A number of studies have manipulated participants' awareness of the conflict between their original attitudes and their counterattitudinal behavior. For our purposes, an important first question is whether the procedure reminded them of their previous attitude, so that the effects would be due to dissonance. Emphasizing the conflict between attitudes and behavior would then be expected to increase change. Elliot Aronson and his associates (Aronson, 1992) have used a "hypocrisy" manipulation to emphasize that people often fail to act in accordance with their principles. These manipulations increase subsequent actions reflecting changed attitudes. In these studies, the effects occur only if the participants have been both reminded of their attitudes and committed to them. As Goethals (1992) notes, the hypocrisy manipulation emphasizes the conflict between actions and attitudes. A more direct example of emphasizing conflict was a study by Blanton, Cooper, Skurnik, and Aronson (1997), who gave participants a bogus personality test and feedback that they were especially "compassionate" immediately after writing a counterattitudinal essay opposing aid to the handicapped. This reminder of the conflict between their essays and their presumed values produced increased attitude change. This study seemed to fit the conditions for dissonance to be the active process, since the participants seemed to be quite aware of their original attitudes before agreeing to the essays: The authors mention that "participants often resisted at first, but then consented after encouragement from the experimenter" (p. 687).

Another group of studies may be seen as making this same point, although admittedly only indirectly. The hottest topic in dissonance research in recent years has been the controversy about what exactly makes a behavior dissonant with an attitude. Among the suggestions are aversive consequences (Cooper & Fazio, 1984), self-consistency (Steele, 1988), and self-evaluation maintenance (Tesser et al., 1989). All of the many studies comparing and disputing these various proposals share a common overall plan. The basic design usually encourages awareness of initial attitude, so change should be mediated by dissonance. Then the experimental variables compare levels of some property, such as aversive consequences. The results are usually that emphasizing awareness of one's actions and their implications increases change, as one would expect if dissonance was at work.

In sum, numerous studies show that emphasizing the conflict between original attitudes and the behavior increases attitude change, if the procedure is one that makes awareness of the original attitudes probable in the first place. Unfortunately, yet hardly surprisingly, I could find no comparable studies in which the awareness of original attitude was minimized but the conflict emphasized, since on the face of it this seems impossible. We cannot emphasize the conflict without quite explicitly implying a reminder of initial attitude. Still, this means that we have only half of the data we would like on this issue.

The arousal research is similarly one-sided but also seems to fit our expectations. All of the studies which showed a link between dissonance and arousal also employed methods which made the conflict between original attitude and induced behavior very explicit. The missing part of the evidence here is some research showing that when original attitudes are not salient, there is no autonomic arousal. The closest approach to that kind of evidence is the fact that no misattribution effects were detectable in Fazio et al.'s "self-perception" condition inside the latitude of acceptance.

The third factor that should be associated with greater change in dissonance-mediated designs is greater dissonance experience. It is interesting that cognitive dissonance researchers have not regularly assessed dissonance experience directly (Elliot & Devine, 1994), relying instead on the very indirect implication of the low-choice comparison conditions. Still, as I noted earlier, a number of studies have attempted to measure dissonance experience. When the design was one that minimized awareness of original attitudes, the usual result is a negative correlation between reported "discomfort and uneasiness" about the counterattitudinal act and change (Duncan & Laird, 1977; Elliot & Devine, 1994; Laird & Berglas, 1975; Wixon & Laird, 1976). On the other hand, when a late reminder occurred after change had taken place, dissonance experience and change were positively correlated (Ross & Shulman, 1973). These results are consistent with the assumption that the first group of studies was demonstrating self-perception but the last was demonstrating dissonance.

As noted earlier, an alternative and perhaps better approach is to manipulate awareness of dissonance and see its consequences. In one such study (Pyszczynski, Greenberg, Solomon, & Sideris, 1993), no pre-measure was employed, so there was little reminder of the participants' original attitudes and the process was likely to be self-perception. After being assigned their counterattitudinal essay topic, half the participants were encouraged to examine and experience their "subtle feelings of anxiety or tension" about writing the essay, and the others were told to ignore such feelings. After writing the essay, the participants who focused on their feelings of anxiety and tension changed their attitudes much less than those who ignored their feelings. Thus, in this study where initial attitudes were not salient, greater attention to dissonance-related feelings led to diminished change.

The major manipulations of the Elliot and Devine study discussed earlier (Elliot & Devine, 1994) are logically similar and yield similar results. Recall that this was one of the studies in which pre-measures were well separated in time and style from the counterattitudinal behavior, so we would expect the effects to be due to self-perception. Their major manipulations consisted of asking participants to report their dissonance feelings ("uncomfortable, uneasy, bothered") either before or after asking them to report their current attitude. Reporting their feelings first seems likely to have encouraged participants to reflect on the procedure; it seemed to have raised awareness of their previous attitude and its conflict with their behavior. Indeed, it is hard to think of why they would have felt discomfort if they had not been reminded of their original attitudes by the affect measure. In two studies, they found that when attitudes were measured first, before participants had been led to think about their conflicted feelings, there were the expected changes in attitudes, but no increase in affect. When dissonance experience was measured first, there were increases in affect, but attitudes did not change. Elliot and Devine interpreted this pattern as showing that attitude change reduced affect, but an equally plausible possibility is that attitude change revised the participants' attitudes to match their behavior, so there was no occasion for feeling discomfort. The same effect occurred in the Wixon and Laird (1976) study discussed earlier. In this study we obtained pre-measures weeks before the induced-compliance session, embedded in a larger questionnaire, which had no apparent connection with the later session. Participants were reminded of their original attitude at various points in the induced-compliance procedure. If they were reminded before they had responded to an attitude questionnaire, they reported no attitude change, but if reminded after the attitude questionnaire, they changed and denied they had ever felt differently.

In sum, a number of aspects of the research on the induced-compliance paradigm are consistent with the awareness interpretation. That is, dissonance occurs when people act in a way that is inconsistent with their original attitudes, and they are aware of their original attitudes at the time of their final attitude assessment. On the other hand, self-perception occurs when people are unaware of their original attitude until after they have used their behavior to draw conclusions about their attitudes. In contrast to Fazio's division of the landscape, these studies all suggest that the critical variable is awareness of original attitude, and factors such as how accessible the attitude is or whether the behavior is inside or outside of the latitude of acceptance function by affecting awareness.

ATTITUDE ACCESSIBILITY

Does this redrawing of the boundaries of partition between the two processes have any real importance? In part the answer must depend on the relative accessibility of attitudes in everyday life. If people are almost always aware of their attitudes, then self-perception would be rare. On the other hand, if even relatively important attitudes are often not accessible, then self-perception processes may be much more common.

Fazio's (1995) work on accessibility implies that attitudes are not always, or even particularly often, accessible. For example, we know that many people are not particularly involved in the political process in the United States, but it is striking that there is sufficient variation in accessibility near the end of a campaign season for this factor to be a significant predictor of actual voting (DeBono & Snyder, 1995). Apparently even after months of politicians' feverish attempts to make political attitudes accessible, these important attitudes remain pretty inaccessible. Certainly this finding suggests that attitudes are sufficiently inaccessible so that there is ample room for self-perception processes to operate frequently in everyday life. How frequently is hard to say, but certainly far more often than just occasionally in the peculiar laboratory concoctions of social psychologists.

SUMMARY ON SELF-PERCEPTION VERSUS COGNITIVE DISSONANCE

We began this lengthy travel through the induced-compliance research with the question of how much of it we can take to be support for the self-perception view of human feelings. At the end of the trip, the answer still seems a bit elusive. For example, Bem (1967) suggested that self-perception theory might explain the results of the first classic dissonance experiment by Festinger and Carlsmith (1959). However, if I am correct about the role of awareness of one's original attitude, then almost certainly this was a real dissonance experiment. Pointlessly performing a boring task for an hour seems almost certain to have made dislike for the task quite salient and accessible, even as the participants were being recruited to tell lies to the next participant. In contrast, the other classic I described, Aronson and Mills's (1959) initiation study, may well have involved self-perception processes, since the participants had no attitude toward the group they were about to join until after they had endured the initiation. The unpleasant initiation may have created an attitude in order to justify the initiation before the participants ever heard the boring discussion. Their judgment of that discussion may well have been filtered through the already established attraction to the group, an attraction generated by enduring the embarrassing initiation. As a consequence, perhaps there was never a real dissonant cognition with which to deal.

Perhaps the best conclusion is that some unknown portion of the experiments that were inspired by dissonance theory were actually demonstrating self-perception effects. For the general thrust of this book, the proportions are not too important. All we really need to know is that some substantial portion of what we usually think of as dissonance experiments actually may be showing that the feelings of liking and disliking, attraction and repulsion, follow the same kinds of self-perception principles as the other feelings I have examined thus far.

INDIVIDUAL DIFFERENCES IN SELF-PERCEPTION AND RESPONSE TO COUNTERATTITUDINAL BEHAVIOR

A few studies make the self-perception case in a very different way. These are studies in which induced-compliance attitude change is predicted from individual difference measures of response to personal cues. Clearly, making speeches and writing essays are actions that belong to the class of personal cues. So we would expect that people who were more responsive to personal cues would also be most likely to change

their attitudes in an appropriately arranged induced-compliance procedure (Laird & Berglas, 1975).

In the first test of this idea, Joan Duncan (Duncan & Laird, 1977) simply
ran participants through the expression manipulation procedure and an
induced-compliance procedure. Her induced-compliance procedure had
been designed to minimize awareness of original attitudes and therefore to
maximize the likelihood that changes would occur through self-perception
processes.

Duncan obtained pre-measures of attitudes on a questionnaire administered to groups 4 to 12 weeks before the induced procedure. These
measures were contained in a larger questionnaire so the particular issue
used in her study was well disguised and participants were unlikely to
connect the questionnaire with the later experiment. When participants
came to the lab for their individual session, they were told the study was
exploring the effect on persuasion of matching personality traits of persuader and audience. They would be making a videotaped speech that
would be shown to groups of students in the next few weeks. They were
told they need not make up the arguments because we had the arguments
ready on cards; all they had to do was to read them as persuasively as possible. At that point the experimenter explained that the video had been
acting up, so to test it we would shoot them making the opening statement; if the video worked we could just go on and shoot the rest. We explained that we had quite a few tapes on one side of the argument, so
would they "be willing to make a speech on [the opposite side of the issue
from the position they endorsed on the pre-measure]?, (and with the tini-
est pause), Good, thank you." At that point we videotaped the participants
saying the opening statement, "I want to tell you why I believe . . . ,"
played it back to them, and said the video was working. Then the arguments seemed to have been misplaced, so the experimenter went off to get
them from her office, and the participants were asked to fill out some
forms that ordinarily came at the end of the session, with the instruction
"you might as well do them now while you're waiting." At this point, the
participants were publicly committed to a counterattitudinal position but
had neither thought up any supporting arguments for their new position
nor heard any supplied by the experimenter. In addition, their awareness
of their original attitude had been minimized. Finally, the "social momentum" of the procedure had elicited their frequent agreement, first with
making a tape, then a tape on a particular issue, then on a particular side
of the issue, all without giving them time to reflect on their own attitudes.
The forms they filled out at this point included a number of filler questions, and the measures of experienced choice, discomfort, and their current attitude, as well as their recall of their prior attitudes.

After the experimenter returned, she said an assistant was looking for
the arguments. In the meantime, she administered the expression manipulation procedure, with the explanation that it was part of the personality
measures to be used to match with audience characteristics.

At frequent intervals participants were reminded they were free to leave the experiment if they chose, and they were asked to agree at every stage of the procedure. Not surprisingly, therefore, all participants felt that they had been completely free to make the speech or not. Many subjects changed their attitudes a great deal, endorsing positions that were well across the midpoint of the scales into territory that was clearly far from their latitude of acceptance, but some did not change much at all. As we would expect in a procedure that was designed to maximize self-perception-based attitude change, those who changed reported no conflict or discomfort about making the speech, and no recollection of ever having had a different attitude position. Those who did not change were more conflicted about making the speech and remembered their old attitudes accurately. Finally, and most important, the participants who changed their attitudes to match their behavior were those who also felt angry when frowning and happy when smiling—those who were most responsive to personal cues.

The same kind of connection was demonstrated in a study by Comer and Rhodewalt (1979) in which, again, participants who were more responsive to the personal cues of their facial expressions also changed their attitudes more in an induced-compliance procedure.

Response to personal cues was a common thread running through the self-perception processes in both the induced-compliance and the expression manipulation procedures. The consistency of the results across the two procedures suggests strongly that similar processes were responsible for generating emotional feelings and new, behavior-congruent attitudes.

UNDISPUTED EFFECTS OF BEHAVIORS ON ATTITUDES

In four additional kinds of experimental situations, self-perception seems certainly to be at work in affecting, or even creating, attitudes—and dissonance theory is not a candidate explanation. These four are (a) the effects of muscle movements on liking and disliking, (b) the effects of ease of processing on liking, (c) the foot-in-the-door phenomenon, and (d) pro-attitudinal behavior.

Muscles and Liking

The leanest, most minimal description of liking and disliking might be as the subjective experiences of approach and avoidance. The obvious self-perception implication of that characterization is that if people could be induced to approach, they should report liking, and if they avoid, they will report disliking. On a smaller scale, if someone is drawing an object toward them, it suggests attraction, whereas pushing the same object away would imply repulsion. Consistent with this conception, people do exert greater extension pressure when contemplating disliked objects and greater contraction with liked objects (Foerster, Higgins, & Idson, 1998; Foerster & Stepper, 2000; Foerster & Strack, 1997, 1998). To test the role of these movements in feelings, Cacioppo, Priester, and Berntson (1993) asked participants to sit in front of an exercise bar and either lift up or press down. The effect of the lifting was to contract the muscles in the arms and shoulders that are used to pull something toward the body, whereas the pressing down contracted muscles involved in pushing away. While lifting or pressing down, the participants were shown a series of Chinese ideographs. The ideographs were chosen because they were relatively complex, plausible stimuli that one might have preferences for, but they were in fact evaluatively neutral. Later the participants were shown pairs made up of one ideograph seen during lifting, and one during pressing down. Ideographs seen while lifting/ pulling were preferred significantly over those seen while pushing down/away. Note that this is a very subtle, small effect that is detectable only as a slight difference in preference for stimuli that have no intrinsic value at all. On the other hand, the manipulation is equally trivial. Unless they were acquainted with self-perception theory, no one would expect light pushing and pulling like this to make any difference at all.

Jens Foerster and Fritz Strack (Foerster, 1998; Foerster & Strack, 1997) have shown similar effects of arm flexion and extension, in a different, and much more seemingly realistic, task. Their participants were asked to name liked and disliked celebrities as rapidly as they could while performing the flexion and extension tasks. The result was a "motor congruency" effect, in which they could name more liked celebrities during flexion and more disliked celebrities during extension.

These motor actions of pulling toward oneself or pushing away also affect other, secondary cognitive processes in ways that seem to reflect the impact of positive and negative feeling states. For example, pulling increases creativity, relative to pushing (Friedman & Foerster, 2000, 2002).

A similar effect was obtained by Foerster and Stepper (2000) with a different kind of movement. They reasoned that positive feelings are associated with upright, erect posture, and negative feelings with lower posture. They asked participants to learn positive and negative words while kneeling or standing upright. They assessed cognitive demands of this learning by performance on a competing simultaneous, finger dexterity task. They found that performance on the finger dexterity task was degraded when the posture and the kind of word to be learned were incompatible.

A similar "congruence effect" was observed when the movement was an apparent approach or withdrawal from a computer screen, and the task was to process positive and negative words. When approaching, positive material is processed more easily; when withdrawing, negative material is easier (Neumann & Strack, 2000).

These last four papers, which describe a dozen or more studies, seem to demonstrate that arm movements, posture, and apparent movement toward or away from an object initiate some rudimentary form of attitude that can then interact with other cognitive tasks to facilitate or interfere. The muscle movements examined in these studies are also "rudimentary" and sufficiently obscure that the small size of the effects and the need for very subtle measurements in the dependent variables are not at all surprising.

A more robust procedure was employed in another, clever study of a more conventional movement, head nodding and shaking (Wells & Petty, 1980). Participants in this study were told that the study concerned the performance of earphones during activity. Under this ruse they were asked to either nod affirmatively or shake their heads negatively while listening to a radio program, which was in fact a persuasive communication. They agreed more with the content they heard while nodding than with the content they heard while shaking their heads. They also seemed to have greater difficulty performing the nods and shakes if the material they were listening to was inconsistent with their attitudes. In a similar procedure, Foerster and Strack (1996) also found an interaction between the participants' evaluations and their head nodding or shaking. When participants were learning positive words while shaking their heads, or negative words while nodding, there was greater interference with a parallel task.

In sum, a number of different tasks have shown that muscle movements that are associated with positive and negative attitudes can generate such attitudes, or components of the attitude process, that can interact with preexisting attitudes. None of these effects are very powerful, but they involve very small components of attitude behavior. And, of course, these effects fit self-perception theory very nicely and dissonance theory only with difficulty.

Fluency and Liking

A robust effect of familiarity on attitudes was first identified by Zajonc (1968). In the first use of the Chinese ideographs mentioned earlier, he showed participants many ideographs. After a delay, he showed them pairs of ideographs, one member of each pair being new and the other member one that they had seen previously. The participants were unable to guess, beyond chance, which was old or new. However, when asked to select the one they liked better, they chose the "old" ideographs significantly more than chance. This basic effect has been replicated many times, with a variety of stimuli, including Turkish words, nonsense syllables, random geometric shapes, and faces (Bornstein, 1989).

The basis of this familiarity effect seems to be that familiar stimuli are processed more rapidly and easily. This increase in speed provides cues for the judgment of familiarity. I have discussed these effects more completely in the chapter on "cognitive feelings," such as feeling of knowing and the tip of the tongue experience. For the moment, one example will illustrate the case for treating these "mere exposure" studies as instances of self-perception. Whittlesea and Williams (2001) manipulated ease of processing in a different way that did not involve prior exposure. They showed participants relatively rapid views of words that the subjects were to rate for attractiveness. The experimenters then subtly degraded the view of some of the words by putting a random array of dots over those pictures. The words were somewhat more difficult to see, but the difference was not large enough to be detectable. The words seen in the degraded display were liked significantly less. Whittlesea and many others (e.g., Bornstein & D'Agostino, 1994; Jacoby & Whitehouse, 1989; Jacoby et al., 1989) have demonstrated that other procedures, such as priming, that increase ease and speed of processing also increase liking.

A particularly cute example of this fluency/liking relationship is a pair of experiments on preferences for letter combinations. Van den Bergh, Vrana, and Eelen (1990) showed typists and nontypists pairs of letter combinations, one of which required a typist to use the same finger to type all the letters. The other combination of the pair was typed with different fingers of both hands and, consequently, was much easier to type. The participants' job was to choose which letter combination they liked better, "for God knows whatever reason" (p. 1155). Nontypists showed no preference between letter combinations, but the typists strongly preferred those that did not need to be typed with one finger. After expressing their preferences, all the participants were asked to pore over the list of combinations and their choices to see if they could identify the factor that differentiated the two or that guided their choices. None even came close.

In fluency studies, liking is derived from observation of one's behavior, but the behavior is markedly different from all those I have discussed thus far: It is mental behavior. That is, we seem to have the capacity to monitor our own perceptual processes and detect properties such as resource requirements and speed. In the absence of other, more powerful determinants of liking and disliking, we seem to use this information to determine our liking. We like the quick and easy.

Foot-in-the-Door

Two groups of suburban householders were approached and asked if they would be willing to have a very large, unsightly sign saying "Drive Carefully" placed in their front yards. For one of these randomly differentiated groups, the large sign request was their first contact about the issue. The other group had been contacted previously, about 2 weeks earlier, and asked to put a small, 3-inch-square "Be a Safe Driver" sign in their window. Since the second sign was large and unsightly, the response of the first group was not surprising: Very few of them agreed. The surprise occurred among the people who had agreed to placing the small sign earlier, three quarters of whom agreed to the large sign.

Freedman and Fraser (1966) called this the "foot-in-the-door" technique of persuasion. Although their first study preceded the development of self-perception theory, they suggested an explanation that sounded very much like self-perception, and ever since that time, self-perception theory has been assumed to be the best explanation of these effects. The first, small favor is experienced as a freely performed behavior from which the self-perception process produces both a positive attitude toward the issue and also a more general self-perception that one is the kind of person who helps out on causes of this sort. Then when the later, larger request comes along, people see it as not unreasonable in light of their (new but not recognized as such) view of themselves.

Since this first foot-in-the-door study, more than 75 others have been performed. A series of meta-analyses by Burger (1999) produced reasonably large effect sizes, and the pattern of results best fits self-perception explanations. He concluded that other factors may contribute to the effect, but the primary cause is self-perception.

One piece of that evidence nicely focuses on the importance of the initial behavior of agreeing with the small request. If that first request is too large, so that people do not agree, then their later compliance with the larger request is undermined even further. Just as people infer a positive attitude from agreeing, they infer a negative attitude from disagreeing.

Why is this not an example of dissonance? Primarily because presumably the person's first agreement comes at a point at which they either have no attitude toward the object or are mildly positive about the issue. They are unlikely to have and become aware of any kind of conflicting attitude. So at that point the manipulation either is pro-attitudinal (and within the latitude of acceptance) or even is creating an attitude.

Based on the self-perception analysis of the foot-in-the-door phenomenon, Jay Wagener (Wagener & Laird, 1980) reasoned that response would be greater for people who were more responsive to personal cues and that people who were not responsive to personal cues would be unaffected. The foot-in-the-door context that he examined was agreeing to participate in psychological research. The participants were initially solicited in a classroom, where half the group was asked to agree to fill out a relatively brief questionnaire. Then both groups were asked to sign up for an experiment that would require about 2 hours of their time. Finally, both groups supplied information about their height and weight.

The height and weight information was used to identify those participants who were overweight. Research discussed in chapter 7 had shown that overweight people were less responsive to personal cues (Edelman, 1984; MacArthur et al., 1980) and more responsive to situational cues, such as experimenters' requests. Hence, in this study we used body weight as an indicator of response to personal cues. Overall, a larger proportion of the overweight participants did volunteer for the larger experiment. However, the proportion of volunteers among the overweight was unaffected by the first, small favor of the questionnaire. In contrast, volunteering by the normal-weight participants was significantly affected by the small favor. The foot-in-the-door effect occurred only among the normal-weight participants and not among the overweight participants, who were presumably not responsive to personal cues from their volunteering behavior.

CONCLUSION

When people say or in some other way act as if they like something, they come to like it, even if they had not previously. Speeches, essays, choices, muscle movements, perceptual fluency, and postures all lead to feelings of liking and disliking. The basic self-perception hypothesis that behavior leads to feelings has certainly been confirmed for attitudes, as it previously has been for emotions and feelings such as confidence. Clearly, attitude-relevant behavior is *sufficient* to alter or produce attitudes.

Missing from all of this research is any evidence that behaviors are also necessary for the formation of attitudes. The reason is surely that unlike emotional feelings, attitudes are assumed to be enduring. So even if people were prevented from saying or doing anything that was relevant to an attitude object, they could still remember the attitude they had developed earlier. That is presumably what Bem had in mind when he spoke of "internal cues."

Also missing from most of this research has been any systematic concern with the possibility that the findings could be reflecting participants' compliance with experimenters' expectations. Again, the reason is not mysterious. Since Festinger began this tradition of research, the experimental hypotheses have been so counterintuitive that it seemed impossible that the participants would be able to produce these results unless they could not help themselves. It is perhaps more curious that there has not been much attention to the possibility of experimenter bias, that the experimenters have induced participants to feel, or report feeling, what they wanted. Generally experimenters are not blind to the participants' condition or their expected behavior. However, the research is so voluminous that even though they are a minority, there are dozens of studies in which the experimenter was effectively blind. We really cannot attribute these effects to experimenter bias.

The final issue that needs to be reviewed is the application of this research to the real world. Here the dissonance literature is a rich source of examples, some of which have been cited earlier. Aronson and his associates have been particularly vigorous in applying dissonance theory to practical matters of everyday life, such as encouraging water conservation (Dickerson et al., 1992) and safer sexual behavior (Aronson et al., 1991; Sakai, 1999; Stone et al., 1994). Dozens of other studies of this sort also exist and indicate clearly that something like the induced-compliance situation does happen often in everyday life when we fit our attitudes to our actions. In the real world, as in the laboratory, we have our usual problem of separating effects produced by cognitive dissonance from those due to self-perception, but a reasonable portion of these studies in reality must belong in self-perception's column.

NOTES

1. Some attitude theorists (e.g., Eagly & Chaiken, 1993) have defined attitudes as hypothetical constructs or "latent variables" with, for example, affective, cognitive, and behavioral components. In this chapter, in keeping with my general focus on feelings, I mean only those aspects of attitudes that are experienced and reported as feelings of liking and disliking.

2. Readers who are not social psychologists may find the extent of deception disquieting. As I discuss the various examples of this kind of research, the need

for considerable deception will become apparent: The theories guiding this research are explicitly contrary to common sense, but they also deal with everyday experiences. As a result, if people were aware of the researcher's expectations, they would be unable to react naturally. Some deception was unavoidable. However, in the last 40 years, standards for the ethical conduct of research have evolved so that many of the research designs from the 1950s and 1960s would probably not be considered appropriate today. For example, all research now is screened by institutional review boards, whose first responsibility is to ensure that no harm comes to participants in psychological research. Of course, in the dissonance experiments participants were certainly not harmed. As a secondary concern, deception must be clearly justified and confined. So, for example, a kind of tacit contract usually is established between participant and researcher, in which the participant agrees to the potential for some deception, but only within the clear boundaries of the experiment, and for good cause. Festinger and Carlsmith's dependent measure probably would not be considered acceptable these days because it was obtained in the hallways, after the tacit contract period had ended.

3. The results of this study were certainly more supportive of self-perception theory but were complex enough that even Bem (1972) felt they were inconclusive.

10

Self-Perception Theory in Full

At the beginning of this book I promised that there would be a very large body of evidence in support of self-perception theory, and indeed there is. All the major groups of feelings have been explored, and in every instance the self-perception case seems somewhere between probable and conclusive. The next major task is to elaborate the basic self-perception premises and the lessons of this research in order to put together a reasonably complete picture of what feelings are, how they work, and how an acceptance of self-perception theory might affect our understanding of human experience and action.

First, however, I think we need a brief overview of the questions identified in the first chapter and the answers suggested by the empirical findings discussed in the other chapters as a frame for the more elaborate discussions. The first four questions that must be answered by self-perception theory are most often raised by professional psychologists. These are as follows:

- Are behaviors *sufficient* to produce feelings? (And, as an important corollary issue/question, can we be sure that supporting evidence was not produced by some sort of experimenter bias?)
- Are behaviors *necessary* for the occurrence of feelings?
- Are the effects demonstrated in experiments *large enough* to account for the intensity of many sorts of feelings?
- Do self-perception effects occur in *real life*?

Three additional objections to self-perception theory arise primarily from common sense and everyday experience, but certainly seem problematic to many psychologists as well. These are as follows:

- If feelings are information, or knowledge about our behaviors, why do feelings not feel like knowledge?
- If feelings are information, and not forces or causes of behavior, why do they seem to be causes?
- If feelings are not the causes of their related behaviors, what are the causes of those behaviors?

In this chapter I will provide answers to all these questions. Some of the answers are very strongly rooted in empirical research; others are just reasonable interpretations. Yet I hope that the whole package will seem to have a coherence and consistency that will recommend it.

ARE BEHAVIORS SUFFICIENT TO PRODUCE FEELINGS?

The most distinctive, most disputed premise of self-perception theory is that behaviors come first and produce the feelings. The direct empirical prediction of this premise is that if we can manipulate the behaviors, then the feelings will follow. Exploring this premise, a wide variety of behaviors have been manipulated, including facial expressions, postures, patterns of gaze and of breathing, hand holding, levels of sympathetic arousal, speeches, essays, various instrumental actions, ease of processing of stimuli, and the amount and fluency with which material comes to mind when remembering. These behaviors have been shown to affect emotional feelings, including anger, happiness, sadness, disgust, guilt, fear, and romantic attraction, as well as feelings of liking and disliking, confidence, pride, boredom, desire or "wanting," familiarity, and "realness." Clearly we have a very broad sample of different kinds of behaviors and of different feelings, and in every case the evidence is that behaviors can indeed produce the corresponding feeling.

A second, equally important, if slightly less disputed, premise of self-perception theory is that the effects of behavior on feelings are not automatic and invariant. Rather, feelings are based on the behaviors *in the context in which they are performed*. Indeed, feelings are the experience of the relationship between behaviors and context. This premise leads to a second well-studied hypothesis, that feelings can be influenced by manipulations of the context as well as by manipulations of behavior. The same behavior in a different context will have a very different meaning. So, for example, arousal experienced in the context of a pill is a meaningless side effect, but in the context of a public performance it is terror. Mutual gaze with a potential romantic partner is romantic attraction, except when it is in the context of counting eyeblinks. Fluency in retrieving a name is experienced as familiarity, except when the context of the fluency is a well-remembered previous encounter with the name. Choosing to play with a toy or engage in a task is experienced as intrinsic pleasure in the toy or task, except when it is in the context of a large incentive. Making a speech or writing an essay is experienced as belief in the position argued, except when the speech or essay is coerced or richly remunerated.

Note that in most of these cases, the default "interpretation" of behaviors is as a feeling. That is, the behaviors are the occasion for feelings, unless they are disqualified by some external constraint. That seems to be the rule for most, if not all, behavior-feeling relationships. The reason seems obvious, too: The context for the behavior is almost always consistent and appropriate. We usually smile at parties, act sad at funerals, and do so without coercion; we also give speeches without excessive payment, and so forth. Bribes and threats that might disqualify our behaviors are rare, fortunately.

We have lots of evidence, then, that the appropriate behaviors in the appropriate contexts are experienced as feelings. Surely the sufficiency question is more than amply answered, at least in a quantitative sense. Earlier I drew the same conclusion when all we had to consider was the research on emotional feelings. Since then, we have added extensive research on motives, attitudes, and cognitive feelings to leave no apparent room for doubt that manipulations of behaviors are sufficient to produce feelings.

EXPERIMENTER BIAS?

Only one uncertainty about the sufficiency question seems possible: that all of these results are due to the subtle influences of experimenter bias. Perhaps the experimenter has induced feelings by other means than the manipulations of behavior, or perhaps the participants have recognized the purpose of the experiment and have obliged the experimenter by claiming feelings they are not actually experiencing. Interestingly, the experimenter bias issue has been raised infrequently except in regard to the self-perception work on emotional feelings. I hope that I dealt adequately with that specific set of complaints in chapter 5, but just as a reminder, there are three good reasons to reject experimenter bias in the research on emotional feelings. The first is that in almost every one of the many studies, extensive and often exceptionally clever efforts were made to disguise the purposes and nature of the manipulations. Efforts were also made to identify and exclude any participants who seemed to be aware of the potential behavior-to-feeling link. Arguably, the degree of attention to the potential for experimenter influence and the variety of strategies to combat it match any other area of research. Second, some studies of facial expressions have employed a "pseudoexperimental control" to measure any influence. In this procedure, some participants are present and perform like the target participants, except that they do not adopt facial expressions. In the two studies that employed this pseudo-experimental control, the participants who did not move their faces also reported no changes in their feelings, although they were equally exposed to the experimenter's behavior (Laird, 1974; Rutledge & Hupka, 1985).

The third set of observations, which in my view provide the most persuasive evidence against experimenter bias, were the "double-blind interaction" studies. In these studies experimenters were blind to participants' standing on some variable that was predicted to interact with the behavioral manipulations. As a consequence, the experimenters could not have influenced some participants' responses in one direction and other participants' responses in the other direction. For example, in two recent studies (Schnall & Laird, 2002), women were asked to adopt facial expressions of smiles and frowns. As usual, we found that some responded to the personal cues of their expressions and felt happier or angrier when adopting the expressions. Others were not affected by their expressions. In a separate procedure we identified which of these women were more or less likely to experience premenstrual tension. At the time the expression manipulation measures were obtained, we had not yet assessed premenstrual tension. In the second study both PMS and cue response were assessed by questionnaires that were administered to a classroom group that had no interaction with the experimenter. Thus, in neither of these studies could the experimenter have known which women to influence in which way during the expression manipulation procedure. And, of course, the experimenter could not influence whether their moods varied with their menstrual cycle. (Recall, too, that the women were not simply reporting whether they believed they sometimes experienced PMS. Actual mood differences across their cycles were measured, either longitudinally or cross-sectionally.)

This kind of "double-blind" interaction has been seen in relationships between responses to personal cues from facial expressions and responses to other personal emotional cues, including postures (Duclos et al., 1989; Flack et al., 1999a; Flack et al., 2000), the effects of gaze on romantic love (Kellerman et al., 1989) and on guilt (Schnall et al., 2000) and arousal (Duncan & Laird, 1980; Genov et al., 2000). Other double-blind interactions cross domains between emotional behaviors and emotional feelings, on the one hand, and other self-perceptions, such as changed attitudes after counterattitudinal behavior (Comer & Rhodewalt, 1979; Duncan & Laird, 1977) and feelings such as confidence (Laird et al., in press), on the other hand. People who differ in response to personal and situational cues also differ in theoretically consistent ways in their sensory acuity (Genov et al., 2000; Stevens et al., 1988). Another related kind of connection is between a self-perception manipulation and a more conventional individual difference measure, such as field dependence (Duncan & Laird, 1977; Edelman, 1984).

Clearly, there are more than enough double-blind interaction studies to rule out experimenter bias, either conscious or unconscious. Experimenter influence always seemed like a last-ditch defense of common sense against the disturbing proposals of self-perception theory, and now it seems clear those defenses have been overrun. Manipulating behavior *is* sufficient to produce feelings.

Of course, sufficiency was never in question in regard to many of the other kinds of feelings I have reviewed. There is, for example, no systematic alternative to the self-perception-like view of the origins of feelings of knowing, the effects of the foot-in-the-door manipulation, or of some of the effects of counterattitudinal behavior on attitudes.

IS BEHAVIOR NECESSARY FOR FEELINGS?

Again, I discussed this at length in chapter 5 when I was pulling together the work on emotional feelings and concluded that the evidence was not as extensive as for sufficiency, but still warranted reasonable confidence in the weaker version of necessity. That is, some kind of emotional behavior seems to be necessary for emotional experience, at least for some people, although no particular kind of behavior is necessary. Emotional feelings can be constructed from expressions, postures, tones of voice, gaze and autonomic arousal, as well as situational expectations about what most people would be feeling in the prevailing circumstances. However, interfering with any of these sources of cues does seem to reduce the intensity of feelings.

In the subsequent sections on other, nonemotional feelings, there has been relatively little direct focus on the necessity question, but we can certainly make some reasonable estimates. For example, most attitude theories explicitly assume that attitudes develop in a variety of ways (e.g., Eagly & Chaiken, 1993; Wood, 2000), not all of which are dependent on prior behavior. A good example is when we acquire an attitude by way of a persuasive communication. The question is whether we could have the feeling of liking or disliking without some underlying behavior. Zajonc's (1980) famous point was that some rudimentary approach or fluency of processing occurs before you have recognized the object in any way that would permit even simple naming. If Zajonc is correct, then even persuasive communications could work through their impact on rudimentary approach behaviors. However, perhaps the safest conclusion about attitudes would be like that for emotions: No single one of the various kinds of cues for attitudes is necessary, but some sorts of cues must be present.

The core empirical observation of the research on intrinsic and extrinsic motives is that the intrinsic motivation to perform an activity can be removed by extrinsic rewards. This finding suggests that some component of motivated, directed behavior is indeed necessary for the feeling of interest in a task, and these behaviors must occur without any recognized external inducement. Similarly, many of the studies of feelings of familiarity and realness demonstrate that the misattribution of fluency to other sources removes any of these cognitive feelings. Fluency that has not been undermined by presumed external sources is essential for the feelings of familiarity and knowing.

In sum, the conclusion proposed earlier for the emotion literature alone seems to apply at least as well to the whole array of feelings: There is enough evidence so that we can be reasonably confident that behaviors are, in the weak sense, necessary. The feelings arise from the self-perception of behaviors and their context; without behavioral or contextual, situational cues, the feelings are diminished or even prevented.

ARE THE EFFECTS OF BEHAVIORS ON FEELINGS "LARGE" ENOUGH?

This question made more sense in regard to emotional feelings than for many of the other feelings I have examined. Some researchers (Matsumoto, 1987) have worried that the effects of behaviors on emotional feelings might be real, but small, as if the feelings produced by laboratory manipulations of expressions, arousal, and so on might be pale imitations of the robust passions of real life. The evidence actually suggests that the impact of emotional behaviors on emotional feelings is more than large enough to provide a reasonable account of real-life passion, especially since emotional cues appear to be additive.

For many other feelings like the "tip of the tongue" or "realness," no weak versions seem to exist. If one feels one has encountered something before, or that a name is that of a famous person, or that the remembered dream really happened, these feelings are identical in intensity to the same feelings in everyday life. In fact, they are indistinguishable from their real-life analogues. (Indeed, we do not ordinarily even think of such feelings as having different intensities.) Similarly, the hunger of restrained eaters in a preloading experiment is the same hunger as any other, and the desire to play with a toy, or to avoid it, is the same desire that initially leads children to playing. In short, the studies of nonemotional feelings strengthen the conclusion that feelings induced in self-perception experiments are just as "large" and intense as the feelings aroused naturally in everyday life. The intensity of feelings that we observe in experiments seems to be limited primarily by the ethical and practical limits on potential experimental manipulations.

DO SELF-PERCEPTION PROCESSES OCCUR IN REAL LIFE?

In the laboratory, behaviors are sufficient and necessary for the occurrence of feelings, and these feelings are as intense as those of everyday life, but do self-perception processes actually occur in real life? Only a few studies of emotional processes have connected directly to real life. One can argue, as I did earlier, that phenomena such as mimicry at the movies (Laird et al., 1994), experiencing pain (Genov et al., 2000), feeling anxious during a public speech (Olson, 1988), or feeling afraid of a snake (Duncan & Laird, 1980) are very close analogues of real-life situations. In the emotion research, though, only the PMS results and perhaps the work on panic disorder explicitly connect to real-life events. However, many of the topics I have discussed in the later chapters strengthen this case. The cognitive feelings, for example, are indistinguishable from feelings of familiarity and "tip of the tongue" in real life. The impact of rewards on motivation and creativity have been applied in the workplace as well as the laboratory (Amabile, 1983). And, eating and weight control are things that happen only in the real world.

Can we conclude that all real-life feelings are produced by self-perception processes? Perhaps that would be a bit daring at this point. Yet all the evidence seems to point that way. If behaviors are certainly sufficient to produce feelings, almost certainly necessary, and probably do so both in laboratories and in real life, then self-perception theory deserves serious attention.

INDIVIDUAL DIFFERENCES IN SELF-PERCEPTION PROCESSES

One issue remains before we can begin to reflect on the larger implications of self-perception theory: the apparently inconvenient fact that in some of this research only some people respond to self-perception manipulations. Some people respond to their own facial expressions, postures, gaze, counterattitudinal speeches, and actions, but others do not. The feelings of those who do not respond instead seem to arise more from their circumstances and their normative expectations about how most people would be responding.

These individual differences have one obviously important implication for our understanding of self-perception theory. Responses to personal or situational cues are consistent across many kinds of feelings and many kinds of behaviors. If people respond to facial expressions, they also respond to arousal changes, emotional actions, gaze, posture, and so forth. Furthermore, people who respond to these emotional cues also respond to their own speeches in the induced-compliance paradigm and to their actions in the foot-in-the-door manipulation. They also do not eat in the "external" pattern characteristic of people who are restraining their eating. These empirical consistencies suggest that the same types of processes are producing this wide array of feelings. Not only do these disparate kinds of research reveal conceptually similar relationships between cues and feelings, but also, they are now connected empirically. Not all feelings and behaviors have been the focus of individual-differences research, so we cannot know if analogous differences in the impact of personal and situational cues will appear everywhere, but at the least they are widespread and appear in the processes that lead to attitudes and motives as well as emotions.

As noted earlier, both personal and situational cues fit logically into the basic self-perception assumptions. Individual differences do not mean that some people are performing as self-perception theory predicts and some as "common sense" would predict. Instead, for both groups, their feelings arise from their behavior and its context, and hence from essentially public information. We have two ways of knowing about how other people may be feeling—how they act and to what it is they are acting in response. We have the same two kinds of cues for ourselves. The individual differences reflect the relative impact of behavior and context when the two are not consistent. Whether the cues arise from behavior or from situational expectations, they are the same kind of public information that you and I can both use to identify my feelings.

Before leaving the discussion of individual differences, I have to underline a recent change in my own thinking, a change that was driven entirely by the accumulation of data. Previously, I believed that people might use both personal and situational cues in many ordinary, real-life situations in which the two were likely to be entirely concordant. Only when the two were discrepant would the differences be important; then, some people would "use" personal cues, and others would use situational cues. However, increasingly it has become clear that the people we have been designating as more responsive to personal cues were also responsive to situational cues. For example, in Joan Kellerman's gaze and love study (Kellerman et al., 1989), the situational cue group was unaffected by the gaze but did respond to the mildly romantic setting. The personal cue group was affected strongly by the gazing, but they also were affected by the romantic setting. Similarly, in Sandi Duclos's recent study (Duclos & Laird, 2001), the personal cue group was affected by manipulations of both personal and situational cues.

The evidence suggests strongly that the differences are primarily in the degree to which people are affected by personal cues. Some people are affected strongly but also respond to situational cues. Others, who I have been describing as responsive to situational cues, are actually best characterized as less responsive to personal cues; usually they must rely only on situational cues.

THE CURRENT STATE OF THE EVIDENCE FOR SELF-PERCEPTION THEORY

I began with four plausible reasons for skepticism about self-perception theory and the studies that were intended to test it. For each of these doubts the evidence is reassuring, and in most cases strongly so. The strongest evidence is directed at the possibility that the effects of behavior on feelings were due to experimental demand, and I believe the effects cannot be plausibly attributed to experimental demand. The effects are also reasonably substantial in size and potentially even stronger in more elaborate procedures. The evidence is somewhat less extensive but still seems adequate to support the conclusion that behaviors are necessary as well as sufficient to produce feelings. Some evidence also indicates that self-perception processes are reflected in important phenomena in the real world. The real-world effects also support the conclusion that self-perception processes do produce relatively strong effects.

Is it time to abandon common sense and embrace self-perception theory or some other neo-Jamesian theory and its view of the "sequence" issue? Probably many people would still be a bit reluctant to make this step. But that reluctance must be tempered by the recognition that literally hundreds of experiments, involving thousands of subjects, have shown that when people are induced to act as if they feel something, they then do feel it. Anyone who attempts to preserve the commonsense view of sequence has substantial theoretical work to do: All these results must be explained, and defenders of common sense cannot use the easy assumption that it is all experimental demand.

My view is that attempts to save the commonsense view of sequence will fail. Indeed, I think they have failed already, and that it is time to embrace the self-perception view: Feelings follow rather than lead behaviors.

FEELINGS ARE KNOWLEDGE

If feelings follow behavior, they cannot be the causes of behavior, since causes must precede their effects. If so, what are feelings? The answer seems to be that they are information about that behavior (Laird, 1989; Schwarz, 1990). When we feel angry, it is a way of knowing that we are scowling, that we are preparing to attack, that our fists are clenched, that our hearts are pounding, and our palms sweating, as our body prepares itself for attack. When we feel attracted to a political candidate, it is our way of knowing that our actions are leading us toward supporting the candidate. When we experience familiarity or tip of the tongue feelings, it is our way of knowing that we are processing the stimuli fluently and easily, as if we had "practiced" in the past.

What is this information "about"? Most generally, it seems to be about ongoing, automatic patterns of behavior that are being launched. In the case of emotions, human beings, like many other animals, seem to be built with a collection of relatively automatic patterns of behavior (Buss, 1999; Cosmides & Tooby, 2000; Plutchik, 1980). These patterns have obvious adaptive significance, such as fleeing danger, confronting and battling rivals, and contentedly continuing an ongoing, successful sequence of actions. The emotional patterns are accompanied by expressive behaviors that communicate to other human beings what actions we are and will be performing. Some emotional, adaptive patterns also involve changes in the state of bodily mobilization for action through changes in sympathetic arousal. When we recognize these patterns occurring, we experience that recognition as an emotional feeling.

Of course, many emotional feelings are more sophisticated and complex, and less universal across cultures (Shaver et al., 1992). Especially complex emotional feelings like nostalgia and awe may well reflect the impact of the culture one grows up in, building upon the basic structure of the evolved emotions. But whatever the debts owed to genetic inheritance and/or to experience, what all these feelings seem to have in common is that they reflect and are "about" ongoing, relatively automatic patterns of action, or of actions that one is "ready" to perform (Frijda, 1986).

Certainly, not all the automatic patterns of behavior that lead to feelings are based on evolved "basic" patterns of action. Complex emotions may well be entirely the result of social constructive processes, and other kinds of feelings seem likely to arise entirely out of the particular experiences of the feeler. Perhaps the clearest examples of feelings that arise from past experience are expert intuitions about how to proceed with a problem. When an expert computer programmer has a feeling about how to proceed with a programming task, the origin of this feeling must depend almost completely on the programmer's experiences with the very latest of cultural artifacts, programming languages. But note that the pattern of behaviors (probably some sort of ease of processing) that lead to this feeling is entirely automatic and outside of conscious experience. It is the automaticity of the pattern that leads us to experience its occurrence as a feeling, not its origins in the history of the species or the individual.

The other feelings I have discussed in the preceding chapters similarly arise in automatic processes. When we feel liking or disliking, we are experiencing our tendencies to approach and avoid. These must be among those behaviors that are most basic and most rooted in evolutionary history. Similarly, the motivational feeling of "wanting" to do something is based on, among other cues, observation of ourselves as engaging in the activity without "extrinsic" reasons. The activities whose fluency produces feelings of familiarity, or of knowing, or even of reality, are more deeply hidden, but they are certainly automatic.

In sum, all the variety of behaviors that lead to feelings seem to be parts of often very elaborate, but always automatic, patterns of behavior. Some of these automatic patterns may emerge more or less fully formed from our genetic endowments, whereas others are undoubtedly learned and eventually overlearned to become automatic. The feelings are our way of knowing that these behaviors are imminent or even have begun.

Ultimately, the evidence is clear and compelling that feelings are not the causes of behavior but rather are knowledge or information about that behavior. However, before I can expect agreement from many readers, I think we must wrestle with several remaining objections to self-perception theory. These objections are not "scientific" or technical. Instead, they arise from the intuitions we all have about feelings, intuitions that make us uncomfortable with self-perception theory.

WHY DON'T FEELINGS FEEL LIKE INFORMATION?

If feelings are information or knowledge, why do they "feel" different? We all know very well what knowing something feels like. We have a metacognitive sense of what it is like to know that the capital of India is New Delhi or that the square root of 25 is 5. A feeling of anger feels very different. Feeling angry just does not seem like the same kind of thing as knowing about India. And indeed, feeling angry *is* not the same kind of thing. The reason that feelings do not feel like ordinary, propositional knowledge is that they are a different kind of knowledge, one that is at the same time totally familiar though often almost unnoticed.

In ordinary experience, we encounter two very different kinds of knowledge that we all have about the world. Both kinds of knowledge are essential, and neither can substitute for the other. One kind was called by Bertrand Russell (1912) "knowledge by description," and the other is "knowledge by acquaintance" (Buck, 1999), or what Fritz Strack has called "noetic" and experiential knowledge. Knowledge by description is verbally encoded and explicit, and it corresponds to the conventional conception of information. It is, for example, the kind of knowledge you would have when I told you that a mango is a fruit, with a sweet, slightly tart, yellow flesh around a central seed. Knowledge by acquaintance, on the other hand, is the kind of knowledge that you acquire by seeing and tasting a mango. The experience can be named, but it cannot be described. It is precisely this kind of knowledge that can only be hinted at, alluded to, or poetically evoked in a description, but with which all of us are quite familiar in our everyday lives. We know the tastes of mangoes, apples, and bananas; we also know the differences between the sound of a clarinet and the sound of a piano. We can recognize the face of the president, and of our loved ones, and the feel of a tire going flat on our car. We can make judgments of this kind with great accuracy; yet we are entirely incapable of saying how or on the basis of what kinds of cues we know these things.

Feelings of joy and anger, of confidence and doubt, or the feeling that one name is familiar and another novel, are all knowledge by acquaintance or experiential knowledge. Precisely for that reason, we can do little more in trying to describe the details of feelings than to name them. If asked what a mango tastes like, we can only say, "Well, it is mango flavored"; similarly, we can only say, "I feel joyful or sad," or "It seems familiar."

We can see now why the most attractive name for this general theoretical position is "self-*perception* theory." Feelings are experiential knowledge, and most, if not all, of our experiential knowledge is perceptual. We are aware only of an integrated whole that comes to us without any knowledge of how we know it. As psychologists using suitable controlled experiments, we may be able to identify the constituents of a perceptual experience and the processes by which these constituents are combined to produce the final experience. But as ordinary human beings and perceivers, we remain unaware of the constituent elements that go into our perceptions and of the processes that generate them. The business of perceptual psychologists has been to identify the processes by which we achieve experiences of mangoes and clarinets. It has thus been the business of feelings researchers and the research reviewed here to identify the processes by which we achieve experiences of despair and delight, caring and confidence, fear and familiarity.

Many "dual process" theories (Chaiken & Trope, 1999) have been proposed recently that describe the differences between the processes that produce either explicit cognitions or intuitive feelings. The process that produces what we all recognize as thoughts or knowledge by description has been called controlled, rational, logical, sequential, resource-limited, available to introspection, and slow. The process that produces feelings or knowledge by acquaintance is automatic, experiential, less logical, pattern-based, less constrained by processing resource limits, opaque to introspection, and fast. The latter is, of course, a perfect description of the system that generates feelings.

In sum, there seem to be many good reasons to view feelings as a kind of knowledge that is experiential, perceptual, or by acquaintance. Feelings serve to inform us about what we are up to; they are about behaviors in context.

FEELINGS AS CONSTRUCTIONS

Behaviors are antecedents but not the causes of feeling, except in the sense that a peach may be said to be the cause of an experience of roundness, fuzziness, and sweetness, all combined to produce "peachness." The behavioral and contextual cues that lead to the experience of an emotion or other feeling are the building blocks from which that experience is constructed, just as the various taste, touch, and appearance sensations are the construction materials for the experience of "peachness."

The constructed nature of feeling experiences deserves extra emphasis. We are quite accustomed to understanding perceptual experiences as "constructed" in the sense that what we actually experience is based on a set of relationships among cues of which we are entirely unaware. Depth perception is an excellent example. We know that the experience of the third dimension of depth depends on a variety of cues. Unless we remember our introductory psychology course, we usually are unaware of what these cues are, and of the process by which they lead to the experience of depth. Our brains combine cues from retinal disparity, linear perspective, gradients of texture and color, movement parallax, and so on to provide us with the immediate perceptual knowledge that Jack is closer than Jill, that the trees are farther than the river, and the like. In this experience, we are unaware both of the kinds of cues and of the processes by which they are combined to produce the experience of depth.

Just as the experience of depth is constructed automatically from retinal disparity, linear perspective, and so forth, the experience of anger is constructed from the proprioceptive feedback from scowls, clenched fists, pounding hearts, and angry voices. Confidence is constructed from erect posture, relaxed muscles, and fluent processing. In both depth and anger, we just experience the final product of the constructive process.

WHY DO FEELINGS FEEL LIKE CAUSES?

A great array of evidence leads to the conclusion that feelings follow and are about our behaviors. Since feelings follow, they cannot be the causes of those behaviors. Why, then, do feelings seem so powerfully to be the causes of our behavior? This is the other objection that our intuitions raise.

Closely linked is the question of what does cause feeling-related behaviors, if the feelings do not.

An attractive answer to both questions is suggested by control theory (Carver & Scheier, 1981, 1998). To understand that answer, we need to spend a bit of time on the general nature of control theory.

The basic conceptual unit of control theory is the familiar negative feedback loop. In its simplest form a control unit consists of four parts: (a) a sensor that can respond to some target feature of the environment, (b) some way to input a reference value for the target feature, (c) a means to compare the observed value of the environmental feature with this reference value, and (d) an effector that can alter the target feature of the environment and that is activated by a discrepancy detected by the comparator (see Figure 10.1 for a schematic example).

The hackneyed (because so apt) example is the system that includes the household thermostat, the furnace, and the room that is heated by the furnace. The thermostat has a reference value, which is the desired temperature, and a sensor, which measures the observed value of the temperature in a room. The sensor is arranged so that if the observed value is below the reference value, the switch in the thermostat turns on the furnace. The furnace in turn heats the house until, eventually, the temperature at the thermostat reaches the reference value; the furnace no longer receives the "on" signal, and it stops. At this point, the house begins to cool, until the temperature again drops below the reference value and the cycle repeats. The result is that the room temperature is controlled so that it stays within a relatively narrow range (see Figure 10.2 for a schematic picture of the thermostat control system).

All control systems consist of loops in which one portion of the loop goes through the world outside the system. As a consequence, the system can be affected by events outside itself, such as a change in the temperature

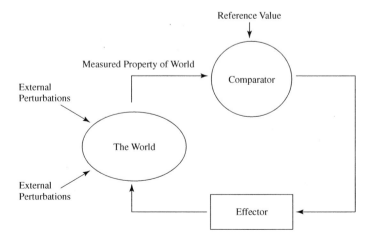

Figure 10.1. The basic functional parts of a simple control system.

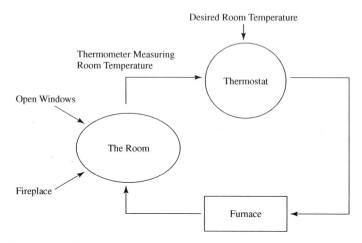

Figure 10.2. The household thermostat and furnace control system.

outside the house, whether one of the children has left the door open, or how well the fire in the fireplace is burning. These latter factors are called environmental perturbations because they affect the observed value of the target variable more or less independently of the activity of the system. The key feature of such a system is that whatever happens with the doors or the fireplace (at least within limits), the house temperature will be regulated to stay close to the reference value. If a window is open, the room does not heat up as rapidly, the temperature of the room does not rise, the thermostat continues to send its "on" signal to the furnace, and the furnace runs much longer. Eventually, the room will warm up (unless, of course, the heat drain exceeds the furnace capacity, at which point the control system has been overwhelmed).

Powers's (1973) book that introduced control systems to much of psychology is called *Behavior: The Control of Perception* because that is the essence of control systems. The effect of the behavior, which in the case of the thermostat is the action of turning on the furnace, the burning of the fuel in the furnace, and the distribution of the resulting heat in the house, is to produce a change in the "perception" of the thermostat. Once that is achieved, the behavior stops. Again, it is important to recognize that what the thermostat "perceives" is not the actions of the system, such as the turning on of the furnace or the burning of oil. The thermostat only perceives a property of the world—its temperature.

Superficially, control systems can be said to govern some property of the environment, such as the temperature of the room. Actually, the thermostat does not really measure the temperature of the room; it only responds to the very local events in the thermostat unit itself. An ice cube on the thermostat, for example, will overheat the room. What is really being controlled is the level of the target variable as assessed by the comparator unit, at the comparator unit.

Powers (1973) seems to have been the first to recognize that in living organisms in particular, control systems like this can be and are organized hierarchically so that the output of the higher system does not affect the environment directly. Rather, the output serves to set the reference value for the lower system.[1] To get a sense of how such a stack of systems might work, imagine that someone wishes to control automatically how long people stay in a room and also wants the people to feel that they have left of their own accord. (In this rather contrived example, I imagine someone who owns a precious painting that is affected badly by the humidity of many people in the room. The owner wants to be able to graciously and unobtrusively minimize the time that any visitors spend in the painting's room.) The room might be heated to a comfortable 70 degrees, like most houses, with a thermostat controlling the temperature. The unusual thing is that the room also is fitted with a motion detector like those that turn on outdoor lights in a backyard. When movement in the room exceeds a certain level, the detector resets the thermostat reference value to 50 degrees. In the absence of motion, the thermostat is set back to 70 degrees. Now, if someone, or even the family dog, enters the room, the motion detector resets the thermostat, the room begins to cool off, and the people (or dog) soon feel uncomfortable and leave. Now we have a two-level system in which the motion detector controls a switch that in turn changes the reference value for the thermostat (see Figure 10.3 for a schematic illustration of this system).

Note that the reference value of the motion detector is the physical size of movement required to trip the output system, and the reference value of the

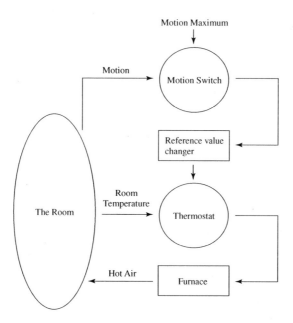

Figure 10.3. A two-level hierarchy of control systems, to keep room visits brief.

thermostat is a temperature, either 50 or 70 degrees. But when combined in this kind of system, the reference value for the whole system is "keeping visits brief."

Powers (1973) pointed out that many human activities can be described by such a hierarchical system, although many more than two levels will be required. For example, at this moment I am trying to present these ideas clearly. At that level, the reference value is some (unfortunately vague) standard of clarity, a clarity that is a property of the "gist" of what I am writing. To achieve this "gist" (the general meaning of the idea of control systems), I write sentences whose meaning I test against some sense of the development of my presentation. As I try to convey ideas clearly, I must first make grammatical and sensible English sentences. This becomes the reference value for the next lower level, in which the output consists of a sentence. Let us say that the output is a sentence like "Feelings are infor-

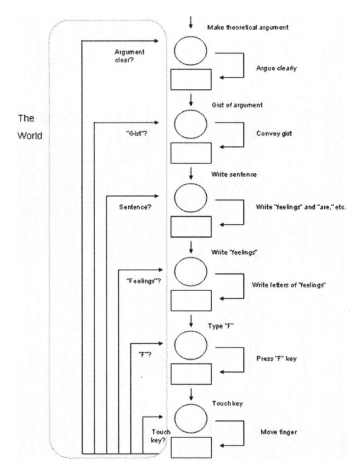

Figure 10.4. The action hierarchy of writing a theoretical argument.

mation about actions in their context." But in order to write that sentence, I must type particular words. The output of the sentence-level loop is to set the reference value for typing particular English words, beginning with *Feelings*. The reference value for a word is my (occasionally unreliable) knowledge of how it is spelled. To type words correctly, I need to strike the correct letters, and the output of the word-level loop is to set a reference level for a succession of particular letters, beginning with an *F* that is capitalized. If that letter does not appear, then I must correct it. And to type the letter, I must set the reference value for a set of finger movements that press the *f* key and the "shift" key (see Figure 10.4).

In this example, we can see a hierarchy of control structures matching a hierarchy of outputs and reference values. Working up from the bottom of those levels are finger movements, then pressing the *F* key, then typing the word *Feelings* and the sentence, and then making this sentence part of a coherent account, and so forth. As one looks "down" in the hierarchy, each lower level consists of a part of the whole, which is the output of the higher level. Looking in the other direction, we can say that in order to match the reference value of each higher level, the lower must be successfully accomplished.

Another important feature of this structure is that each higher level may, and almost always must, have many lower level loops whose reference values are controlled by it. These lower level loops are engaged either sequentially or simultaneously. An example of a sequential group of loops would be those that control the spelling of each of the words in the sentence. One such loop is followed by another and another, the *Feelings* loop by the *are* loop, and so on. The control of the key press module is a good example of the control of a number of feedback loops simultaneously, as the finger muscles must be coordinated with the wrist position muscles.

We can readily identify higher and lower levels than those described thus far. At the upper end are outputs, appropriate reference values and comparators for "Writing a book" and, above that, "Being a psychologist." At the lower end, we could identify the muscle movements involved in striking particular keys. How far "up" or "down" it is possible or useful to go is not entirely clear, although it may depend largely on one's purposes. Certainly, to understand ordinary action, the levels depicted in the examples seem adequate.

Emotional processes exhibit the same kind of hierarchical structure. For example, suppose that one is confronted with a rival, a situation that seems to call for the "fight" response. The reference value for behavior at this level might be set at "attack," and action will be adjusted until it meets this value. The attack system contains a number of separate parts that are all activated simultaneously, which is to say that the reference values of these subordinate systems are all reset. For simplicity, we can think of them as three systems, involving autonomic response, expressive behavior, and overt action. The output of the higher level attack system sets the reference value for the autonomic system to a high level of sympathetic activity, the overt behavior system is set to punch and kick, and the expressive behavior system is set to scowl, clench fists, and so on. Looking only at the expressive behavior system, the output of the scowl system is to set the reference value for the frontalis and corrugator muscles to high tension.

We see, then, at least three distinct levels in this anger example, starting with "attack," then "scowl," then "contract corrugator." Or, if we follow a different branch, we begin with "attack," then "punch," then "contract arm and back muscles." These are also particularly clear examples of the expanding numbers of feedback systems whose reference values are set by the higher levels. The attack system resets the reference values for at least three systems, sympathetic arousal response, expressive behavior, and action. Each of these also controls a group of other, lower level systems. In the sympathetic arousal system, there are modules controlling, for example, heart rate, blood pressure, skin conductance, and epinephrine secretion.

Finally, we are in a position to step back from these hierarchical structures of control processes and look at how these phenomena connect to self-perception theory. If one looks at all the structures described so far, we can see that they represent two streams, which are represented most clearly in Figure 10.4.

Going down is a series of outputs, or signals from comparators that cause output mechanisms to "do" something like burn oil, press a key, or tense a muscle. However, at every level but the bottom, the "action" is accomplished by resetting the reference value for a lower level system. On the left side of the figures is an upward flow of information. Crudely, we could say that the right, downward side corresponds to action, and the left, upward side to informational feedback that is the value compared with the reference until the actions have brought this information to the level specified in the reference value.

In common sense, we have traditionally—if only implicitly—identified feelings with the right, downstream side of these figures. That is, we have assumed that in some way feelings were "causing" outputs. Instead, we now can see that feelings must be part of the left, upstream informational side of these structures. When we "feel," we are aware of the information about a particular kind of behavior. The feeling of anger, for example, is the information that some or all of the following are happening: We are scowling, our hearts are pounding, and/or we are drawing back a fist. See Figure 10.5.

Although feelings are not causes, feelings do have a central role in controlling behavior. Just as behaviors control perceptions, including feelings, the feelings in turn affect the behaviors. That is what it means to call this a feedback *loop*. The information that is borne by feelings is compared to the reference values. Depending on the feeling and the reference value, this information may lead directly to alteration in behavior. If I become aware through my feeling of anger that I am about to punch someone, and my reference value for such behavior is that assault is undesirable, I will inhibit my punch. If, on the other hand, I have a reference value that encourages attack, I may redouble my assault.

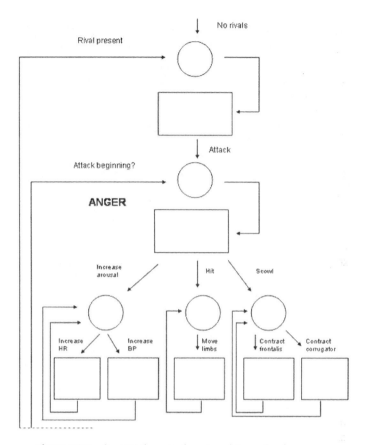

Figure 10.5. A partial control system hierarchy for anger.

Now we have arrived at the answer to why feelings feel like the causes of action. Information in the form of feelings *does* affect behavior. Indeed, it is essential for adaptive, coherent behavior; but information does not "cause" behavior in the billiard ball sense. Rather, it is grist for the comparator and its reference value, and the consequence of any feeling is uncertain until we know those values. However, feelings are part of the system that generates action, so they are easily misperceived as "causes" if the control system properties of organisms are not recognized.

An additional reason that feelings seem so obviously to be causes is that they are the most experientially recognizable portions of the various nested feedback loops. In fact, they are in many cases the only components of the systems that are experienced. If, as we believe, a control systems account of the role of feelings is correct, then it is not surprising that feelings have been misidentified with the downstream, more or less causal, aspects of the system rather than with the correct, upstream, informational side.

IF FEELINGS DON'T CAUSE BEHAVIOR, WHAT DOES?

As a nice corollary of the control systems view, we can now provide an account of why we can act without the causal impetus of our feelings, why we smile before we are happy, and our hearts pound before we are afraid. Those things happen because they are parts of ongoing control systems that operate routinely without our conscious awareness. Human beings, and doubtless all organisms, seem to be built to perform complex actions through the action of these systems (Carver & Scheier, 1998).

SOME OTHER OBJECTIONS

A few other objections are sometimes raised against the self-perception account of feelings. One is that there seems to be no room for hiding or disguising one's feelings, or for pretending. If self-perception theory is correct, then if we pretend to feel something, we should feel it. Of course, we have all had many experiences of hiding or simulating feelings in order to meet the demands of social situations. Does this mean that self-perception theory is somehow wrong? The answer is probably not, for at least four reasons. First of all, the necessary movements of, for example, facial expressions may be extremely subtle. In one study that very nicely matches some of the conditions of everyday pretense, participants were induced to adopt facial expressions that were so small that they were undetectable by observers, although they were revealed by EMG recordings (McCanne & Anderson, 1987). Despite being undetectable, these mini-expressions were sufficient to produce changes in feelings. If these research participants had been suppressing a laugh at their boss's expense, they would have saved their jobs and still felt mirth.

Furthermore, the intention to suppress one's expressive behavior has a second, paradoxical effect (Wegner, 1997; Wegner, Schneider, Carter, & White, 1987) of increasing one's focus and awareness on the tiny "leakage" (Ekman, 2001) of expression that seems inevitably to occur. The effects of tiny twitches of expression may be multiplied by this focus.

In addition to our increased attention and response to inhibited or false expressions, some of our other response systems may be providing cues for our actual but hidden feelings. Most notoriously, the autonomic nervous system responds without much opportunity for us to control it. Since autonomic activity is usually very difficult for observers to recognize, our autonomic responses rarely betray us, unless perhaps we are hooked up to a polygraph. Still, while we are controlling our expressions and actions, autonomic responses that are ongoing during our pretense may contribute to our real—if hidden—experience.

Finally, many people report that pretending to feel something does in fact lead them to feel it, even though they may later disavow those feelings. Many actors report that initially as they begin to learn a role they feel nothing, but as the actions and speeches become automatic, they begin to experience the feelings of their characters (although they rarely carry those feelings home with them after the performance). Similarly, supposedly one of the hazards of spying is that the constant, almost 24-hour need to play a role leads eventually to the role seeming more real than the spy's previous life.

These explanations of how we can act as if we felt something when we do not in fact do so are only plausible. Perhaps further research will undermine these particular accounts of how we do this interesting trick. But at a minimum, the plausible objection derived from everyday experience has been met with at least equally plausible explanations. Perhaps we should judge the situation with respect to this objection a draw.

Before leaving the issue of pretending to feel, we should recognize that pretending but not feeling is indeed a trick or a skill. Small children have some difficulty in performing it, which is why games in which adults "chase" a small child often escalate into tears for the child. Pretending to be a big dinosaur chasing a small one is a skill we adults have learned but do not sufficiently appreciate in ourselves.

CONCLUSION

William James promised to upset common sense by reversing the direction of the connection between expressive behaviors and emotional feelings. Self-perception theory broadens that attack to include all feelings. As it turns out, this first disruption of common sense leads on to two more, even deeper attacks on the commonsense view of humanity.

The second, further assault on common sense follows directly from the recognition that feelings follow behaviors. If they follow, then feelings cannot be causes. In fact, feelings do not seem to be the kind of thing that "causes" at all. Instead, feelings appear to be information about those behaviors. Common sense assumes an analogy between feelings and physical forces. In the commonsense view, feelings had energy and momentum, and thus compelled action. Common sense views human beings as essentially like machines in which our human activities are seen as caused by antecedent mental events and as though feelings were those causes. But if feelings are information, they cannot be causes. The analogy with physical energy simply will not hold.

The final, broadest assault on common sense follows because if feelings are not causes of behavior, we are left with no obvious way to construct a simple causal account of much of human behavior. Common sense views human beings as mechanisms, albeit extremely complicated mechanisms, and feelings have been assumed to be the intermediate causes that lie between environmental instigations and final behaviors. Once this mechanistic model of human beings begins to crumble and we can no longer treat human beings as clockwork machines, we need a different kind of model. The most attractive alternative is the cybernetic, interactive, and essentially noncausal model of control systems. As human beings, we are extremely complex integrated systems of feedback loops with information at the very core of our being.

Certainly these three revisions of common sense have received differing amounts of support. The first, sequence point, has been amply confirmed. The second, that feelings are a kind of information, is a very plausible interpretation, but surely not as certain as the first. Finally, the control systems view is the most reasonable-seeming way of resolving the problems posed by the first two points, but other resolutions may well be developed.

In this chapter I have been tacitly assuming that just as control systems are organized hierarchically, the world must contain some kind of hierarchically organized entities to be controlled. The ontological implication is clear: that reality is a hierarchically organized structure. In the next and final chapter that point is made explicit.

NOTE

1. The meaning of *higher* and *lower* here simply refers to which one controls the other. There is no implication that one is more powerful or developed, or in any other way better. It is simply a matter of arrangement.

11

Self-Perception, Levels of Organization, and the Mind-Body Relation

This chapter is the end of a journey (or at least as far as I am prepared to go in this book), one that began with quite narrow empirical tests of a single, simple empirical hypothesis derived from William James's theory of emotion. His theory says that feelings are the results, not the causes, of emotional behaviors. The straightforward implication of his theory is that if one manipulates the behaviors, the feeling should occur. A large body of evidence supports the Jamesian, self-perception view that feelings arise from actions, including not just emotional feelings but all sorts of other feelings. This conclusion leads to a set of conceptual problems about the nature of feelings. The most attractive solution seems to be that feelings are a kind of knowledge "by acquaintance" about our ongoing behavior. That conclusion in turn raises new questions, because if feelings are a kind of knowledge and follow the behavior, then they cannot be the causes of behavior. Therefore, we need to answer two further questions as to why feelings so powerfully seem to be causes of action and how actions arise if they are not caused by feelings. The most attractive answer to those questions leads us to a conception of human beings (and indeed all living creatures) as consisting of hierarchically "stacked" control systems. Finally, the hierarchical control systems view generates a particular view of the nature of "mind" and how mind is related to body. The elaboration of this final conceptual step is the purpose of this chapter. Of course, as we have moved farther and farther from the direct empirical evidence, alternative interpretations become more and more plausible. However, I find the view I will describe here most attractive and hope that the reader also will find it has some charms.

In the previous chapter I pointed out that a "stack" of control systems produces a hierarchy of outputs—for example, movements, key presses, letters, words, sentences, and meanings. Each of these outputs is compared to reference values, and performance is adjusted until each output produces changes in the world that match its reference value. If we look at a stack of control systems, we see a consistent change in the perceptual, informational side that matches the changes in reference values and outputs. There is a "stack" of properties in the world that are compared to a "stack" of reference values to produce a "stack" of outputs. The whole system of behaviors and perceptions moves "upward" toward increasing complexity and organization. Note that the perceptual levels in the hierarchy are outside the person. That is, the information that is acquired and compared with the reference values is information that is external to the person. They are properties of the external, real world and are not just our increasingly complicated ideas. When I compare the spelling of the word *hierarchicle* with the reference spelling, the misspelled word *hierarchicle* is really out there in the world, on my computer screen. And so are the letters appearing on my computer screen, the words they make up, the sentences made up of words, and the ideas expressed in the sentences. In short, the hierarchical control systems view of people implicitly assumes that the world contains a hierarchy of levels of existence that are independent of any observer. The things at every level are "really" out there.

The idea that there are many levels of existence is, of course, not at all unusual. Hierarchical conceptions appear in many places, one of which is one of the original theoretical sources of self-perception theory, Gilbert Ryle's attempt to resolve the mind-body problem. His major work, *The Concept of Mind* (1949), was primarily a critical attack on the logic of conventional mind-body dualism. However, Ryle recognized that his self-perception-like approach led toward a need to see the world as hierarchically organized, and in some later work (Ryle, 1971) he developed these ideas. My main purpose in this chapter is to present arguments fashioned after Ryle, that the world does indeed consist of many levels of organization "stacked" hierarchically, and to argue for Ryle's alternative to mind-body dualism. With this alternative in clear view, its advantages over dualism will I hope be clear, and perhaps we can embrace both self-perception theory and the larger, hierarchical levels-of-organization approach.

THE PROBLEM OF IMMATERIAL EXISTENCE

Commonsense dualism holds that people consist of two interacting but very different kinds of things: mental and physical, mind and body. The problem with dualism is that mind and body seem too different from each other to ever be able to interact. For example, physical, material objects exist in particular places and times. In contrast, mental entities are not so clearly locatable in space and time. Where, for example, is my fondness for mystery stories or my ability to speak and write English? These are just not the sort of things that have clearly specifiable durations or locations. One way of characterizing mind and body is to say that physical objects have extension in space and time, whereas mental objects do not. Mental objects are sometimes described instead as having intension—they exist only as they are known through experience, and, most important, it is the hallmark of mental objects that they have no extension in space and time.

Because mind and body seem so deeply different, and their interaction so improbable, many thinkers have chosen to adopt "monist" positions, either that everything was mind or, more commonly in modern times, that everything was matter. The most common view of mind and body these days is materialism, the doctrine that nothing really exists except "matter and its relations." The very name *materialism* suggests that a particular kind of existence is the most basic and that everything else, including "mind," is built from this basic level through "relations." Obviously the basic level that is "privileged" by materialism is the physical world of objects, of bodies, but also rocks and water, mountains and oceans, automobiles and arms, billiard balls and bathtubs. As we will see later, the apparently special status of the level of physical objects seems less special on careful examination, but we certainly need to begin there, with physical objects, in the home grounds of materialism.

Physical, but Impalpable and Invisible

We tend to take for granted the existence of physical objects. Indeed, what we mean by "existing" seems to be what mountains and rocks do—they just *are*. To a considerable extent, what we mean by "exist" is to be available to the senses, to be directly observable, and to be the kind of thing that you could bang your shins on. This is the hallmark of the physical, that physical objects are somewhere and "somewhen." If this kind of palpable objectness is intuitively taken to be the paradigm of existing, then the existence of mental entities like an emotion of anger or an ability to solve calculus problems seems remarkably different and problematic.

Ryle (1949) observed that the apparent radical differences between mental and physical entities began to disappear if we looked closely at our ideas about the physical world. Before proceeding to describe Ryle's suggestions, I should point out that what I will be saying in the next few sections may well seem stunningly obvious to any speaker of English, or indeed any language. However, by working through a series of things that we all know about our language and our world, we do arrive at a kind of mundane but satisfying understanding of the nature of things in the world, both material and immaterial, including mind and body. In the end, this understanding may well seem to be something the reader has known all along. I think indeed we all do, in some sense, know these things, but nonetheless a slow buildup toward an explicit statement does bear some fruit.

A convenient place to start on a Rylean analysis of mind and body is with a very ordinary physical object. Consider the cup that is sitting beside my computer as I write this. There it is, in all its "thingness." I can see it, touch it, and even bang it on my shins. We might call it "perceptually observable," to indicate that we have only to look if we want to reassure ourselves that it exists. We can hear it clink against the table, feel its weight and smoothness, and taste the remnants of its contents. The cup certainly has the essential attributes of physical existence, a specific location in time and space. It is right here, right now.

Now consider another cup next to it, equally "thingy" and real. The second cup is larger than the first. "Larger" is certainly a property of one cup in relation to the other, and is therefore a property of the physical, material realm ("matter and its relations"). But notice that "larger" does not possess the supposed attributes of the physical realm. It has no location—if I put a still larger cup on the desk, "largerness" would not move abruptly to the new one. Nor, if I move the cups in relation to each other, right and left, does "largerness" change in any way. The obvious point is that the property of "larger" is something about the physical world, but it is not located in a particular place. It refers to a particular relationship between objects. The objects have locations, but the relationship of "larger" has no location itself.

Largerness also lacks any necessary location or duration in time. For example, you can compare the size of the cup on my desk with the long-smashed cup that you had as a child. Is the largerness of your childhood cup temporally located in your childhood, in the present, or in the many years between, when neither cup existed at all? Clearly none of these answers makes much sense, precisely because larger is not the kind of thing that has any particular span of time, just as it does not have a location in space.

Of course, none of these observations about the concept of "larger" are surprising to anyone who speaks our language. Observations like these only remind us that there are many concepts like "larger" that we clearly need to describe aspects of the physical, material world, but that equally clearly lack what initially seemed to be one of the hallmarks of physical existence, a specific locus in space and time. The concept of "larger" is just a simple, clear example of the second part of the definition of materialism, which is that reality consists of matter and *its relations*. Larger is a relation between material objects.

Now consider a variation on one of Ryle's favorite examples. In a moment of inattention, I push both my cups over the edge of the desk. A new concept presents itself, namely, "falling." Surely falling is a physical concept, a proper and reasonable inhabitant of the physical realm. But notice that, like "larger," "falling" does not have a fixed space-time locus. Instead, it is precisely the nature of the concept of falling that it describes a systematic change in spatial locus through a span of time. Furthermore, "falling" is not directly observable in quite the way that the objectness of each cup is. Instead, when we experience an object as falling, we are experiencing the relationship between a series of those object experiences.

Numerous psychological experiments demonstrate that, for example, if two nearby lights flash, first above and then below, you and I will not experience two stationary blinking lights. Instead, we will experience a single light, moving down, or "falling." This phenomenon demonstrates that movement is the perception of the relationship among a series of object experiences (Grossberg, 1993). More important, movement is a series of transformations of space-time loci and has no space-time locus of its own. Again, the physical realm is seen to contain two kinds of phenomena, one that has a particular space-time locus, and another that consists of relationships between those space-time loci.

The falling cups have not waited for this lengthy analysis and thus strike the floor. One breaks into two pieces. "Breaking" is a concept of a different and more complicated sort from "falling." That is, it represents a relationship between two kinds of movement, of each piece relative to the other as they fall apart.

An additional complexity presents itself, because although both cups hit the floor together, one cup broke and the other did not. The broken cup was porcelain, but the other was plastic. Why did the porcelain cup break? It broke because, obviously, unlike the plastic cup, it was brittle.

Here we have a new feature of the physical realm, "brittleness," which is even more divorced from space-time loci and the "thingness" of objects. The nature of the observations required for brittleness is important to recognize. We cannot see brittleness as easily or directly as we could see the cup or its falling, but we certainly can observe whether or not a cup is brittle. However, the necessary observations are complicated because they are three times removed from the object of cup. The first step is to movements of cups, the second to breaking, and finally to comparing cups that break with cups that do not.

The space-time locus of "brittleness" is even more ambiguous, or perhaps irrelevant, than the space-time loci of falling or breaking. In a sense the brittleness is associated with the cup, but it is not exactly clear where. For example, is the cup brittle only along the joint where it in fact came apart? The temporal dimension is equally slippery here. Was the cup brittle all the time it was sitting safely on my desk? Would the cup be brittle if somehow it was preserved forever like an archaeological exhibit and never broke?

Clearly, once again we have a good, sensible, useful idea about physical existence that does not have the properties that we previously thought defined that realm. Brittleness is not directly observable, has no specific space-time locus, and certainly could not directly affect our shins. In short, brittleness is beginning to sound very much like a mental rather than a physical property. This was the first step of Ryle's argument: the supposed difference between the physical and mental realms begins to dissolve as we look carefully at the physical realm itself.

A second point is equally important: that these observable aspects of the physical world are ordered. At the "bottom" in this example is the physical object that can be touched, seen, and tasted. We could call this level "perceptually observable" to indicate that we can check on an object's existence by using our senses, by looking, touching, and so forth. At the next level are other physical things like "falling," which is a relationship between object experiences. Next is "breaking," which is a particular kind of movement of parts relative to the whole, and finally we reach "brittle."

These different kinds of ideas and things represent different logical categories (Russell, 1912). These logical categories are ordered because the content of one kind of category consists of relations between the objects of the next "lower" level. So, we might expand the definition of materialism to read that everything real consists of matter and its relations, and relations between its relations, and relations between relations between relations, and so on, potentially ad infinitum.

LEVELS OF ORGANIZATION

A convenient label for these differences is that they represent different levels of organization (e.g., Greenberg & Tobach, 1987). The level part of this term describes the fact that these logical categories are ordered, with each succeeding level being built on the preceding. The organization part of the label emphasizes that each level consists precisely of an organization of the elements of the next level below. Note that the ordering of levels does not imply any value judgments about the levels. Higher levels are not better, or more sophisticated, or more developed. Levels are ordered simply because a higher level consists of relationships among lower level elements.

The most familiar example of hierarchical levels of organization, partly developed in chapter 10, is the written language. At the lowest level are marks on a page of paper. Some, but not all, such marks are letters. In all written alphabets, particular patterns of marking are taken to be letters, and others are just scribbles. The letters of one language may be the scribbles of another. So, the "letterness" consists of particular patterns of marks; at the next level are words. These consist of letters in particular patterns or orders. The difference between "dog" and "god" as words is entirely in the relationship between the letters. At the next level are sentences (and meaningful sentence fragments) that are said to have meaning. Their meaning depends, once again, on the organization of the words that make them up. "The dog worshiped the god" and "The god worshiped the dog" obviously have very different meanings. In this case, then, we can see four levels—marks, letters, words, and sentences—each of which consists of relationships between the elements of the next lower level.[1]

Levels of Organization and Human Behavior

Now that our ordinary understanding of levels of organization has been made explicit (we did know this stuff all along), we can turn to human beings and their activities. Consider another example that I also used earlier in the discussion of "stacks" of control systems. Then the point was to exemplify how control systems could be organized, but now I want to focus on the ontological implications of the levels-of-organization idea. The example is me at this moment, still sitting at my typewriter, trying to make some sense appear on the page. Let us begin with my "finger." It is certainly a physical object, like a cup or a rock. Now my finger "wiggles" downward, an event like falling that is a relationship between finger locations. My finger does not just move downward, however. As it wiggles, it "presses" a key, a relationship between the movement and the object nearby. Since the key is part of the computer, I am "typing." And although I could be entering numbers into a spreadsheet, I am actually "writing." While writing, I could be making a grocery list, or plans for my vacation, but I am actually "composing a theoretical argument/explanation." Since I am a psychologist composing arguments for other psychologists, I am "being a psychologist."

Each of the seven terms in quotation marks—finger, wiggle, pressing, typing, writing, composing theory, being a psychologist—describes something currently true and real about me. And these descriptions range from a clearly physical kind of existence, like "finger," to a clearly mental kind of existence, like "composing theory." Notice, however, that there is not a natural division between the mental and physical kinds of thing. Instead, in this hierarchy, we see a span of terms that are obviously mental or physical only at the extremes.

This was the central point of Ryle's analysis, that the materialists and idealists had gone in the wrong direction in trying to resolve the mind-body problem. The problem with dualism was not that it assumed too many kinds of existence, but rather that it recognized too few. Instead of two things, mind and body, in this example at least seven kinds of thing can be identified, ranging smoothly between the clearly bodily and the clearly mental, with no natural division anywhere.

The nature of levels and their relationships will become more explicit if we explore this example a bit more. First, we need to look at what constitutes each level. The many descriptions spanning the levels between "finger" and "psychologizing" are all ways of understanding what I am doing right now. However, as Ryle pointed out, even though I can be understood to be doing seven things at the same time, these seven are not different in the way that a circus performer simultaneously juggling, balancing a plate on a stick, playing an accordion and cymbals, singing, dancing, and winking is doing seven things. Instead, they are seven increasingly highly organized ways of thinking about what I am doing. Ryle (1971) referred to these differences as between "thin" and "thick" descriptions of action.

It is tempting and sometimes convenient to say that these are seven different ways of thinking about the same event. Notice, however, that these seven ways of thinking about my actions are not really describing the same event. What counts as "the event" varies systematically with each level. The event of a key press is only a tiny part of the event of "writing," which is only a tiny part of "being a psychologist." Since each level is constituted by relationships among elements of the next lower level, the lower level elements are, in a sense, contained within the higher. However, the higher also contains those other elements whose relationships constitute the level. Most important, the higher level is not simply a collection of elements but rather the organized relationship among them; actually, "contain" is not at all the correct word. Instead, each higher level is constituted from the elements of the lower level. Thus, there is only a limited sense in which it is appropriate to say that these are all ways of thinking about the same event. At each level, the definition of an event changes, too. Although all are legitimate answers to the question, "What are you doing now?" the "now" is different for each answer. When I respond that I am pressing a key, the "now" is a fraction of a second. When I respond that I am describing a theory, the "now" may extend over months (though of course with a few interruptions) and certainly has no clear beginning or end.

This same notion of a hierarchical structure of ways of thinking about actions has been developed in psychological research by Vallacher and Wegner (1987), who have demonstrated systematic differences in the ways people become aware of actions depending on the context of awareness and the kind of person. At least one principle guiding which level we are aware of is what is most useful to us at the moment (Mullener & Laird, 1974). If we can think about our actions at many levels, it is precisely because many levels of action actually do exist.

Social/Cultural Contexts

In the system of levels of my action, the higher level understandings depend on more than just my doings and me. Even at the relatively low level of pressing a key, my key-pressing activity requires a key. At the higher levels, the relationships with the world around me are equally necessary— to type, the key must be attached to a word processor, and to be writing requires an audience who might read.

As we ascend these levels, many activities that we characteristically think of as belonging to a single person actually require a social and cultural context. For example, when I compose an argument, I have some kind of audience in mind. If what I write is incomprehensible to everyone who does or could exist, it cannot be said to be an argument. (Certainly, at merit raise time, the university administrators would not consider it a constituent of "being a psychologist.") The point is that at the higher levels of organization, many patterns of what we usually call "my" action actually involve other people as well. At these levels, the actions are intrinsically social and interpersonal—we literally cannot talk about higher levels of organization and the person without talking about the social world as well (e.g., Wertsch, 1985). How, for example, could one speak of someone as a Democrat unless there was a system of elections and parties? To be a Democrat, one must live in a social system that includes Republicans! Or at a somewhat lower level, one could not speak of a person as generous without other people who would be the recipients of his generosity. Many, perhaps all, higher levels consist precisely of interactions and transactions between people or groups of people. In addition, still higher levels, like "democracy" or "gross national product," are so far removed from the activities of individual people that we no longer even think of individuals.

In sum, Ryle's solution to the problem of immaterial existence was to recognize that there are many levels of organization of existence ordered between the levels we see as prototypically physical and the levels we see as prototypically mental. The origins of the mind-body problem lay in the failure to recognize the existence of the many levels that extend in small steps between the conventionally mental and conventionally physical realms (and also beyond in either direction).

All Levels Are Real

The reality of these levels has been assumed thus far, but the question deserves explicit attention. Some people might be inclined to say that only the level of palpable objects is truly real, and that perhaps all the other levels are "just" our interpretations or constructions of the world. This position seems to arise from at least two sources. One is the common-sense tendency to equate "real" with "palpable" and therefore "material." Hopefully the discussion of "falling," "breaking," and "brittle" has already demonstrated the error of this confusion. How could one deny reality to concepts like "larger," "falling," or "brittle," all of which are as real as cups, but a great deal less palpable?

A second reason that higher levels sometimes seem less "real" is the diversity of experiences we can all have of what seem to be the same events. We all assume that there is only one reality, so if you and I have widely different but equally valid-seeming perceptions when we observe "the same thing," it seems that what we perceive must depend on how we look at it rather than what it is. Furthermore, if two opposing claims about the world seem equally valid, both cannot be true, so at least one and perhaps both of the views must be no more than "constructions" by the observers. Like all creative products, such constructions could be neither true nor false. Following this line of reasoning, the problem of multiple truths is solved by denying truth to all.

Although this constructivist view has its attractions, I think it is mistaken. We can see an alternative, and I think better, resolution to the problem of multiple truths if we look closely at an example of differing experiences of the "same" thing. Consider the standard illustration that appears in many introductory psychology texts. This is the picture (see Figure 11.1) that can be seen as either a young woman or an old crone. In the same picture, we can experience two very different things, both of which seem, and indeed are, equally accurate. One demonstration of that fact is that in time, each of us will see the alternative, and then will be able to switch between them.

Because we can see either the crone or the young woman in "the same" picture, is neither the crone nor the young woman real? Surely not, but how, then, can the same, single thing be two things? The apparent theoretical

Figure 11.1. An example of two equally "good" views of a single thing.
*Source: American Journal of Psy*chology. Copyright 1930 by the Board of Trustees
of the University of Illinois. Used with permission of the University of Illinois
Press.

difficulty arises from a misunderstanding of what constitutes "the same
event." What is the same are not the old woman and the young one. Instead, what is the same is at a lower level—patterns of black and white on a
page. Higher levels might organize those lower levels in a variety of higher
level patterns. So, in a real sense, when you see the picture as an old
woman, you are responding to a different object—a different organization
of those patches of black and white—than when I see it as a young woman.
And both of these organizations are different from the patches of ink,

which are at a lower level. At the level of ink on the page, there is one thing; at the higher level of old and young women, there are two. It is precisely the trick of pictures like this that they contain two equally good higher level organizations of a single array of black and white.

All the examples of differing interpretation seem to fit this example. In every case, the sameness is defined at a lower level than the level at which differences are seen. So, when you see a fumbling president and I see an aimless, self-serving Congress, we may both be fitting the "same," sad, political events into different higher level patterns that really exist in the world.

Note that this permissive view of multiple higher order truths is not unlimited. The implication of this analysis is that there are both genuinely true and genuinely false perceptions of the world. Even if there are many real, higher level organizations that can be constructed from a particular lower level set of elements, there are an even larger number of imaginable organizations that are not true and do not correspond to the actuality of the lower levels. Both the young woman and the old woman are true perceptions of the real organizations of that figure, but if someone claimed it was a picture of a pig playing a tuba or a model of economic development, those "perceptions" would be wrong.

In sum, all levels of organization seem equally real in the sense that they belong equally to our worlds. If we are going to accord realness to any levels, then we have no basis for arbitrarily deciding that realness has vanished at some point in the smoothly ascending system of levels. Only palpability is confined to a single level.

LEVELS OF ORGANIZATION AND MATERIALISM

As I have said already a number of times, the levels-of-organization view is no more than a version of materialism because each of the succeeding levels is rooted in material existence. The first level consists of material objects, such as fingers and cups, the next level consists of relations between material objects, the next level yet consists of relations between relations between material objects, and so on.

Sometimes materialists explicitly claim a special existential status for the level of material objects. It is what is "really real," and the rest, including what is usually understood as mental, is somehow secondary or derived. Even if not explicit, the assumption that material objects are special is the source of the name for this position, *materialism*.

In contrast, from the levels-of-organization perspective, the only thing special about the level of physical objects is that it is about the lowest level that human beings can readily experience. The levels above are no less, and no more, real.

When we look in the other direction of the hierarchical structure, we see some additional problems with according special status to the level of physical objects. Because I began this discussion with commonsense dualism, the lowest levels of experience we have looked at so far have been ordinary objects like cups and fingers. Objects of this sort are the lowest level of organization that we are ordinarily aware of in our commonsense dealings with the world. However, cups and fingers can easily be recognized as made up from lower levels of organization, such as the cells of a finger. In fact, many modern materialists identify the material ground for mental phenomena as at the level of fingers, although they prefer a different organ—the brain—and the nervous system. Of course, the brain and nervous system are essentially involved in psychological events, in somewhat the same way that we could not talk about one cup being larger than another unless there were two cups to be compared. However, one can attribute special status to the level of organization of the nervous system only temporarily. Inconveniently for any notion that neurons are special, the scientific understanding that licenses our talk about neurons also includes the fact that neurons are themselves made up of smaller structures such as mitochondria, cell walls, and sodium gates. Thus, those scientific arguments that give neurons some claim to be more "real" than key presses or thoughts simultaneously undermine the distinctiveness of neurons. Furthermore, our science recognizes that mitochondria, cell walls, and the like are constituted from molecules, which are constituted from atoms, which are constituted from subatomic particles, which are constituted from quarks, and so forth. Once we make the step of recognizing a level of existence that lies below everyday object-experiences, we must recognize a whole series of levels of existence that descend as smoothly from cups toward quarks as other levels ascend from cups toward joy and poetry.[2]

In sum, no single level or kind of existence seems to be clearly material or mental, much less special. Instead, we see a range of levels, from electron orbits to enjoying symphonic music to cultural diffusion, all equally real, all different. Within this range of levels, a wide span is what we usually mean by material, another wide region is what we usually mean by mental, and the two regions shade gradually into each other with a substantial amount of overlap.[3] Furthermore, no obvious criterion seems to exist to identify one of the many levels as special and different in its existential status.

SO SHOULD WE CALL THIS MATERIALISM?

Materialism is defined as holding that the only things that are real are matter and its relations. Certainly, this is an apt description of the theory that recognizes the multitude of hierarchically organized levels. However, the label of "materialism" seems to be confusing and to foster an error, since it tends to give special status to one of the many levels when nothing about our understanding of levels suggests anything special about that particular level, the level of palpable experience of objects. At most, the "material" level is special only because it is the lowest level we human beings readily experience. The best part of the "materialism" label is that it implies a rejection of the far worse idea that mind and the material body are radically different. But it seems far better to think always of levels of organization, stretching unknown distances upward yet also downward from our everyday experiences.

Ontological Realism-Epistemological Constructivism

Implicit up to now has been the distinction between the levels of organization of things in the world and the levels of organization of our experience. As the example of the picture of the young woman and the old woman makes clear, although we detect real organizations of the external world, we must play an active role in this process. A reasonable question is whether we should view the process of understanding as extracting information (Gibson, 1979) or constructing it. Both descriptions are metaphoric, and each metaphor has its charms. The word *extracting* carries the meanings Gibson intended, that even very high levels of organization are real and out there in the world, that high-level information about the world is really there in the sensory stream, and that we are naturally built to detect these high levels. The charm of the construction metaphor is that it nicely focuses on the process in which the products of each lower level are in some sense the building blocks of the next, both in reality and in our understanding of reality. The drawback to the constructing metaphor is its recent history of implying that whatever is constructed is therefore a kind of fiction that has nothing to do with an external reality. Despite its drawbacks, I will use a construction metaphor for the rest of this chapter to emphasize the work that must be done to become aware at higher levels. The implications of Gibson's label are equally correct in that no level is more or less real than any other, and also that people are constructed to extract automatically and "naturally" very complex levels of information from the sensory stream.[4]

Earlier I suggested that we would all feel that we had known about levels of organization all along. I do not mean here to try to persuade simply by asserting that "everyone knows this," but rather that the basic ideas are familiar even if not previously encountered in just this form. The central idea, of course, is that the world consists of many levels of organization and that the recognition of these levels makes it easy to see many classic problems as not really problematic at all. In the previous chapter we saw the clarity that seems to emerge from a control systems understanding of hierarchical organization: The nature of feelings and their role in behavior become quite straightforward and obvious. In this chapter we have also seen that one of the major difficulties of dualism dissolves under the light of hierarchical organization. Mind and body are, indeed, both real and equally real—but neither is even a single level. Instead, what we ordinarily call mind and what we ordinarily call matter are both best seen as a region or span of levels of organization. These levels ascend smoothly without any natural division from what dualists would call body to what they would call mind, from the material ground to the social constructions of democracy and gross domestic product.

Two problems of dualism remain, and an analysis of hierarchical organization suggests some useful ways of thinking about them. The first of these is the problem of the privacy of mind and mental contents and acts. The second is the problem of "qualia," which is that it is not clear why our experiences and feelings should be just the way they are. Why does the experience of red feel the way it does? Or even, perhaps, could my experience of red be the same as your experience of green?

THE "PRIVACY" OF MENTAL EVENTS, ACTIONS, AND CAUSES

Common sense and many more formal theories of mind assume that the mental realm is absolutely private: No one but ourselves can know our minds. And other people are not just handicapped by lack of facts (or interest) about us. In this view, no amount of observing, by any imaginable technique, could yield more than reasonable inferences about the workings of our minds. The nature of mind is to be accessible only to introspection. The mental world is as intrinsically private as the physical is public.

To anticipate the hierarchical organization response to this problem, if the dichotomy of physical and mental is too crude, probably we should be equally suspicious of a simple division into public and private. Consistent with the levels-of-organization discussion in the preceding section, private versus public seems best seen as a continuous series of levels, not an either-or dichotomy. Rather than two separate realms of the private and the public, the events of our psychological life are entirely public at low levels and, for very practical reasons, become increasingly inaccessible to others as we move up to higher and higher levels. At the higher levels, an outside observer of us becomes increasingly handicapped by lack of information, but not because these higher levels are disappearing behind the curtains of the private mind. And, of course, the notion that bodies and material things are public and minds are private arises from the familiar error of failing to recognize the many gradations that lie between the prototypical material and the prototypical mental.

Before unpacking this idea, I must note that our everyday experience includes two kinds of mental "stuff," each of which seems private in a somewhat different way. One kind of stuff might be called mental objects and includes such things as emotions, motives, desires, attitudes, and beliefs. We know these mental objects by "feeling" them, an experience that is direct and apparently unmediated. The other kind of mental phenomenon that needs explanation consists of mental actions, such as thinking, perceiving, and remembering. These two aspects of mind involve somewhat different senses of privacy and require somewhat different analysis. They will thus be treated separately.

The Privacy of Mental "Objects"

The "privacy" of emotions, motives, and so forth can be dispensed with quickly. As I have discussed at great length already, the basic point of self-perception theory is that the whole idea of private mental feelings observable only through introspection is mistaken. Instead, our feelings are interpretations of our ongoing behaviors and the contexts in which they are occurring. Most of the earlier chapters have been devoted to reviewing literally hundreds of experiments that support this view. My brief formula to describe the basic self-perception hypothesis is as follows: Feelings do not cause behaviors; they follow, are based on, and are information about those behaviors and the context in which they are being enacted. So, there are no mental objects, private or otherwise, because there are just behaviors and contexts. Both behaviors and contexts are essentially public.

The feelings are not just about the behaviors, however. The feelings are actually at a level above the level of the behavior and the context. That is, feelings consist precisely of the relationship between the behavior, such as a smile, and the context, such as meeting a friend. A smile in that context is happiness. An approving speech in the context of an apparent free expression of opinion is a positive attitude. A feeling of fluency in the absence of any other explanation is familiarity. However, just as the behaviors are public, so, too, are the contexts. They are, after all, no more than social systems and settings.

Why, then, do mental properties seem to be private? Some of the apparent privateness arises from the importance of the context and other higher level relations. As patterns or patterns of patterns of action in context, emotions and other psychological states are all observable. The necessary observations are not easy, but the difficulty arises because the patterns are complex and abstract, not because the events observed are occurring in some inner, intrinsically private space. In particular, the behaviors that are one of the kinds of constituents of the pattern may be readily observable, as, for example, when we can see a smile or frown, hear a speech, or watch someone approach an object. However, some of the other components of the pattern may be much less easily observed. For example, we may not be able to tell whether someone was paid or asked to do these things, or whether the target persons are actors performing according to a script or just ordinary people pretending interests and desires to avoid social embarrassment. Without these essential pieces of contextual information, we cannot interpret the more easily observed behaviors correctly. Notice that none of these additional, essential kinds of information are intrinsically private. They are just more difficult to observe at the moment the target person is acting. Returning to the analogy of the old woman/young women picture, it would be very difficult for you to know which organization I am experiencing at this moment, because they are equally likely. But there is nothing mysteriously impossible or intrinsically private about my experiences, which are, after all, just experiences of a drawing.

Furthermore, as we ascend from the perceptually observable level, the complexity of the observations confers increasing amounts of a practical kind of privacy. For example, consider a hierarchy of awarenesses that has near its top the trait of being patriotic. Low in such a hierarchy might be three levels consisting of "drawing back the corners of my mouth," then "smiling," and then "happy." Still higher would be "being happy at the

sight of the flag" and, finally, being pleased by any instances of my country's success or being "patriotic." This hierarchy begins with a very public
kind of behavior. You may well be in a better position than I to notice that
the corners of my mouth are drawn back. That this is a smile, rather than
a grimace to expose my teeth to the dentist, requires a bit more interpretation, but you are probably in a reasonable position to recognize that. To
know that I am happy, rather than faking to avoid offending my neighbor,
requires a great deal more information of a kind that is increasingly hard
for you to obtain. For one thing, you would probably need to have observed a history of interactions with my neighbor. However, this information, too, is ultimately public, if historical. Finally, if you observe me
expressing positive feelings toward my country over some span of time,
you will judge that I am a patriot. Of course, to know about the many
other occasions I have lauded my country would require that you have
spent a great deal of time with me.[5]

Now, suppose that I am actually a spy, planted in this country to infil-
trate my university and discover its important secrets. I may make all sorts
of persuasive public displays of patriotism but all the while actually be
pretending. I might go undetected for a lifetime, but not because my true
national affections exist only in some hidden recess of my mind. My actual
allegiances would be well known to my spymasters, and hiding them
would be evidence of great care and skill, but not of the nature of mind.
The actual point at which true and phony patriots diverge is at the level of
the context for the expression of positive feelings. If my context is to reveal
freely my opinion of my country, then the positive statements, smiles, and
happy postures are experienced as patriotic feelings. If my context is to
appear fond of my country to avoid detection, then my statements and
smiles will be "disqualified" as in misattribution experiments, and I will
feel no fondness for my country.

As this example makes clear, the increasing privacy is practical. It arises
because of the difficulty of sharing the increasingly complex matrix of information that is necessary to "see" the same patterns that the actor sees.
Knowing all about another person's emotions, beliefs, and desires is not a
matter of a logical impossibility. However, the practical barriers to our
knowledge of others, and their knowledge of us, are in many cases strong
enough so that we can all feel secure. They also seem strong enough to
have fostered the erroneous belief in intrinsically private knowledge.

Mental Processes

Now we can turn to examine the processes such as thinking, imagining,
remembering, puzzling, and solving, all of which seem to involve a different kind of privacy. When I wonder if I am actually foolish or happy, my
answer seems to be derived entirely from the self-perception of the complex patterns of my public behavior. I may not be any better at recognizing
those patterns than anyone else, but whether I am at this moment thinking
about my foolishness or my happiness, no one can know unless I tell

them. And when I sit at my desk, no one else can tell whether I am think-ing about a psychological problem or about what I will eat for lunch. Thinking is private in the sense that one person often cannot guess *about* what it is another is thinking.

Is there, then, a way of understanding thinking that connects our pri-vate musings with publicly observable events? One approach to this ques-tion is attractive because of its fit with the previous discussion of levels of organization of actions, but unfortunately, as we will see, this approach seems too simple. One example of this too-simple hierarchical idea ap-pears in Ryle's paper subtitled "What Is Le Penseur Doing?" (1971). He points out that Le Penseur might be Euclid working on some theorem. So what is he doing? We might describe him as moving muscles in his mouth and throat, as talking to himself, as thinking about a math problem, and perhaps as solving it, and finally as being a great mathematician. All these are possibly true, all at different levels of organization. It is our familiar "stack" of hierarchically ordered organizations.

If this were an accurate picture of what thinking consists of, it would provide just the kind of hierarchical explanation we would like and ex-pect. At the bottom of this set of levels, Le Penseur's behavior is obviously public. Even though he sits motionless, as outside observers we could readily notice the twitching muscles in Le Penseur's throat. Almost equally easily we could infer that he is talking to himself. Perhaps with great effort we could learn to decode these mumblings and twitches and even know what he is saying. This is the familiar subvocal theory of thought that was popular among behaviorists a while ago.

Unfortunately, as Ryle recognized, the evidence is inconsistent with the assumption that when Le Penseur (or any of us) thinks, he must be liter-ally talking to himself, even "subvocally"—after all, many of us can think and chew gum at the same time. Consequently, we cannot find the public ground for thinking so easily.

Still, thinking and speaking must have some connection (Dennett, 1991). Often when we are thinking especially hard, we do speak phrases and sentences to ourselves. Many of us have had the experience of being led to a new understanding of something during the attempt to describe it to someone else, either in speech or in writing. Finally, although we may be able to think and chew gum at the same time, speaking about one thing while thinking about another is beyond us, at least if the topics are chal-lenging. The most we can manage is to alternate rapidly between the two topics of thought. At a minimum, speech does seem to be involved in thought in some way.

The development of thinking supports this notion, too. Children seem to progress from a stage at which they do some kinds of thinking by speak-ing aloud, and then to a stage of telegraphic mumbles to themselves, and finally to quiet thought with no external manifestations (Vygotsky, 1962; Wertsch, 1985). This developmental sequence provides a historical link of thinking with the public activity of speaking.

Learning to read is a parallel example of the progression from an activity that is clearly public to an activity that is private in practice if not principle. When children learn to read, they begin with identifying individual letters and their sounds. Once they can identify letters, they move on to small words and learn to make their sounds. They often need to hear themselves "sounding out" the word in order to identify it. Usually when they can say the words fluidly, they still must say them and listen to their speech to acquire the sense of sentences. Then they learn to read silently, although often their teachers must remind them not to move their lips. Finally, many people become able to "speed-read" and acquire the sense of a text without any appreciable knowledge of the words that supplied the sense.

Notice there are two processes here. One is the progression through the levels from letters, to words, to sentences, to sense (or gist). The other is a separate process that consists of learning to give up the full vocal speech, to just moving one's lips, to eventually reading so fast that no one's lips could move fast enough. The second of these is what Vygotsky noted in regard to thinking. If the reading example is truly parallel, it is essential in order to free thinking from the pace of lip and throat muscle movements.

If the parallel holds, then we should expect the first process to occur as well. That is, the developing child might be expected to acquire the ability to think about higher and higher levels of organization. Adults, then, might be said to think in "gists" rather than words much of the time. But just as a particularly difficult book may slow us down to word-by-word reading, when the problems are tough, we sometimes think in obviously verbal ways, including sometimes talking to ourselves.

When we speed-read, we are only aware of the sense of the material. However, clearly there must be nonconscious, parallel processes working at lower levels of organization that identify letters, words, and sentences to feed upward to the higher level gist-detecting processes. Similarly, although our conscious experience of thought may be in gists, there probably are many lower level processes working in parallel that correspond to processes in the domain of reading that lead to letter and word recognition.

When we adults think (or speed-read), all the lower level processes that permit operating on gists have been so automatized that we are unaware of their occurrence. Consequently, we are equally unaware of the essentially public lower level processes that provide the components from which higher level organizations of thought are constituted.

The final point of this view of thinking is that higher level components like gists or meanings are very abstract, high-level organizations of lower level activities. These meanings and gists are not "hidden" because they are mental but because they are highly abstract. If instead of just thinking, I was to speak my thoughts out loud, the sounds would be public, and you could observe them with your sensory organs. But the gist of my thoughts would never be something you could directly hear, see, or in any other way directly observe, because gists are at too high a level of abstraction. A gist consists precisely of a relation, between relations between relations, between relations between relations between relations between sounds. This is not to say that the gist is not in the sensory flow, the patterns of sounds reaching our ears. Rather, as Gibson (1979) pointed out, these higher level organizations are contained in the patterns of physical energies at very much higher levels of organization.

Images

In addition to speech and language-related concepts, we also use images in our thinking (Shepard & Cooper, 1986). Just as the gist is a high-level organization of the material read or heard, images clearly preserve some higher level aspects of visual displays without including much that was originally present. A mental map is very much like a real map in that it represents a few things, such as the ways towns and roads are connected, without including most other features of the world, such as the trees and bushes, or the beauty of the villages, or even whether the road runs up- or downhill. Similarly, images contain highly abstracted spatial information, just as gists contain highly abstracted linguistic information. Using either of these kinds of high-level representation is a considerable skill that has developed out of much clearly public looking and saying.

As one consequence of the increasing freedom of thinking from speaking, we acquire the capacity for deliberate deception, even mild deceptions like the impassive, glazed look of many people at meetings. As the examples of reading and of inner speech make clear, thinking so covertly seems to be a considerable accomplishment, one that young children have not yet achieved.

Remembering

Memory may seem inconsistent with this public view of cognition, since memories seem to exist in some more or less permanent but private form for as much as a lifetime. It is difficult to avoid assuming that these memories must be stored somewhere until we need them. The storehouse seems at first glance to be the kind of place that only introspection can examine. The storehouse must, it seems, be full of sensations, thoughts, and feelings waiting to be retrieved on demand, a kind of warehouse of videotapes of our lives.

In some sense, this must indeed be true—the organism must have changed in some way that makes remembering possible. We go astray here in thinking of memories rather than the act of remembering. When we recall a childhood picnic or the multiplication tables, we are performing an action, we are doing something. If we had not been transformed in some way by our pasts, we could not now perform these actions. However, the changes do not need to correspond to our current rememberings. What is preserved is not a replica of our past, private experiences or a page from a mathematics book, like images on a TV screen.[6] What is preserved is something that makes it possible for us to perform these actions of recollection now. These changes are almost certainly in our neuronal connections and activities, but they are not pictures and sounds.

The video is actually a perfect analogy here. If we had videotaped the picnic, we could see and hear it again and again. But the videotape does not look anything like the events "captured" on it. The videotape is a strip of plastic. Examined more closely (and technologically), all we could see would be a magnetic coating with patterns of electrical charges. Only by playing the tape through a VCR can these charges be organized into pictures and sounds. What this means for a video is that the sounds and sights of the video are neither "on the tape" nor in the machine but are instead higher order forms that are produced by the interaction of tape and machine. Similarly, our memories are undoubtedly preserved in some essentially public form of neuronal activity or structure. They become increasingly private in the practical sense only as they are organized into higher and higher levels of activity that we can eventually experience. We would not call the scenes of a videotape private because we can only observe a strip of plastic instead of sights and sounds, and similarly, memories stored as neuron changes are no more private. These changes in the "storage" neurons and the activities of those parts of the brain that "read" these stored neurons are brought together to produce recollections. Once the storage neurons are replayed as acts of remembering, they are no more or less private than any other thoughts.

In sum, both feelings and thoughts are relatively high-order patterns of publicly observable events. Or they are patterns of activity that were rooted in public actions and that we have learned with difficulty to hide. Thus, one of the supposed properties distinguishing the mind from the body, that mind was inherently private, seems to be true—but only in a practical, not logical, sense. It is certainly true that increasingly higher levels of organization of experience or thought are private for all practical purposes.

QUALIA, OR HOW PHYSICAL STIMULI PRODUCE PERCEPTUAL EXPERIENCES

In the last chapter I discussed the way in which mental contents like emotions, desires, and attitudes can lead to action. We might think of this as the "downward" problem of how higher order properties affect lower level actions. The corresponding problem is that of "upward" causation, of how physical energies and events can produce the mental experiences we have of the world. One way this problem is confronted is around the issue of qualia. A quale is the direct, immediate experience of something, such as the color red in our perception of an apple. While we all know that our experience of red derives from the wavelengths of light falling on our retina (in relation to the wavelengths reflected from other parts of the visual field), we also know that indescribable feeling of redness. The problem is that the two seem to have nothing in common. There seem to be two parallel kinds of "stuff," electromagnetic radiation and redness; how the two can be connected is difficult to imagine. One way of stating this problem is that it is unclear why red objects should feel just "this way, the way red objects feel." The apparent arbitrariness of this connection even makes creepily plausible the otherwise silly-sounding idea that the feeling or quale of redness could be attached instead to green objects and vice versa.

The route toward an answer to this problem seems to be the same as the answer we have found for the other problems of dualism. In every case, the appearance of a problem depends on focusing our attention on widely separated, prototypically material and prototypically mental portions of the range of levels. These distant end points then seemed too far away from each other to share any kind of reality, to be known by the same public or private means, or to affect one another in any way. The qualia version of this question is, How could electromagnetic radiation out there lead to my distinctive experience of redness? So far, in each case, we saw that between these distant strangers were a gradual series of steps that bridged all these gaps without difficulty. The same kind of insight bridges the apparent chasm between physical energies and qualia. We just need to follow each of the small steps that lie between, and the mystery dissolves.

Not all the steps between electromagnetic radiation and experienced qualia are known; in the example depicted in Figure 11.2, however, we can trace much of the route (e.g., Hubel & Wiesel, 1979). When you or I look at a Neckar cube, we see it as three-dimensional. We just see it that way, and that three-dimensional quality, that distinctive feeling of depth, is surely a reasonable example of a quale. Here the problem is how that feeling of depth could arise from a pattern of black and white ink on the page and the photons that reach some, but not all, parts of our eyes as we look at it.

The first step is, of course, the transduction of the light photons into neural energy in the receptor cells of the retina. These receptor cells respond to the presence or absence of light energy. The next step is the response to relative light and dark at the ganglion cells of the retina. A number of

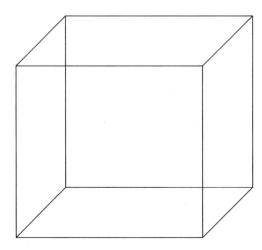

Figure 11.2. A Neckar Cube, in which we automatically perceive the "quale" of depth.

receptor cells affect the activity of a single ganglion cell, and the ganglion cell fires in response to relationships among these receptor cells. Some ganglion cells fire most actively if the receptor cells in its region are illuminated while those around them are dark. In effect, then, the ganglion cells are responding to a relationship, to a point of light on a field of black (or to some other relationship among receptor cells). This ganglion cell response is clearly a relation and at the next level of organization above the simple light/no light response of the rods and cones. The ganglion cell is responding with something like "more light on the receptors in the middle of my field than on the outside ring." So, before the information of the visual display has even left the retina, it has been processed into a higher level of organization.[7]

At the next set of synapses in the optic tract a variety of higher order patterns among ganglion cell outputs begin to take shape (Grossberg, 1993). For example, one group of cells respond to combinations of these ganglion cell points that form lines or edges. These cells are responding to a higher order relationship between a number of points that arrange themselves, for example, into a horizontal line. This step of organization takes place in the thalamus, before the visual information has even reached the visual cortex. At the next step, in the occipital cortex of the brain, are cells that respond to relationships between lines that form corners, for example. The final product of perceived depth is a still more complex integration of these patterns. (In parallel with these patterns are other higher order organizations that detect movement, forms, and colors.)

Notice, then, the visual system is a clear, unambiguous example of a hierarchically organized system. At every step, information is extracted and organized into increasingly abstract properties of the visual world.

We do not know the exact set of neurons in the visual cortex that detect how objects are arrayed in three-dimensional space, but this is the only step we do not already understand. Although not quite completely closed, the gap between electromagnetic energies and the qualities of experience no longer seems so mysterious. If the visual system builds perceptual experiences in this way, then the final "product" that we experience as a quale is certainly constituted from lower level activities, like squarenesses and corners, which will not seem so difficult to relate to the quale of depth. And these lower order things will be constituted from still lower things, like lines, until, following the hierarchical organizational process in the other direction, we reemerge at the retina and the response to electromagnetic energies. A similar account, with perhaps a few more gaps, could be provided for any of the qualia. Although this explanation is undoubtedly too simple, in essence we see here a process in which information is organized in higher and higher levels, until at the end of the process is a group of neurons, or some other brain structure, that is active in one way for far objects and in another way for near objects.

The only question that might remain is at the very last stage, why depth *feels* the way it does, why the color red that we have detected *feels* as it

Location	Conditions for Activity
Photons	Reflected from world into eye, to receptor cells
Receptor Cells	Active if photon strikes photo-pigment
Ganglion Cells	Active if receptor cells in center are active and surround cells are not
Thalamus	Active if ganglion cells in a simple pattern are active; e.g., a line
Occipital Cortex	Active if thalamic cells are active in a complex pattern; e.g., lines meeting at a right angle, or parallel lines
Visual Association Areas??	Active if combinations of lines in parallel and at angles, etc., make a Neckar Cube

Figure 11.3. The series of integrative steps in the visual system that build an experience of depth from the impact of photons. The column labeled Location lists the places in the visual pathway where the integrative activity takes place. The column labeled Conditions for Activity describes the relationship of the lower level elements that produces activity at this level.

does, why the activity of the last neuron or group of neurons in the sequence, those that detect "far" or "near," should feel as it does.

Perhaps the best answer to this question is another question: How else would depth or redness feel? When we become aware of information about the world, we have to experience it somehow, and this is just the way we do (Dennett, 1991). The feeling quality of depth or redness is just what it is. The original mystery was why electromagnetic radiation falling on our eye could produce such experiences. Now the mystery has at least been reduced to that last stage of how relatively high levels of organization of information could be experienced differently. Indeed, the question begins to sound silly. If the final quale that we need to explain is the experience that the cube is three-dimensional, then the answer is, at best, "That's the way that three-dimensional objects feel."

The same insight applies to the red/green qualia question. At the second stage of the perceptual system are ganglion cells that respond to a different set of relationships between receptor cells. Among those receptor cells are some that fire most often to light at 559 nanometers, while others are most sensitive to light at 530 nanometers. If the 559 cells are more active than the 530 cells, the ganglion cell's "message" is "red." That is in fact the only meaning that the experience of redness really has. Because we are unable to experience any of the intermediate steps from electromagnetic radiation to the experience, the feeling of redness seems mysterious.

In sum, events at the lower, "physical" levels can cause events at the higher, "mental" levels because the perceptual systems are built to detect incoming sensory energies, but equally are built to detect patterns within these energies, and patterns within these patterns, and so forth, as Gibson (1979) argued. At the end of this process emerge experiences and qualia. The apparent strangeness of the connection between the physical energies and the experiences seems to be largely a product of our ignorance of the intermediate steps that lie between them. Most of the mystery disappears when we understand that system.

RELATIONS BETWEEN HIGHER AND LOWER LEVELS: ANALYTIC, CONSTITUTIVE, AND CAUSAL RELATIONS

Before leaving the question of how entities at different levels may interact, a few general principles are worth emphasizing. Across levels, two kinds of relationship occur, upward and downward. What is true at one level imposes some constraints on what must be true of levels above and below, but these constraints are loose and do not absolutely determine what is true above or below.

We can see how these constraints operate in the well-worked example of my activity right now: finger, wiggling, pressing a key, typing, writing, arguing, psychologizing, and so on. If I am wiggling my finger, there is no necessity that it presses a key. However, if it is near a keyboard, it will press, whereas remaining motionless or lifting my finger could not press a key. Thus, what is true at the lower level—wiggling—changes the possibilities of what could be true at higher levels without requiring that anything be so. Similarly, if I am writing, I could be arguing. I am more likely to be arguing than if I was dribbling a basketball, but my writing need not constitute an argument. Still, if I am writing, the range of possibilities is limited: arguments or grocery lists, but not three-point baskets or cooking supper.

The same kind of partial constraint applies downward as well. If I am arguing, I do not need to be writing. But I do have to be doing something like speaking, gesturing, or grimacing. That is, I must be doing something communicative, although I need not be communicating in any particular way. If I am writing, I could be using a pencil instead of a word processor. If I press a key, I am most likely to do it by wiggling my finger, but I could use my nose, or a pencil held in my mouth, or my toes. These sorts of relationships are constitutive in the sense that some of the components of a higher level fact must be present in order to constitute that fact. Without the proper lower level construction materials, a higher level relationship between those materials cannot exist.

In sum, if we know that something is true at a particular level, then that fact restricts the kinds of things that might exist at higher levels and requires that some kinds of things be true at lower levels. Both kinds of requirements are loose, however, and permit a variety of alternatives. And neither the upward nor downward kinds of constraint fit our notion of a causal relationship.

Causation and Within-Level Relationships

The paradigm of a causal relationship is billiard balls colliding on a table: The red ball moves *because* it was struck by the white ball. The movement of the white ball and its collision with the red ball are the cause; the movement of the red ball is the effect. In this example, the terms of cause and effect are at exactly the same level. There is a red ball and a white ball, the movement of one and the movement of the other. As Hume pointed out long ago, we do not in fact observe causation here in the same way that we observe the balls and their contiguous movements. Balls are at one level, their movements at the next higher level, and causation is at a still higher level, the relationship between the movements of the balls.

Although the paradigmatic case for causation is at the level of movements of perceptually observable objects, we also use causal statements at other levels as well. If I ask for the cause of someone feeling angry, the report that they were just insulted seems a reasonable, genuinely causal answer. It describes the immediately antecedent, sufficient event. In the same way, the statement that changes in the Federal Reserve interest rate policy cause changes in levels of economic activity seems plausibly causal. The hypothesis that the rise of Protestantism caused the Industrial Revolution also seems to be a reasonable causal connection. Although any of these might be wrong, they do not seem illegitimate. The reason is that in all these examples, the cause and the effect are at the same level of organization, or at least so it seems.

Ryle (1949) pointed out that cause and effect must be at the same level or we will commit a "category error." That is, we may talk sense, but not causal sense, and we should be careful not to think we are talking about causes. For example, the answer that "the red ball moved because it was elastic" or that "Frank was angry because he is a crabby person" are not causal explanations of the same sort as "the ball moved because it was struck" or "Frank was angry because he was insulted." Elastic and crabby are higher level dispositions, indicating that the person in question is the sort who would be angry if insulted, and perhaps even when not, or the ball is the sort of thing that would move if something else collided with it. No one would look for an immediately antecedent instance of elasticity to explain the ball movement, nor should they look for an immediately antecedent instance of crabbiness. In sum, to avoid category errors, we must be careful to talk about causes only when both cause and effect are at the same level.

Causal analysis is complicated in an additional, different way. The nature of the within-level, plausibly causal relationship changes with different levels. At the perceptually observable object level of billiard balls, the connection seems invariant and inexorable. However, at increasingly higher levels the connections between cause and effect seem looser and less precise.

Why does a causal connection between two events seem different as one moves to higher levels? It is because the entities that are being connected are no longer those with exact locations in time and space. Our prototypical understanding of causation is an immediately antecedent event that occurs in a particular place like the point of contact between the billiard balls. But higher level phenomena by their nature have less precise spatial and temporal loci, so they cannot be "immediately" antecedent in the same way. Things like in-

terest rates and economic activity, or religion and industrial growth have neither precise beginnings and endings nor precise locations. Hence, the whole
notion of "immediately antecedent" loosens. Similarly, the "point of contact"
of cause and effect is impossible to specify in the same way.

In sum, causation is a kind of relationship between things at the same
level of organization in which one is the necessary and sufficient antecedent
of the other. The prototypical example of causation is the within-level relationship between the movements of perceptually observable objects.
While similar within-level relationships occur at other levels, they are not
precisely identical; they involve objects with different kinds of spatial and
temporal properties, if any.

Causation is not the only kind of within-level relationship, of course.
Another is similarity, the basis for categorization. Temporal succession, as
in a narrative of events, is another. Like causation, similarity and succession seem most at home at the level of perceptually observable objects and
become somewhat different at higher levels. For example, similarity at
higher levels is far more complex and difficult to define than at the lower
levels. Although we know what we mean when we say that the daughter is
similar to the mother, we do not know precisely what the basis for our
judgment of similarity is.

Succession also becomes a looser concept as the temporal locus of concepts becomes less clear. We may describe infancy, childhood, and adolescence as following each other, but of course the boundaries between these
times are extremely imprecise. The succession is more approximate than,
for example, yesterday, today, and tomorrow, or the white ball moved, the
white ball struck the red ball, and the red ball moved.

Note also that the concept of cause also changes, ultimately transform-
ing into something very different as one goes "down" in the levels of organization of existence. At the subatomic levels of quantum mechanics the
ideas of location, duration, succession, and causation are all very different
from anything like our homey, commonsense ideas based in the world of
palpable objects and their movements. For that reason, concepts like causation seem very strange.

CONCLUSION

The key idea in all this is that the world is organized in many levels. In
this book we came to this recognition through self-perception theory and
its supporting research, but of course, that is by no means the only possible route. The hierarchical structure of levels of organization has been noticed and discussed frequently by others. In this chapter we have been
looking at one set of implications that flow from the hierarchical systems
theory, a conception of how mind and body are related that seems to
avoid most of the problems of dualism and simple forms of materialism.
Most of the mysteries of mind dissolve when the smooth progression of
levels between the prototypically physical and prototypically mental are

recognized. Of course, the hierarchical levels-of-organization perspective also leads to our starting place, self-perception theory.

The levels-of-organization perspective has some other attractive implications. One of these is to locate the many subdisciplines of psychology (and, indeed, all sciences) relative to each other and in the process, with any luck, legitimizing each to the others. No genuine grounds exist for rivalry between neuroscientists and social psychologists or those who study perception and those who study culture. Rather than competing visions of the nature of the discipline and of human beings, we are just working at different levels in the hierarchy. In fact, eventually the connections among all of these will be as much a part of our knowledge as the elements within each part.

A particular benefit is the light the levels conception throws on methodology. Methods that are appropriate to the causal analysis of neurophysiological events, for example, would obviously be inappropriate for phenomena at higher levels, where the very concept of causation is different. Discourse analysis may be appropriate to some levels, experimental manipulations to another, and so forth.

Another attractive implication of the levels-of-organization view is that it may shift our search for the explanation of human actions to new and potentially more fertile ground. The traditional way to explain any action has been to search for some inner, "mental" property such as a feeling that was supposed to be its cause. However, feelings of emotion, desire, and liking seem to be information about our ongoing actions. They cannot, then, be the causes of those very actions, and we will have to find a different kind of explanation for action.

NOTES

1. Many people who have commented on such hierarchies have described the properties of higher levels as "emerging" from the lower levels (e.g., Bunge, 1980; Popper & Eccles, 1977). So, for example, life is said to be an emergent property of certain configurations of chemicals, and wetness is said to be an emergent property of the combination of hydrogen and oxygen. This seems to be a dangerous way of conceiving of level relations, since it implies that as one property emerges, something else may stay the same and be present at the higher level. Instead, the higher level actually consists of these "emergent" properties. As this example makes clear, a word does not emerge from the letters, but rather consists of a particular order of those letters.

2. Just because brains and neurons do not have any special existential status does not mean that neuroscience is not important to the understanding of human beings. The levels-of-organization perspective suggests that we need to be clearer about what an understanding of the mechanisms of the brain can and cannot do. Neuroscience is a bit like automotive engineering. If I know how my car works, then I can drive more efficiently and safely and can repair any breakdowns. However, if I cannot drive to the store, it may not be because my car is broken, but instead because I do not know the way. No amount of knowledge of automotive engineering will reveal the route.

3. The same argument applies to behaviorism as well. Behaviorists seem to have talked happily about many lower levels of organization of human activity and only objected to talk about the higher levels. But none of these levels seems to deserve a privileged position in our theorizing. Each has its own methodological challenges and opportunities, but all are equally real and part of what we human beings are.

4. Of course, existing higher level structures may affect lower level processes to produce "top-down" effects in perception.

5. That is the reason that spouses and family members are better at knowing our thoughts and feelings, because they have that necessary context.

6. Eidetic imagery seems to be an exception to this claim, and perhaps some people can, with substantial effort, retain a complete visual image of a page in a book. Nonetheless, these memories are the exception rather than the rule for the eidetickers, too (Stromeyer, 1970).

7. Note the contrast with the videotape that actually records just the patterns of light and dark without any organization of the information in the image. Just as the visual information leaves the retina in the optic nerve, it is already more complex and organized than a videotape signal.

References

Adelman, P. K., & Zajonc, R. B. (1989). Facial efference and the experience of emotion. *Annual Review of Psychology, 40,* 249–280.

Allport, F. H. (1924). *Social psychology.* Boston: Houghton Mifflin.

Amabile, T. M. (1979). Effects of external evaluation on artistic creativity. *Journal of Personality and Social Psychology, 37,* 221–233.

Amabile, T. M. (1983). *The social psychology of creativity.* New York: Springer-Verlag.

Amabile, T. M., Hennessey, B. A., & Grossman, B. S. (1986). Social influences on creativity: The effects of contracted-for reward. *Journal of Personality and Social Psychology, 50,* 14–23.

Arnold, M. B. (1960). *Emotion and personality: Vol. 1. Psychological aspects.* New York: Columbia University Press.

Aronson, E. (1992). The return of the repressed: Dissonance theory makes a comeback. *Psychological Inquiry, 3,* 303–311.

Aronson, E., Fried, C., & Stone, J. (1991). AIDS prevention and dissonance: A new twist on an old theory. *American Journal of Public Health, 81,* 1636–1638.

Aronson, E., & Mills, J. (1959). The effect of severity of initiation on liking for a group. *Journal of Abnormal and Social Psychology, 59,* 177–181.

Aronson, E., & Carlsmith, J. M. (1963). Effect of the severity of threat on the devaluation of forbidden behavior. *Journal of Abnormal and Social Psychology, 66,* 584–588.

Axsom, D. (1989). Cognitive dissonance and behavior change in psychotherapy. *Journal of Personality and Social Psychology, 25,* 234–252.

Bandler, R. J., Madaras, G. R., & Bem, D. J. (1968). Self observation as a source of pain perception. *Journal of Personality and Social Psychology, 9,* 205–209.

Banse, R., & Scherer, K. R. (1996). Acoustic profiles in vocal emotion expression. *Journal of Personality and Social Psychology, 70,* 614–636.

Bargh, J. A. (1997). The automaticity of everyday life. In R. S. Wyer Jr. (Ed.), *Advances in social cognition* (Vol. 9, pp. 1–62). Mahwah, NJ: Erlbaum.

Baumeister, R. F., Hutton, D. G., & Tice, D. M. (1989). Cognitive processes during deliberate self-presentation: How self-presenters alter and misinterpret the behavior of their interaction partners. *Journal of Experimental Social Psychology, 25,* 59–78.

Bem, D. J. (1965). An experimental analysis of self-persuasion. *Journal of Personality and Social Psychology, 1,* 199–218.

Bem, D. J. (1966). Inducing belief in false confessions. *Journal of Personality and Social Psychology, 3,* 707–710.

Bem, D. J. (1967). Self-perception: An alternative interpretation of cognitive dissonance phenomena. *Psychological Review, 74,* 183–200.

Bem, D. J. (1972). Self-perception theory. In L. Berkowitz (Ed.), *Advances in experimental social psychology* (Vol. 6, pp. 1–62). New York: Academic Press.

Bem, D. J., & McConnell, H. K. (1970). Testing the self-perception explanation of dissonance phenomena: On the salience of premanipulation attitudes. *Journal of Personality and Social Psychology, 14,* 23–31.

Berglas, S., & Laird, J. D. (1972, April). *The experience of dissonance and "dissonance induced" change.* Paper presented at the annual meeting of the Eastern Psychological Association, Boston, MA.

Berkowitz, L. (1990). On the formation and regulation of anger and aggression: A cognitive-neoassociationistic analysis. *American Psychologist, 45,* 494–503.

Berkowitz, L. (1993). *Aggression: Its causes, consequences and control.* New York: McGraw-Hill.

Berkowitz, L. (1994). Is something missing? Some observations prompted by the cognitive-neoassociationist view of anger and emotional aggression. In L. R. Huesmann (Ed.), *Aggressive behavior: Current perspectives* (pp. 35–58). New York: Plenum.

Berlyne, D. E. (1960). *Conflict, arousal and curiosity.* New York: McGraw-Hill.

Bermond, B., Nieuwenhuyse, B., Fasotti, L., & Schuerman, J. (1991). Spinal cord lesions, peripheral feedback, and intensities of emotional feelings. *Cognition and Emotion, 10,* 201–220.

Berscheid, E. W., & Walster, E. (1974). A little bit about love. In T. Huston (Ed.), *Foundations of interpersonal attraction* (pp. 356–379). New York: Academic Press.

Blaney, P. H. (1986). Affect and memory: A review. *Psychological Bulletin, 99,* 229–246.

Blanton, H., Cooper, J., Skurnik, I., & Aronson, J. (1997). When bad things happen to good feedback: Exacerbating the need for self-justification with self-affirmations. *Personality and Social Psychology Bulletin, 23,* 684–692.

Bloch, S., Lemeignan, M., & Aguilera, N. (1991). Specific respiratory patterns distinguish among human basic emotions. *International Journal of Psychophysiology, 11,* 141–154.

Bornstein, R. F. (1989). Exposure and affect: Overview and meta-analysis of research, 1967–1987. *Psychological Bulletin, 106,* 265–289.

Bornstein, R. F., & D'Agostino, P. R. (1994). The attribution and discounting of perceptual fluency: Preliminary tests of a perceptual fluency/attributional model of the mere exposure effect. *Social Cognition, 12,* 103–128.

Bower, G. H. (1980). Mood and memory. *American Psychologist, 36,* 129–148.

Brehm, J. W. (1960). Attitudinal consequences of commitment to unpleasant behavior. *Journal of Abnormal and Social Psychology, 60,* 384–389.

Bresler, C. (1984). *Sad, or maybe just a little tired?* Unpublished doctoral dissertation, Clark University.

Bresler, C., & Laird, J. D. (1983, April). *Short-term stability and discriminant validity of the "self-situational" cue dimension.* Paper presented at the meeting of the Eastern Psychological Association, Philadelphia, PA.

Brown, R., & McNeill, D. (1966). The "tip of the tongue" phenomenon. *Journal of Verbal Learning and Verbal Behavior, 5,* 325–337.

Buck, R. (1985). Prime theory: An integrated view of motivation and emotion. *Psychological Review, 92,* 389–413.

Buck, R. (1999). The biological affects: A typology. *Psychological Review, 106,* 301–336.

Bunge, M. (1980). *The mind-body problem.* Oxford, England: Pergamon.

Burger, J. M. (1999). The foot-in-the-door compliance procedure: A multiple-process analysis and review. *Personality and Social Psychology Review, 3,* 303–325.

Bushman, B. J., Baumeiseter, R. F., & Stock, A. D. (1999). Catharsis, aggression, and persuasive influence: Self-fulfilling or self-defeating prophecies? *Journal of Personality and Social Psychology, 76,* 367–376.

Buss, D. M. (1999). *Evolutionary psychology: The new science of the mind.* Needham Heights, MA: Allyn and Bacon.

Cabanac, M., Duclaux, R., & Spector, N. H. (1971). Sensory feedback in regulation of body weight: Is there a ponderstat? *Nature, 229,* 125–127.

Cacioppo, J. T., Priester, J. R., & Berntson, G. G. (1993). Rudimentary determinants of attitudes. II: Arm flexion and extension have differential effects on attitudes. *Journal of Personality and Social Psychology, 65,* 5–17.

Cameron, J., & Pierce, W. D. (1994). Reinforcement, reward and intrinsic motivation: A meta-analysis. *Review of Educational Research, 64,* 363–423.

Cannon, W. B. (1927). The James-Lange theory of emotions: A critical examination and an alternative theory. *American Journal of Psychology, 39,* 106–124.

Cannon, W. B. (1936). *Bodily changes in pain, hunger, fear and rage.* New York: Appleton-Century-Crofts.

Capella, J. N. (1993). The facial feedback hypothesis in human interaction: Review and speculation. *Journal of Language and Social Psychology, 12,* 13–29.

Carver, C. S., Antoni, M. H., & Scheier, M. F. (1985). Self-consciousness and self-assessment. *Journal of Personality and Social Psychology, 48,* 117–124.

Carver, C. S., & Scheier, M. F. (1981). *Attention and self-regulation: A control-theory approach to human behavior.* New York: Springer-Verlag.

Carver, C. S., & Scheier, M. F. (1998). *On the self-regulation of behavior.* New York: Cambridge University Press.

Chaiken, S., & Trope, Y. (Eds.). (1999). *Dual-process theories in social psychology.* New York: Guilford.

Chisholm, J. S. (1999). *Death, hope, and sex: Steps to an evolutionary ecology of mind and morality.* New York: Cambridge University Press.

Churchland, P. M. (1988). *Matter and consciousness.* Cambridge, MA: Bradford.

Chwalisz, K., Diener, E., & Gallagher, D. (1988). Autonomic arousal feedback and emotional experience: Evidence from the spinal cord injured. *Journal of Personality and Social Psychology, 54,* 820–828.

Clynes, M. (1977). *Sentics: The touch of emotions.* Oxford, England: Anchor Press.

Clynes, M., Jurisevic, S., & Rynn, M. (1990). Inherent cognitive substrates of specific emotions: Love is blocked by lying but not anger. *Perceptual and Motor Skills, 70,* 195–206.

Colby, C. Z., Lanzetta, J. T., & Kleck, R. E. (1977). Effects of expression of pain on autonomic and pain tolerance responses to subject-controlled pain. *Psychophysiology, 14,* 537–540.

Comer, R., & Laird, J. D. (1975). Choosing to suffer as a consequence of expecting to suffer: Why do people do it? *Journal of Personality and Social Psychology, 32*, 92–101.

Comer, R., & Rhodewalt, F. (1979). Cue utilization in the self-attribution of emotions and attitudes. *Personality and Social Psychology Bulletin, 5*, 320–324.

Connor, L. T., Balota, D. A., & Neely, J. H. (1992). On the relation between feeling of knowing and lexical decision: Persistent sub-threshold activation or topic familiarity? *Journal of Experimental Psychology: Learning, Memory and Cognition, 18*, 544–554.

Convoy, J. L., & Laird, J. D. (1984, April). *Projecting what you feel: The effects of emotion on story content.* Paper presented at the annual meeting of the Eastern Psychological Association, Baltimore, MD.

Cooper, J. (1980). Reducing fear and increasing assertiveness: The role of dissonance reduction. *Journal of Experimental Social Psychology, 16*, 199–213.

Cooper, J., & Fazio, R. H. (1984). A new look at dissonance theory. In L. Berkowitz (Ed.), *Advances in experimental social psychology* (Vol. 17, pp. 229–266). New York: Academic Press.

Cooper, J., Zanna, M., & Taves, P. A. (1978). Arousal as a necessary condition for attitude change following induced compliance. *Journal of Personality and Social Psychology, 36*, 1101–1106.

Cornelius, R. R. (1991). Gregorio Maranon's two-factor theory of emotion. *Personality and Social Psychology Bulletin, 17*, 65–69.

Cosmides, L., & Tooby, J. (2000). Evolutionary psychology and the emotions. In M. Lewis & J. M. Haviland-Jones (Eds.), *Handbook of emotions* (2nd ed., pp. 147–173). New York: Guilford.

Cotton, J. (1981). A review of research on Schachter's theory of emotion and the misattribution of arousal. *European Journal of Social Psychology, 11*, 365–397.

Cotton, J. L., Baron, R. S., & Borkovec, T. D. (1980). Caffeine ingestion, misattribution therapy, and speech anxiety. *Journal of Research in Personality, 14*, 196–206.

Critchley, H. D., Mathias, C. J., & Dolan, R. J. (2002). Fear conditioning in humans: The influence of awareness and autonomic arousal on functional neuroanatomy. *Neuron, 33*, 653–663.

Crockett, W. H. (1974). Balance, agreement, and subjective evaluations of the p-o-x triads. *Journal of Personality and Social Psychology, 29*, 102–110.

Crouch, A., & Degelman, D. (1998). Influence of female body images in printed advertising on self-ratings of physical attractiveness by adolescent girls. *Perceptual and Motor Skills, 87*, 585–586.

Crowe, R. R., (1985). Mitral valve prolapse and panic disorder. *Psychiatric Clinics of North America, 8*, 119–132.

Croyle, R., & Cooper, J. (1983). Dissonance arousal: Physiological evidence. *Journal of Personality and Social Psychology, 45*, 782–791.

Damasio, A. R. (1994). *Descartes' error.* New York: Avon Books.

Damasio, A. R. (1999). *The feeling of what happens: Body and emotion in the making of consciousness.* New York: Harcourt Brace.

Damrad-Frye, R., & Laird, J. D. (1989). The experience of boredom: The role of the self-perception of attention. *Journal of Personality and Social Psychology, 57*, 315–320.

Darwin, C. R. (1872). *The expression of emotions in man and animals.* London: Albemarle.

Davidson, R. J. (1992). Prolegomenon to the structure of emotion: Gleanings from neuropsychology. *Cognition and Emotion, 6*, 245–268.

Davies, M., & Humphreys, G. W. (Eds.). (1993). *Consciousness: Psychological and philosophical essays.* Malden, MA: Blackwell.

DeBono, K. G., & Snyder, M. (1995). Acting on one's attitudes: The role of a history of choosing situations. *Personality and Social Psychology Bulletin, 21,* 620–628.

Deci, E. L. (1971). Effects of externally mediated rewards on intrinsic motivation. *Journal of Personality and Social Psychology, 18,* 108–115.

Deci, E. L., & Ryan, R. M. (1985). *Intrinsic motivation and self-determination in human behavior.* New York: Plenum.

Dennett, D. C. (1991). *Consciousness explained.* Boston: Little, Brown.

deRivera, J. (1977). A structural theory of the emotions. *Psychological Issues, 10*(4, Monograph 40).

Descartes, R. (1641/1990). *Mediations on first philosophy* (G. Heffernan, Trans.). Notre Dame, IN: University of Notre Dame Press.

Dickerson, C., Thoidbodeau, R., Aronson, E., & Miller, D. (1992). Using cognitive dissonance to encourage water conservation. *Journal of Applied Social Psychology, 22,* 841–854.

Dimberg, U., Thunberg, M., & Elmehed, K. (2000). Unconsious facial reactions to emotional facial expressions. *Psychological Science, 11*(1), 86–89.

Dimsdale, E., Newton, P. P. & Joist, T. (1989). Neuropsychological side effects of beta-blockers. *Archives of Internal Medicine, 149,* 514–525.

Dion, K., Berscheid, E., & Walster, E. (1972). What is beautiful is good. *Journal of Personality and Social Psychology, 24,* 285–290.

Duclos, S. E., & Laird, J. D. (2001). The deliberate control of emotional experience through control of expressions. *Cognition and Emotion, 15,* 27–56.

Duclos, S. E., Laird, J. D., Schneider, E., Sexter, M., Stern, L., & Van Lighten, O. (1989). Emotion-specific effects of facial expressions and postures on emotional experience. *Journal of Personality and Social Psychology, 57,* 100–108.

Duncan, J. W., & Laird, J. D. (1977). Cross-modality consistencies in individual differences in self-attribution. *Journal of Personality, 45,* 191–206.

Duncan, J. W., & Laird, J. D. (1980). Positive and reverse placebo effects as a function of differences in cues used in self-perception. *Journal of Personality and Social Psychology, 39,* 1024–1036.

Dunlosky, J., & Nelson, T. O. (1992). Importance of the kind of cue for judgments of learning (JOL) and the delayed-JOL effect. *Memory and Cognition, 20,* 374–380.

Dutton, D., & Aron, A. (1974). Some evidence for heightened sexual attraction under conditions of high anxiety. *Journal of Personality and Social Psychology, 30,* 510–517.

Eagly, A. H., & Chaiken, S. (1993). *The psychology of attitudes.* Fort Worth, TX: Harcourt Brace Jovanovich.

Ebbesen, E., Duncan, B., & Konecni, V. (1975). Effects of content of verbal aggression on future verbal aggression: A field experiment. *Journal of Experimental Social Psychology, 11,* 192–204.

Edelman, B. (1984). A multiple-factor of body weight control. *Journal of General Psychology, 110,* 99–114.

Eisenberger, R., & Cameron, J. (1996). Detrimental effects of reward: Reality or myth? *American Psychologist, 51,* 1153–1166.

Eisenberger, R., & Cameron, J. (1998). Reward, intrinsic interest and creativity: New findings. *American Psychologist, 53,* 676–679.

Ekman, P. (1992a). An argument for basic emotions. *Cognition and Emotion, 34,* 169–200.

Ekman, P. (1992b). Facial expressions of emotion: New findings, new questions. *Psychological Science, 3,* 34–38.

Ekman, P. (1993). Facial expression and emotion. *American Psychologist, 48,* 384–392.

Ekman, P. (2001). *Telling lies: Clues to deceit in the marketplace, politics, and marriage.* New York: Norton.

Ekman, P., Davidson, R. J., & Friesen, W. V. (1990). The Duchenne smile: Emotional expression and brain physiology II. *Journal of Personality and Social Psychology, 58,* 342–353.

Ekman, P., & Friesen, W. V. (1978). *Facial action coding system.* Palo Alto, CA: Consulting Psychologists Press.

Ekman, P., Levenson, R. W., & Friesen, W. V. (1983). Autonomic nervous system activity distinguishes among emotions. *Science, 221,* 1208–1210.

Elkin, R. A., & Leippe, M. R. (1986). Physiological arousal, dissonance, and attitude change: Evidence for a dissonance-arousal link and a "don't remind me" effect. *Journal of Personality and Social Psychology, 51,* 55–65.

Elliot, A. J., & Devine, P. G. (1994). On the motivational nature of cognitive dissonance: Dissonance as psychological discomfort. *Journal of Personality and Social Psychology, 67,* 382–394.

Esses, V. M., & Herman, C. P. (1984). Palatability of sucrose before and after glucose ingestion in dieters and nondieters. *Physiology and Behavior, 32,* 711–715.

Eysenck, H. J. (1970). *Readings in extraversion-introversion: I. Theoretical and methodological issues.* Oxford, England: Wiley-Interscience.

Fabrigar, L. R., Priester, J. R., Petty, R. E., & Wegener, D. T. (1998). The impact of attitude accessibility on elaboration of persuasive messages. *Personality and Social Psychology Bulletin, 24,* 339–352.

Fazio, R. H. (1987). Self-perception theory: A current perspective. In M. P. Zanna, J. M. Olson, & C. P. Herman (Eds.), *Social influence: The Ontario symposium* (Vol. 5, pp. 129–150). Hillsdale, NJ: Erlbaum.

Fazio, R. H. (1995). Attitudes as object-evaluation associations: Determinants, consequences, and correlates of attitude accessibility. In R. E. Petty & J. A. Krosnick (Eds.)., *Attitude strength: Antecedents and consequences. Ohio State University series on attitudes and persuasion* (Vol. 4, pp. 247–282). Hillsdale, NJ: Erlbaum.

Fazio, R. H. (2000). Accessible attitudes as tools for object appraisal: Their costs and benefits. In G. R. Maio & J. M. Olson (Eds.), *Why we evaluate: Functions of attitudes* (pp. 1–36). Mahwah, NJ: Erlbaum.

Fazio, R. H., & Powell, M. C. (1997). On the value of knowing one's likes and dislikes: Attitude accessibility, stress, and health in college. *Psychological Science, 8,* 430–436.

Fazio, R. H., Powell, M. C., & Williams, C. J. (1989). The role of attitude accessibility in the attitude-to-behavior process. *Journal of Consumer Research, 16,* 280–288.

Fazio, R. H., Sherman, S. J., & Herr, P. M. (1982). The feature-positive effect in the self-perception process: Does not doing matter as much as doing? *Journal of Personality and Social Psychology, 42,* 404–411.

Fazio, R. H., Zanna, M. P., & Cooper, J. (1977). Dissonance and self-perception: An integrative view of each theory's proper domain of application. *Journal of Experimental Social Psychology, 13,* 464–479.

Feldman-Barrett, L., & Russell, J. A. (1998). Independence and bipolarity in the structure of current affect. *Journal of Personality and Social Psychology, 74,* 967–984.

Fenigstein, A., Scheier, M. F., & Buss, A. H. (1975). Public and private self-consciousness: Assessment and theory. *Journal of Consulting and Clinical Psychology, 43,* 522–527.

Festinger, L. (1957). *A theory of cognitive dissonance.* Stanford, CA: Stanford University Press.

Festinger, L., & Carlsmith, J. M. (1959). Cognitive consequences of forced compliance. *Journal of Abnormal and Social Psychology, 58,* 203–211.

Fishbein, M. J., & Laird, J. D. (1979). Concealment and disclosure: Some effects of information control on the person who controls. *Journal of Experimental Social Psychology, 15,* 114–121.

Flack, W. F., Jr., Cavallaro, L. A., & Laird, J. D. (1997, April). *Effects of facial expressions, bodily postures, and vocal expressions on emotional feelings in schizophrenia and depression.* Paper presented at annual meeting of the Eastern Psychological Association, Washington, DC.

Flack, W. F., Jr., Laird, J. D., & Cavallaro, L. A. (1999a). Additive effects of facial expressions and postures on emotional feelings. *European Journal of Social Psychology, 29,* 203–217.

Flack, W. F., Jr., Laird, J. D., & Cavallaro, L. A. (1999b). Emotional expression and feeling in schizophrenia: Effects of expressive behavior on emotional experience. *Journal of Clinical Psychology, 55,* 1–20.

Flack, W. F., Jr., Laird, J. D., Cavallaro, L., & Pelletier, C. M. (2000, April). Effects of disguised and deliberate facial expressions, bodily postures, and vocal expressions on emotional experiences in schizophrenia and depression. Paper presented at the annual meeting of the Eastern Psychological Association.

Flack, W. F., Jr., & Martin, A. H. (2004, July). *Emotional experience and expression in eating disorders.* Paper presented at the annual meeting of the International Society for Research on Emotion, New York.

Foerster, J. (1998). Der einfluss motorischer perzeptionen auf sympathie-urteile attraktiver und unattraktiver portraits (The influence of motor perception on likeability judgments of attractive and unattractive portraits). *Zeitschrift für Experimentelle Psychologie, 45,* 167–182.

Foerster, J., Higgins, E. T., & Idson, L. C. (1998). Approach and avoidance strength during goal attainment: Regulatory focus and the "goal looms larger" effect. *Journal of Personality and Social Psychology, 75,* 1115–1131.

Foerster, J., & Stepper, S. (2000). Compatibility between approach/avoidance stimulation and valenced information determines residual attention during the process of encoding. *European Journal of Social Psychology, 30,* 853–871.

Foerster, J., & Strack, F. (1996). Influence of overt head movements on memory for valenced words: A case of conceptual-motor compatibility. *Journal of Personality and Social Psychology, 71,* 421–430.

Foerster, J., & Strack, F. (1997). Motor actions in retrieval of valenced information: A motor congruence effect. *Perceptual and Motor Skills, 85*(3, Pt. 2), 1419–1427.

Foerster, J., & Strack, F. (1998). Motor actions in retrieval of valenced information: II. Boundary conditions for motor congruence effects. *Perceptual and Motor Skills, 86*(3, Pt. 2), 1423–1426.

Forgas, J. P. (1995). Mood and judgment: The affect infusion model (aim). *Psychological Bulletin, 117,* 39–66.

Foster, C. A., Witcher, B. S., Campbell, W. K., & Green, J. D. (1998). Arousal and attraction: Evidence for automatic and controlled processes. *Journal of Personality and Social Psychology, 74,* 86–101.

Foxman, J., & Radtke, R. C. (1970). Negative expectancy and the choice of an aversive task. *Journal of Personality and Social Psychology, 15,* 253–257.

Freedman, J. L., & Fraser, S. C. (1966). Compliance without pressure: The foot-in-the-door technique. *Journal of Personality and Social Psychology, 4*, 195–202.

Fridlund, A. J. (1994). *Human facial expression*. San Diego, CA: Academic Press.

Friedman, R. S., & Foerster, J. (2000). The effects of approach and avoidance motor actions on the elements of creative insight. *Journal of Personality and Social Psychology, 79*, 477–492.

Friedman, R. S., & Foerster, J. (2002). The influence of approach and avoidance motor actions on creative cognition. *Journal of Experimental Social Psychology, 38*, 41–55.

Frijda, N. H. (1986). *The emotions*. Cambridge, England: Cambridge University Press.

Frijda, N. H., Kuipers, P., & ter Shure, E. (1989). Relations among emotion, appraisal, and emotional action readiness. *Journal of Personality and Social Psychology, 57*, 212–228.

Geiwitz, P. J. (1966). Structure of boredom. *Journal of Personality and Social Psychology, 3*, 592–600.

Genov, A. (2000). *Autonomic and situational determinants of the subjective experience of emotion: An individual differences approach*. Unpublished doctoral dissertation, Clark University.

Genov, A., Pietrzak, R., Laird, J. D., Bemis, M., & Fortunato, C. (2000). *Pain perception is affected by differential responsiveness to bodily vs. situational cues*. Manuscript in preparation.

Gibson, J. J. (1979). *The ecological approach to visual perception*. Boston: Houghton Mifflin.

Gigerenzer, G., & Goldstein, D. G. (1996). Reasoning the fast and frugal way: Models of bounded rationality. *Psychological Review, 103*, 650–669.

Gigerenzer, G., & Todd, P. M. (1999). *Simple heuristics that make us smart*. New York: Oxford University Press.

Gilbert, D. T. (1989). Thinking lightly about others: Automatic components of the social inference process. In J. S. Uleman & J. A. Bargh (Eds.), *Unintended thought: Causes and consequences for judgment, emotion, and behavior* (pp. 154–186). New York: Guilford.

Goethals, G. R. (1992). Dissonance and self-justification. *Psychological Inquiry, 3*, 327–329.

Goethals, G. R., & Reckman, R. F. (1973). The perception of consistency in attitudes. *Journal of Experimental Social Psychology, 9*, 491–501.

Gold, A. E., MacLeod, K. M., Frier, B. M., & Dreary, I. J. (1995). Changes in mood during acute hypoglycemia in healthy participants. *Journal of Personality and Social Psychology, 68*(3), 498–504.

Greenberg, G., & Tobach, E. (1987). *Cognition, language and consciousness: Integrative levels*. Hillsdale, NJ: Erlbaum.

Greenwald, A. G. (1975). On the inconclusiveness of "crucial" cognitive tests of dissonance versus self-perception theories. *Journal of Experimental Social Psychology, 11*, 490–499.

Gross, J. J. (1998). Antecedent- and response-focused emotion regulation: Divergent consequences for experience, expression, and physiology. *Journal of Personality and Social Psychology, 74*, 224–237.

Gross, J. J., & Levenson, R. W. (1993). Emotional suppression: Physiology, self-report, and expressive behavior. *Journal of Personality and Social Psychology, 64*, 970–986.

Gross, J. J., & Levenson, R. W. (1997). Hiding feelings: The acute effects of inhibiting negative and positive emotion. *Journal of Abnormal Psychology, 106*, 95–103.

Grossberg, S. (1993). Neural facades: Visual representations of static and moving form-and-color-and-depth. In G. Humphreys (Ed.), *Understanding vision*. Oxford, England: Blackwell.

Hamilton, J. C., & Laird, J. D. (1981). *The effects of self-descriptions of ability on task performance: Boasting helps*. Paper presented at the Eastern Psychological Association, New York.

Harmon-Jones, E., Brehm, J. W., Greenberg, J., Simon, L., & Nelson, D. E. (1996). Evidence that the production of aversive consequences is not necessary to create cognitive dissonance. *Journal of Personality and Social Psychology, 70*, 5–16.

Harmon-Jones, E., & Mills, J. (Eds.). (1999). *Cognitive dissonance: Progress on a pivotal theory in social psychology*. Washington, DC: American Psychological Association.

Harris, M. B. (1991). Sex differences in stereotypes of spectacles. *Journal of Applied Social Psychology, 21*, 1659–1680.

Hart, J. T. (1967). Memory and the memory-monitoring process. *Journal of Verbal Learning and Behavior, 6*, 685–691.

Hatfield, E., Cacioppo, J. T., & Rapson, R. L. (1994). *Emotional contagion*. New York: Cambridge University Press.

Hatfield, E., Hsee, C. K., Costello, J., & Weisman, M. S. (1995). The impact of vocal feedback on emotional experience and expression. *Journal of Social Behavior and Personality, 10*, 293–312.

Hatfield, E., & Sprecher, S. (1986). Measuring passionate love in intimate relationships. *Journal of Adolescence, 9*, 383–410.

Hazaleus, S. L., & Deffenbacher, J. T. (1986). Relaxation and cognitive treatments of anger. *Journal of Consulting and Clinical Psychology, 54*, 222–226.

Heatherton, T. F., Polivy, J., & Herman, C. P. (1989). Restraint and internal responsiveness: Effects of placebo manipulations of hunger state on eating. *Journal of Abnormal Psychology, 98*, 89–92.

Hebb, D. O. (1958). *A textbook of psychology*. Oxford, England: Saunders.

Hennessey, B. A., Amabile, T. M., & Martinage, M. (1989). Immunizing children against the negative effects of reward. *Contemporary Educational Psychology, 14*, 212–227.

Hepburn, D. A., Deary, I. J., Munoz, M., & Frier, B. M. (1995). Physiological manipulation of psychometric mood factors using acute insulin-induced hypoglycaemia in humans. *Personality and Individual Differences, 18*(3), 385–391.

Herman, C. P., Olmsted, M. P., & Polivy, J. (1983). Obesity, externality, and susceptibility to social influence: An integrated analysis. *Journal of Personality and Social Psychology, 45*, 926–934.

Herman, C. P., & Polivy, J. (1975). Anxiety, restraint and eating behavior. *Journal of Abnormal Psychology, 84*, 666–672.

Hess, U., Kappas, A., McHugo, G. J., Lanzetta, J. T. & Kleck, R. E. (1992). The facilitative effect of facial expression on the self-generation of emotion. *International Journal of Psychophysiology, 12*, 251–265.

Higgins, T. L. (1999). The influence of ease of retrieval and amount retrieved on metamemory judgments and decisions. *Dissertation Abstracts International: B. The Sciences and Engineering, 59*(9B), 5124.

Hohmann, G. W. (1966). Some effects of spinal cord lesions on experienced emotional feelings. *Psychophysiology, 3*, 526–534.

Hopmeyer, A. S., & Stevens, D. A. (1989). Individual differences in psychophysical responses to chemical stimuli. *Chemical Senses, 14*, 711.

Hubel, D. H., & Wiesel, T. N. (1979). Brain mechanisms of vision. *Scientific American, 241*, 150–168.

Isen, A. M. (1990). The influence of positive and negative affect on cognitive organization: Some implications for development. In N. L. Stein, H. Leventhal, & R. A. Bennett (Eds.), *Psychological and biological approaches to emotion* (pp. 75–94). Hillsdale, NJ: Erlbaum.

Izard, C. E. (1977). *Human emotions*. New York: Plenum.

Izard, C. E. (1990). Facial expressions and the regulation of emotions. *Journal of Personality and Social Psychology, 58*, 487–498.

Izard, C. E. (1993). Four systems for emotion activation: Cognitive and noncognitive processes. *Psychological Review, 100*, 68–90.

Jackson, L. A., & Ervin, K. S. (1992). Height stereotypes of women and men: The liabilities of shortness for both sexes. *Journal of Social Psychology, 132*, 433–445.

Jacoby, L. L., & Kelley, C. M. (1987). Unconscious influences of memory for a prior event. *Personality and Social Psychology Bulletin, 13*, 314–336.

Jacoby, L. L., Kelley, C. M., Brown, J., & Jasechko, J. (1989). Becoming famous overnight: Limits on the ability to avoid unconscious influences of the past. *Journal of Personality and Social Psychology, 56*, 326–338.

Jacoby, L. L., & Whitehouse, K. (1989). An illusion of memory: False recognition influenced by unconscious perception. *Journal of Experimental Psychology: General, 118*, 126–135.

Jacoby, L. L., Woloshyn, V., & Kelley, C. M. (1989). Becoming famous without being recognized: Unconscious influences of memory produced by dividing attention. *Journal of Experimental Psychology: General, 118*, 115–125.

James, W. (1890). *Principles of psychology*. New York: Holt.

James, W. (1884). What is an emotion? *Mind, 19*, 188–205.

Janis, I. L., & Mann, L. (1977). *Decision making: A psychological analysis of conflict, choice, and commitment*. New York: Free Press.

Janoff-Bulman, R. (1992). *Shattered assumptions: Towards a new psychology of trauma*. New York: Free Press.

Jasnos, T. M., & Hakmiller, K. L. (1975). Some effects of lesion level and emotional cues on affective expression in spinal cord patients. *Psychological Reports, 37*, 859–870.

Jaynes, J. (1976). *The origin of consciousness in the breakdown of the bicameral mind*. Reading, MA: Addison-Wesley.

Johnson, M. K., Foley, M. A., & Leach, K. (1988). The consequences for memory of imagining in another person's voice. *Memory and Cognition, 16*, 337–342.

Johnson, M. K., Hashtroudi, S., & Lindsay, D. S. (1993). Source monitoring. *Psychological Bulletin, 114*, 3–28.

Johnstone, T., Van Reekum, C. M., & Scherer, K. R. (2001). Vocal expression correlates of appraisal processes. In K. R. Scherer & A. Schorr (Eds.), *Appraisal processes in emotion: Theory, methods, research* (pp. 271–284). London: Oxford University Press.

Jones, R. A., Linder, D. E., Kiesler, C. A., Zanna, M., & Brehm, J. W. (1968). Internal states or external stimuli: Observers' attitude judgments and the dissonance theory—self-persuasion controversy. *Journal of Experimental Social Psychology, 4*, 247–269.

Kahn, M. (1966). The physiology of catharsis. *Journal of Personality and Social Psychology, 3*, 278–286.

Kahneman, D., Slovic, P., & Tversky, A. (1982). *Judgment under uncertainty: Heuristics and biases*. Cambridge, England: Cambridge University Press.

Kahneman, D., & Tversky, A. (1996). On the reality of cognitive illusions. *Psychological Review, 103,* 582–591.

Kahneman, D., & Tversky, A. (1972). On the psychology of prediction. *Psychological Review, 80,* 237–251.

Kaiser, S., & Scherer, K. R. (1998). Models of "normal" emotions applied to facial and vocal expression in clinical disorders. In W. F. Flack Jr. & J. D. Laird (Eds.), *Emotions in psychopathology: Theory and research* (pp. 81–98). New York: Oxford University Press.

Kaplan, R. (1975). The cathartic value of self-expression: Testing catharsis, dissonance and interference explanations. *Journal of Social Psychology, 97,* 195–208.

Kellerman, J., & Laird, J. D. (1982). The effect of appearance on self-perception. *Journal of Personality, 50,* 296–315.

Kellerman, J., Lewis, J., & Laird, J. D. (1989). Looking and loving: The effects of mutual gaze on feelings of romantic love. *Journal of Research in Personality, 23,* 145–161.

Kelley, C. M., & Jacoby, L. L. (1998). Subjective reports and process dissociation: Fluency, knowing and feeling. *Acta Psychologica, 98,* 127–140.

Kelley, H. H. (1967). Attribution theory in social psychology. In D. Levine (Ed.), *Nebraska Symposium on Motivation* (Vol. 15, pp. 192–241). Lincoln: University of Nebraska Press.

Kellogg, R., & Baron, R. S. (1975). Attribution theory, insomnia, and the reverse placebo effect: A reversal of Storm's and Nisbett's findings. *Journal of Personality and Social Psychology, 32,* 231–236.

Kiesler, C. A., Nisbett, R. E., & Zanna, M. (1969). On inferring one's beliefs from one's behavior. *Journal of Personality and Social Psychology, 11,* 321–327.

Kleck, R. E., Vaughan, R. C., Cartwright-Smith, J., Vaughan, K. B., Colby, C. Z., & Lanzetta, J. T. (1976). Effects of being observed on expressive, subjective, and physiological responses to painful stimuli. *Journal of Personality and Social Psychology, 34,* 1211–1218.

Kleinke, C. L., Peterson, T. R., & Rutledge, T. R. (1998). Effects of self-generated facial expressions on mood. *Journal of Personality and Social Psychology, 74,* 272–279.

Knight, L., & Boland, F. (1989). Restrained eating: An experimental disentanglement of the disinhibiting variables of calories and food type. *Journal of Abnormal Psychology, 98,* 412–420.

Koriat, A. (1993). How do we know that we know? The accessibility model of the feeling of knowing. *Psychological Review, 100,* 609–639.

Koriat, A. (1995). Dissociating knowing and the feeling of knowing: Further evidence for the accessibility model. *Journal of Experimental Psychology: General, 3,* 311–333.

Kraut, R. E. (1982). Social presence, facial feedback, and emotion. *Journal of Personality and Social Psychology, 42,* 853–863.

Kuvalanka, K., Grubstein, L., Kim, T. H., Nagaraja, T., & Laird, J. D. (1994, April). *Posture and confidence: Standing and sitting tall, feeling good.* Paper presented at the annual meeting of the Eastern Psychological Association, Providence, RI.

Lacey, J. I., & Lacey, B. C. (1958). Verification and extension of the principle of autonomic response-stereotypy. *American Journal of Psychology, 71,* 50–73.

Laird, J. D. (1967). *William James and the role of the face in emotional feelings.* Unpublished doctoral dissertation, University of Rochester.

Laird, J. D. (1974). Self-attribution of emotion: The effects of expressive behavior on the quality of emotional experience. *Journal of Personality and Social Psychology, 33,* 475–486.

Laird, J. D. (1984). The real role of facial response in experience of emotion: A reply to Tourangeau and Ellsworth, and others. *Journal of Personality and Social Psychology, 47,* 909–917.

Laird, J. D. (1989). Mood affects memory because feelings *are* cognitions. *Journal of Social Behavior and Personality, 4,* 33–38.

Laird, J. D., Alibozak, T., Davainis, D., Deignan, K., Fontanella, K., Hong, J., et al. (1994). Individual differences in the effects of spontaneous mimicry on emotional contagion. *Motivation and Emotion, 18,* 231–246.

Laird, J. D., & Berglas, S. (1975). Individual differences in the effects of engaging in counter-attitudinal behavior. *Journal of Personality, 43,* 286–304.

Laird, J. D., & Bresler, C. (1990). William James and the mechanisms of emotional experience. *Personality and Social Psychology Bulletin, 16,* 636–651.

Laird, J. D., & Bresler, C. (1992). The process of emotional experience: A self-perception theory. In M. S. Clark (Ed.), *Emotion: Vol. 13, Review of personality and social psychology* (pp. 213–234). Newbury Park, CA: Sage.

Laird, J. D., & Crosby, M. (1974). Individual differences in self-attribution of emotion. In H. London & R. Nisbett (Eds.), *Thinking and feeling: The cognitive alteration of feeling states* (pp. 44–59). Chicago: Aldine-Atherton.

Laird, J. D., Cuniff, M., Sheehan, K., Shulman, D., & Strum, G. (1989). Emotion-specific effects of facial expressions on memory for life events. *Journal of Social Behavior and Personality, 4,* 87–98.

Laird, J. D., Kuvalanka, K., Grubstein, L., Kim, T. H., & Nagaraja, T. (in press). Posture and confidence: Standing (and sitting) tall, makes you feel good. *Journal of Nonverbal Behavior.*

Laird, J. D., Wagener, J. J., Halal, M., & Szegda, M. (1982). Remembering what you feel: The effects of emotion on memory. *Journal of Personality and Social Psychology, 42,* 646–658.

Lambie, J. A., & Marcel, A. J. (2002). Consciousness and the varieties of emotion experience: A theoretical framework. *Psychological Review, 109,* 219–259.

Landis, C., & Hunt, W. A. (1932). Adrenalin and emotion. *Psychological Review, 39,* 467–485.

Lange, C. (1922). The emotions: A psychophysiological study. In W. James & C. Lange (Eds.), *The emotions* (pp. 33–90). Baltimore: Williams and Wilkins.

Lanzetta, J. T., Cartwright-Smith, J., & Kleck, R. E. (1976). Effects of nonverbal dissimulation on emotional experience and autonomic arousal. *Journal of Personality and Social Psychology, 33,* 354–370.

Larsen, R., & Sinnett, L. M. (1991). Meta-analysis of experimental manipulations: Some factors affecting the *velten* mood induction procedure. *Personality and Social Psychology Bulletin, 17,* 323–334.

Larsen, R. J., Kasimatis, M., & Frey, K. (1992). Facilitating the furrowed brow: An unobtrusive test of the facial feedback hypothesis applied to unpleasant affect. *Cognition and Emotion, 6,* 321–338.

LeDoux, J. E. (1996). *The emotional brain.* New York: Simon and Schuster.

Lepper, M. R., Greene, D., & Nisbett, R. (1973). Undermining children's intrinsic interest with extrinsic rewards: A test of the "overjustification" hypothesis. *Journal of Personality and Social Psychology, 28,* 129–137.

Levenson, R. W. (1992). Autonomic nervous system differences among emotions. *Psychological Science, 3,* 23–27.

Levenson, R. W., Carstensen, L. L., Friesen, W. V., & Ekman, P. (1991). Emotion, physiology and expression in old age. *Psychology and Aging, 6,* 28–35.

Levenson, R. W., Ekman, P., & Friesen, W. V. (1990). Voluntary facial action generates emotion-specific nervous system activity. *Psychophysiology, 27,* 363–384.

Levenson, R. W., Ekman, P., Heider, K., & Friesen, W. V. (1992). Emotion and autonomic nervous system activity in the Minangkabau of West Sumatra. *Journal of Personality and Social Psychology, 62,* 972–988.

Leventhal, H. (1980). Toward a comprehensive theory of emotion. In L. Berkowitz (Ed.), *Advances in experimental social psychology* (pp. 149–207). London: Academic Press.

Lindsay, D. S. (1990). Misleading suggestions can impair eyewitnesses' ability to remember event details. *Journal of Experimental Psychology: Learning, Memory and Cognition, 16,* 1077–1083.

Loftus, E. F. (1979). *Eyewitness testimony.* Cambridge, MA: Harvard University Press.

Loftus, E. F., Miller, D., & Burns, H. (1973). Semantic integration of verbal information into visual memory. *Journal of Experimental Psychology: Learning and Memory, 4,* 19–31.

London, H., & Monello, L. (1974). Cognitive manipulations of boredom. In H. London & R. Nisbett (Eds.), *Thought and feeling* (pp. 44–59). Chicago: Aldine.

Losch, M. E., & Cacioppo, J. T. (1990). Cognitive dissonance may enhance sympathetic tonus, but attitudes are changed to reduce negative affect rather than arousal. *Journal of Experimental Social Psychology, 26,* 289–304.

Loveland, K. K., & Olley, J. G. (1979). The effect of external reward on interest and quality of task performance in children of high and low intrinsic motivation. *Child Development, 50,* 1207–1210.

Lowe, M. R. (1992). The effects of dieting on eating behavior: A three-factor model. *Psychological Review, 114,* 100–121.

Lowe, J., & Carroll, D. (1985). The effects of spinal injury on the intensity of emotional experience. *British Journal of Clinical Psychology, 24,* 135–136.

MacArthur, L. A., Solomon, M. R., & Jaffee, R. H. (1980). Weight and sex differences in emotional responsiveness to proprioceptive and pictorial stimuli. *Journal of Personality and Social Psychology, 39,* 308–319.

Mallick, S. K., & McCandless, B. R. (1966) A study of catharsis aggression. *Journal of Personality and Social Psychology, 4,* 591–596.

Manstead, A. S. R., & Wagner, H. L. (1981). Arousal, cognition and emotion: An appraisal of two-factor theory. *Current Psychological Reviews, 1,* 35–54.

Maranon, G. (1924). Contribution a l'etude de l'action emotive de l'adrenaline. *Review Francaise d'Endocrinologie, 2,* 301.

Marshall, G. D., & Zimbardo, P. G. (1979). Affective consequences of inadequately explained psychological arousal. *Journal of Personality and Social Psychology, 37,* 970–988.

Martin, L. L., Harlow, T. F., & Strack, F. (1992). The role of one's own bodily sensations in the evaluation of social events. *Personality and Social Psychology Bulletin, 18,* 412–419.

Maslach, C. (1979). Negative emotional biasing and unexplained arousal. *Journal of Personality and Social Psychology, 37,* 953–969.

Matsumoto, D. (1987). The role of facial response in the experience of emotion: More methodological problems and a meta-analysis. *Journal of Personality and Social Psychology, 52,* 769–774.

Mattes, J. A. (1985). Metaprolol for intermittent explosive disorder. *American Journal of Psychiatry, 142,* 1108–1109.

Mauro, R., Sato, K., & Tucker, J. (1992). The role of appraisal in human emotions: A cross-cultural study. *Journal of Personality and Social Psychology, 62,* 301–317.

McAllister, H. A. (1980). Self-disclosure and liking: Effects for senders and receivers. *Journal of Personality, 48,* 409–418.

McCanne, T. R., & Anderson, J. A. (1987). Emotional responding following experimental manipulation of facial electromyographic activity. *Journal of Personality and Social Psychology, 52,* 759–768.

McClanahan, K. K., Gold, J. A., Lenney, E., Ryckman, R. M., & Kuhlberg, K. (1990). Infatuation and attraction to a dissimilar other: Why is love blind? *Journal of Social Psychology, 130,* 433–445.

McCrimmon, R. J., Frier, B. M., & Dreary, I. J. (1999). Appraisal of mood and personality during hypoglycemia in human subjects. *Physiology & Behavior, 67*(1), 27–33.

McFarlane, T., Polivy, J., & Herman, C. P. (1998). Effects of false weight feedback on mood, self-evaluation, and food intake in restrained and unrestrained eaters. *Journal of Abnormal Psychology, 107,* 312–318.

McIntosh, D. N. (1996). Facial feedback hypotheses: Evidence, implications, and directions. *Motivation and Emotion, 20,* 121–147.

McLoyd, V. C. (1979). The effects of extrinsic rewards of differential value on high and low interest. *Child Development, 50,* 1010–1019.

McNally, R. J. (1990). Psychological approaches to panic disorder: A review. *Psychological Bulletin, 108,* 403–419.

Mehrabian, A. (1968). Inference of attitudes from the posture, orientation, and distance of a communicator. *Journal of Consulting and Clinical Psychology, 32,* 296–308.

Mehrabian, A. (1969). Significance of posture and position in the communication of attitude and status relationships. *Psychological Bulletin, 71,* 359–372.

Metcalfe, J. (1996). Metacognitive processes. In E. L. Bjork & R. A. Byork (Eds.), *The handbook of perception and cognition, Vol. 10: Memory* (pp. 383–411). San Diego: Academic Press.

Metcalfe, J. (1998). Cognitive optimism: Self-deception or memory-based processing heuristics? *Personality and Social Psychology Review, 2,* 100–110.

Montada, L., & Lerner, M. J. (Eds.). (1998). *Responses to victimizations and belief in a just world.* New York: Plenum.

Montepare, J. M. (1995). The impact of variations in height on young children's impressions of men and women. *Journal of Nonverbal Behavior, 19,* 31–47.

Mullener, N., & Laird, J. D. (1974, April). *Levels of awareness of persons.* Paper presented at the annual meeting of the Eastern Psychological Association, Washington, DC.

Neumann, R., & Strack, F. (2000). Approach and avoidance: The influence of proprioceptive and exteroceptive cues on encoding of affective information. *Journal of Personality and Social Psychology, 79,* 39–48.

Newman, F., Stein, M. B., Tretlau, J. R., Coppola, R., & Uhde, T. W. (1992). Quantitative electroencephalographic effects of caffeine in panic disorder. *Psychiatry Research, 45,* 105–113.

Nisbett, R. E. (1968a). Determinants of food intake in human obesity. *Science, 159,* 1254–1255.

Nisbett, R. E. (1968b). Taste, deprivation and weight determinants of eating behavior. *Journal of Personality and Social Psychology, 10,* 107–116.

Nisbett, R. E., & Schachter, S. (1966). Cognitive manipulation of pain. *Journal of Experimental Social Psychology, 2,* 227–236.

Nisbett, R. E., & Wilson, T. D. (1977). Telling more than we can know: Verbal reports on mental processes. *Psychological Review, 87,* 231–259.

Noyes, R. J. (1985). Beta-adrenergic drugs in anxiety and stress. *Psychiatric Clinics of North America, 8,* 119–132.

Oatley, K., & Jenkins, J. M. (1992). Human emotions: Function and dysfunction. *Annual Review of Psychology, 43,* 55–85.

Olson, J. M. (1988). Misattribution, preparatory information, and speech anxiety. *Journal of Personality and Social Psychology, 54,* 758–767.

Olson, J. M., & Ross, M. (1988). False feedback about placebo effectiveness: Consequences for the misattribution of speech anxiety. *Journal of Experimental Social Psychology, 24,* 275–291.

Ortony, A:, Clore, G. L., & Collins, A. (1988). *The cognitive structure of emotions.* Cambridge, England: Cambridge University Press.

Osgood, C. E., Suci, G. J., & Tannenbaum, P. H. (1957). *The measurement of meaning.* Urbana: University of Illinois Press.

Ottaviani, R., & Beck, A. T. (1987). Cognitive aspects of panic disorders. *Journal of Anxiety Disorders, 1,* 15–28.

Pennebaker, J. (1982). *The psychology of physical symptoms.* New York: Springer Verlag.

Philippot, P., Chapelle, G., & Blairy, S. (2002). Respiratory feedback in the generation of emotion. *Cognition & Emotion, 16,* 605–627.

Pietrzak, R. H., DeVylder, E. K., Laird, J. D., Genov, A., Fernandes, B., & Bemis, M. (2001, April). *Individual and sex differences in human jealousy: Evolution, physiology, and emotion.* Paper presented at the annual meeting of the Eastern Psychological Association, Washington, DC.

Pinhas, L., Toner, B. B., Ali, A., Garfinkel, P. E., & Stuckless, N. (1999). The effects of the ideal of female beauty on mood and body satisfaction. *International Journal of Eating Disorders, 25,* 223–226.

Pittman, T. S. (1975). Attribution of arousal as a mediator in dissonance reduction. *Journal of Experimental Social Psychology, 11,* 53–63.

Pliner, P. L. (1973). Effect of liquid and solid preloads on eating behavior of obese and normal persons. *Physiology and Behavior, 11,* 285–290.

Plutchik, R. (1980). *Emotion: A psychoevolutionary synthesis.* New York: Harper and Row.

Polivy, J. (1998). The effects of behavioral inhibition: Integrating internal cues, cognition, behavior and affect. *Psychological Inquiry, 9,* 181–204.

Polivy, J., Herman, C. P., & Warsh, S. (1978). Internal and external components of emotionality in restrained and unrestrained eaters. *Journal of Abnormal Psychology, 87,* 497–504.

Popper, K. R., & Eccles, J. C. (1977). *The self and its brain.* Oxford, England: Springer-Verlag.

Posavac, H. D., Posavac, S. S., & Posavac, E. J. (1998). Exposure to media images of female attractiveness and concern with body weight among young women. *Sex Roles, 38,* 187–201.

Powers, W. T. (1973). *Behavior: The control of perception.* Chicago: Aldine.

Prinz, J. J. (2004). *Gut reactions: A perceptual theory of emotion.* New York: Oxford University Press.

Pyszczynski, T., Greenberg, J., Solomon, S., & Sideris, J. (1993). Emotional expression and the reduction of motivated cognitive bias: Evidence from cognitive dissonance and distancing from victims' paradigms. *Journal of Personality and Social Psychology, 64,* 177–186.

Ratey, J. J., Sorgi, P., O'Driscoll, G. A., Sands, S., Daehler, M. L., Fletcher, J. R., et al. (1992). Nadolol to treat aggression and psychiatric symptomatology in chronic psychiatric inpatients: A double-blind, placebo-controlled study. *Journal of Clinical Psychiatry, 53,* 41–45.

Reisenzein, R. (1983). The Schachter theory of emotion: Two decades later. *Psychological Bulletin, 94,* 239–264.

Reisenzein, R. (1994). The functional significance of somatic changes for emotional experience. In D. Nutzinger, L. Harte, & H. G. Napotsky (Eds.), *Somatoform disorders* (pp. 142–166). New York: Wiley.

Reisenzein, R., & Schonpflug, W. (1992). Stumpf's cognitive-evaluative theory of emotion. *American Psychologist, 47,* 34–45.

Rhodewalt, F., & Comer, R. (1979). Induced-compliance attitude change: Once more with feeling. *Journal of Experimental Social Psychology, 15,* 35–47.

Richards, J. M., & Gross, J. J. (2000). Emotion regulation and memory: The cognitive costs of keeping one's cool. *Journal of Personality and Social Psychology, 79*(3), 410–424.

Rime, B., & Giovanni, D. (1986). The physiological patterns of reported emotional states. In K. R. Scherer, H. G. Walbott & A. B. Summerfield (Eds.), *Experiencing emotion: A cross-cultural study* (pp. 84–97). Cambridge, England: Cambridge University Press.

Riskind, J. H. (1983). Nonverbal expressions and the accessibility of life experience memories: A congruence hypothesis. *Social Cognition, 2,* 62–86.

Riskind, J. H. (1984). They stoop to conquer: Guiding and self-regulatory functions of physical posture after success and failure. *Journal of Personality and Social Psychology, 47,* 479–493.

Riskind, J. H., & Gotay, C. C. (1982). Physical posture: Could it have regulatory or feedback effects on motivation and emotion? *Motivation and Emotion, 6,* 273–298.

Rodin, J. (1981). Current status of the internal-external hypothesis for obesity: What went wrong? *American Psychologist, 36,* 361–372.

Rodin, J., & Slochower, J. (1974). Fat chance for a favor: Obese-normal differences in compliance and incidental learning. *Journal of Personality and Social Psychology, 29,* 557–565.

Rodin, J., Slochower, J., & Fleming, B. (1977). Effects of degree of obesity, age of onset and weight loss on responsiveness to sensory and external stimuli. *Journal of Comparative and Physiological Psychology, 91,* 586–597.

Rogers, R. W., & Deckner, C. W. (1975). Effects of fear appeals and physiological arousal upon emotion, attitudes, and cigarette smoking. *Journal of Personality and Social Psychology, 32*(2), 222–230.

Rosen, R., & Kostis, J. (1985). Biobehavioral sequelae associated with adrenergic-inhibiting antihypertensive agents: A critical review. *Health Psychology, 4,* 579–604.

Rosenthal, R. (1991). *Meta-analytic procedures for social research* (Rev. ed.). Newbury Park, CA: Sage.

Ross, M. (1975). Salience of reward and intrinsic motivation. *Journal of Personality and Social Psychology, 32,* 245–254.

Ross, M. (1989). Relation of implicit theories to the construction of personal histories. *Psychological Review, 96,* 341–357.

Ross, M., & Olson, J. M. (1981). An expectancy-attribution model of the effects of placebos. *Psychological Review, 88,* 408–437.

Ross, M., & Shulman, R. F. (1973). Increasing the salience of initial attitudes: Dissonance versus self-perception theory. *Journal of Personality and Social Psychology, 28,* 138–144.

Rotter, J. B. (1990). Internal versus external control of reinforcement: A case history of a variable. *American Psychologist, 45,* 489–493.

Rubin, Z. (1973). *Liking and loving.* New York: Holt, Rinehart and Winston.

Russell, B. N. Y. (1912). *Problems of philosophy.* New York: Oxford University Press.

Russell, J. A., & Bullock, M. (1985). Multidimensional scaling of emotional facial expressions: Similarity from preschoolers to adults. *Journal of Personality and Psychology, 48,* 1290–1298.

Rutledge, L. L., & Hupka, R. B. (1985). The facial feedback hypothesis: Methodological concerns and new supportive evidence. *Motivation and Emotion, 9,* 219–240.

Ryle, G. (1949). *The concept of mind.* New York: Norton.

Ryle, G. (1971). The thinking of thoughts: What is Le Penseur doing? In *Collected papers.* New York: Barnes and Noble.

Sakai, H. (1999). A multiplicative power-function model of cognitive dissonance: Toward an integrated theory of cognition, emotion, and behavior after Leon Festinger. In E. Harmon-Jones & J. Mills (Eds.), *Cognitive dissonance: Progress on a pivotal theory in social psychology* (pp. 267–294). Washington, DC: American Psychological Association.

Salancik, G. R. (1974). Inference of one's attitude from behavior recalled under linguistically manipulated cognitive sets. *Journal of Experimental Social Psychology, 10,* 415–427.

Schachter, S. (1964). The interaction of cognitive and physiological determinants of emotional state. In L. Berkowitz (Ed.), *Advances in experimental social psychology* (pp. 49–80). New York: Academic Press.

Schachter, S. (1968). Internal and external cues differentially affect the eating behaviors of obese and normal subjects. *Science, 161,* 751–756.

Schachter, S., Goldman, R., & Gordon, A. (1968). Effects of fear, food deprivation, and obesity on eating. *Journal of Personality and Social Psychology, 10,* 91–97.

Schachter, S., & Gross, L. (1968). Manipulated time and eating behavior. *Journal of Personality and Social Psychology, 10,* 98–106.

Schachter, S., & Rodin, J. (1974). *Obese humans and rats.* Washington, DC: Erlbaum/Halstead.

Schachter, S., & Singer, J. E. (1962). Cognitive, social and physiological determinants of emotional state. *Psychological Review, 69,* 379–399.

Schachter, S., & Wheeler, L. (1962). Epinephrine, chlorpromazine, and amusement. *Journal of Abnormal and Social Psychology, 65,* 121–128.

Scherer, K. R. (1986). Vocal affect expression: A review and a model for future research. *Psychological Bulletin, 99,* 143–165.

Schlenker, B., & Trudeau, J. (1990). Impact of self-presentations on private self-beliefs. *Journal of Personality and Social Psychology, 58,* 22–33.

Schnall, S., Abrahamson, A., & Laird, J. D. (2002). Premenstrual tension is an error of self-perception processes: An individual differences perspective. *Basic and Applied Social Psychology, 24,* 214–227.

Schnall, S., & Laird, J. D. (2002). Keep smiling: Enduring effects of facial expressions and postures on emotional experience and memory. *Cognition and Emotion, 15,* 27–56.

Schnall, S., Laird, J. D., Campbell, L., Hwang, H., Silverman, S., & Sullivan, D. (2000, October). *More than meets the eye: Avoiding gaze makes you feel guilty.* Paper presented at the annual meeting of the Society for Personality and Social Psychology, Nashville, TN.

Schuette, R. A., & Fazio, R. H. (1995). Attitude accessibility and motivation as determinants of biased processing: A test of the mode model. *Personality and Social Psychology Bulletin, 21,* 704–710.

Schwartz, B. L. (1998). Illusory tip-of-the-tongue states. *Memory, 6,* 623–642.

Schwartz, B. L., Travis, D. M., Castro, A. M., & Smith, S. M. (2000). The phenomenology of real and illusory tip-of-the-tongue states. *Memory and Cognition, 28,* 18–27.

Schwartz, G. E., Weinberger, D. A., & Singer, J. A. (1981). Cardiovascular differentiation of happiness, sadness, anger and fear following imagery and exercise. *Psychosomatic Medicine, 43,* 343–364.

Schwarz, N. (1990). Feelings as information: Informational and motivational functions of affective states. In E. T. Higgins & R. M. Sorrentino (Eds.), *Handbook of motivation and cognition* (Vol. 2, pp. 527–561). New York: Guilford.

Schwarz, N., Bless, H., Strack, F., Klumpp, G., Rittenauer-Schatka, H., & Simons, A. (1991). Ease of retrieval as information: Another look as the availability heuristic. *Journal of Personality and Social Psychology, 61,* 195–202.

Schwarz, N., & Clore, G. L. (1988). How do I feel about it? The informative function of affective states. In K. Fiedler & J. Forgas (Eds.), *Affect, cognition and social behavior* (pp. 159–176). Toronto, Ontario, Canada: Hogrefe International.

Searle, J. R. (1992). *The rediscovery of the mind.* Cambridge, MA: MIT Press.

Seligman, C., Fazio, R. H., & Zanna, M. P. (1980). Effects of salience of extrinsic rewards on liking and loving. *Journal of Personality and Social Psychology, 38,* 453–460.

Shaver, P., Wu, S., & Schwartz, J. C. (1992). Cross-cultural similarities and differences in emotion and its representation: A prototype approach. In M. S. Clark (Ed.), *Review of personality and social psychology: Emotion* (Vol. 13, pp. 175–212). Newbury Park, CA: Sage.

Shepard, R. N., & Cooper, L. A. (1986). *Mental images and their transformations.* Cambridge, MA: MIT Press.

Siegman, A. W., & Boyle, S. (1993). Voices of fear and anxiety and sadness and depression: The effects of speech rate and loudness on fear and anxiety and sadness and depression. *Journal of Abnormal Psychology, 102,* 430–437.

Singerman, K. J., Borkovec, T. D., & Baron, R. S. (1976). Failure of a "misattribution therapy" manipulation with a clinically relevant target behavior. *Behavior Therapy, 7,* 306–316.

Skinner, B. F. (1957). *Verbal behavior.* Englewood Cliffs, NJ: Prentice Hall.

Slivken, K. E., & Buss, A. H. (1984). Misattribution and speech anxiety. *Journal of Personality and Social Psychology, 47,* 396–402.

Snell, B. A. (1982). *The discovery of the mind in early Greek philosophy and literature.* Mineola, NY: Dover.

Snyder, M. (1974). Self-monitoring of expressive behavior. *Journal of Personality and Social Psychology, 30,* 526–537.

Snyder, M., & Ebbesen, E. (1972). Dissonance awareness: A test of dissonance theory versus self-perception theory. *Journal of Experimental Social Psychology, 8,* 502–517.

Soussignan, R. (2002). Duchenne smile, emotional experience, and autonomic reactivity: A test of the facial feedback hypothesis. *Emotion, 2*(1), 52–74.

Sprecher, S., & Metts, S. (1989). Development of the "romantic beliefs scale" and examination of the effects of gender and gender-role orientation. *Journal of Social and Personal Relationships, 6,* 387–411.

Steele, C. M. (1988). The psychology of self-affirmation: Sustaining the integrity of the self. In L. Berkowitz (Ed.), *Advances in experimental social psychology* (Vol. 21, pp. 261–302). San Diego, CA: Academic Press.

Stepper, S., & Strack, F. (1993). Proprioceptive determinants of emotional and nonemotional feelings. *Journal of Personality and Social Psychology, 64,* 211–220.

Stevens, D. A., Dooley, D. A., & Laird, J. D. (1988). Explaining individual differences in flavor perception and food acceptance. In D. M. H. Thomson (Ed.), *Food acceptability* (pp. 173–180). London: Elsevier.

Stone, J., Aronson, E., Crain, A. L., & Winslow, M. P. (1994). Inducing hypocrisy as a means of encouraging young adults to use condoms. *Personality and Social Psychology Bulletin, 20,* 116–128.

Storms, M. D., & Nisbett, R. E. (1970). Insomnia and the attribution process. *Journal of Personality and Social Psychology, 16,* 219–228.

Strack, F., Martin, L. L., & Stepper, S. (1988). Inhibiting and facilitating conditions of facial expressions: A non-obtrusive test of the facial feedback hypothesis. *Journal of Personality and Social Psychology, 54,* 768–776.

Strack, F., & Neumann, R. (2000). Furrowing the brow may undermine perceived fame: The role of facial feedback in judgments of celebrity. *Personality and Social Psychology Bulletin, 26,* 762–768.

Stromeyer, C. F. I. (1970). Eidetikers. *Psychology Today,* pp. 76–80.

Strout, S. L., Bush, S. E., & Laird, J. D. (2004, August). *Differences in the experience of emotion.* Paper presented at the annual meeting of the International Society for Research on Emotion, New York.

Strout, S. L., Sokol, R. I., Thompson, N. S., & Laird, J. D. (2004, May). *A preliminary investigation of the relationship between attachment and emotion perception.* Paper presented at the annual meeting of the Human Behavior and Evolution Society, Frankfurt, Germany.

Tang, S. H., & Hall, V. C. (1995a). Even with problems, meta-analysis contributes. *Applied Cognitive Psychology, 9,* 423–424.

Tang, S. H., & Hall, V. C. (1995b). The overjustification effect: A meta-analysis. *Applied Cognitive Psychology, 9,* 365–404.

Tavris, C. (1984). On the wisdom of counting to ten: Personal and social dangers of anger expression. In P. Shaver (Ed.), *Review of personality and social psychology* (Vol. 5, pp. 170–191). Beverly Hills, CA: Sage.

Tesser, A., Pilkington, C. J. & McIntosh, W. D. (1989). Self-evaluation maintenance and the mediational role of emotion: The perception of friends and strangers. *Journal of Personality and Social Psychology, 57,* 441–456.

Thayer, R. E. (1996). *The origin of everyday moods: Managing energy, tension, and stress.* New York: Oxford University Press.

Tomkins, S. S. (1962). *Affect, imagery, consciousness* (Vol. 1). New York: Springer.

Tomkins, S. S. (1963). *Affect, imagery, consciousness* (Vol. 2). New York: Springer.

Tomkins, S. S. (1982). Affect theory. In P. Ekman (Ed.), *Emotion in the human face* (2nd ed., pp. 353–395). Cambridge, England: Cambridge University Press.

Tulving, E. (1985). How many memory systems are there? *American Psychologist, 40,* 385–398.

Tversky, A., & Kahneman, D. (1973). Availability: A heuristic for judging frequency and probability. *Cognitive Psychology, 5,* 207–232.

Tversky, A., & Kahneman, D. (1974). Judgment under uncertainty: Heuristics and biases. *Science, 185,* 1124–1131.

Vallacher, R. R., & Wegner, D. M. (1987). What do people think they are doing? Action identification and human behavior. *Psychological Review, 94,* 2–15.

Van den Bergh, O., Vrana, S., & Eelen, P. (1990). Letters from the heart: Affective categorization of letter combinations in typists and nontypists. *Journal of Experimental Psychology: Learning, Memory and Cognition, 16,* 1153–1161.

Vaughan, K. B., & Lanzetta, J. T. (1980). Vicarious instigation and conditioning of facial expressive and autonomic responses to a model's expressive display of pain. *Journal of Personality and Social Psychology, 38,* 909–923.

Vaughan, K. B., & Lanzetta, J. T. (1981). The effect of modification of expressive displays on vicarious emotional arousal. *Journal of Experimental Social Psychology, 17,* 16–30.

Velten, E. (1968). A laboratory task for induction of mood states. *Behaviour Research and Therapy, 6,* 473–482.

Volavka, J. (1988). Can aggressive behavior in humans be modified by beta-blockers? *Postgraduate Medicine, 29,* 163–168.

Vygotsky, L. S. (1962). *Thought and language.* Cambridge, MA: MIT Press.

Wagener, J. J., & Laird, J. D. (1980a). The experimenter's foot-in-the-door: Self-perception, body weight and volunteering. *Personality and Social Psychology Bulletin, 6,* 441–446.

Wagener, J. J., & Laird, J. D. (1980b, April). *A "new look" at judgments about emotion in others: The effects of the emotional experience of the judge.* Paper presented at the annual meeting of the Eastern Psychological Association, Hartford, CT.

Wapner, S., & Demick, J. (Eds.). (1991). *Field dependence-independence: Cognitive style across the life span.* Hillsdale, NJ: Erlbaum.

Watson, D., & Tellegen, A. (1985). Toward a consensual structure of mood. *Psychological Bulletin, 98,* 219–235.

Wegner, D. M. (1997). Why the mind wanders. In J. D. Cohen & J. W. Schooler (Eds.), *Scientific approaches to consciousness* (pp. 295–315). Hillsdale, NJ: Erlbaum.

Wegner, D. M., Schneider, D. J., Carter, S. R., & White, T. L. (1987). Paradoxical effects of thought suppression. *Journal of Personality and Social Psychology, 53,* 5–13.

Wells, G. L., & Petty, R. E. (1980). The effects of overt head movements on persuasion: Compatibility and incompatibility of responses. *Basic and Applied Social Psychology, 1,* 219–230.

Wertsch, J. V. (1985). *Vygotsky and the social formation of mind.* Cambridge, MA: Harvard University Press.

White, G. L., & Kight, T. D. (1984). Misattribution of arousal and attraction: Effects of salience of explanations of arousal. *Journal of Personality and Social Psychology, 20,* 55–64.

White, L., Fishbein, S., & Rutstein, J. (1981). Passionate love and the misattribution of arousal. *Journal of Personality and Social Psychology, 41,* 56–62.

Whittlesea, B. W. A. (1993). Illusions of familiarity. *Journal of Experimental Psychology: Learning, Memory and Cognition, 19,* 1235–1253.

Whittlesea, B. W. A., & Williams, L. D. (1998). Why do strangers feel familiar, but friends don't? A discrepancy-attribution account of feelings of familiarity. *Acta Psychologica, 98,* 141–165.

Whittlesea, B. W. A., & Williams, L. D. (2001). The discrepancy-attribution hypothesis: I. The heuristic basis of feelings and familiarity. *Journal of Experimental Psychology: Learning, Memory, and Cognition, 27,* 3–13.

Wicklund, R. A., & Brehm, J. W. (1976). *Perspectives on cognitive dissonance.* Hillsdale, NJ: Erlbaum.

Wilcox, K., & Laird, J. D. (2000). The impact of media images of super-slender women on women's self-esteem: Identification, social comparison, and self-perception. *Journal of Research in Personality, 34,* 278–286.

Williams, G. P., & Kleinke, C. L. (1993). Effects of mutual gaze and touch on attraction, mood and cardiovascular reactivity. *Journal of Research in Personality, 27,* 170–183.

Wilson, P. R. (1968). Perceptual distortion of height as a function of ascribed academic status. *Journal of Social Psychology, 74,* 97–102.

Winton, W. M. (1986). The role of facial response in self-reports of emotion: A critique of Laird. *Journal of Personality and Social Psychology, 50,* 808–812.

Winton, W. M. (1990). Jamesian aspects of misattribution research. *Personality and Social Psychology Bulletin, 16,* 652–664.

Wittgenstein, L. (1953). *Philosophical investigations.* New York: Macmillan.

Wixon, D. R., & Laird, J. D. (1976). Awareness and attitude change in the forced compliance paradigm: The importance of when. *Journal of Personality and Social Psychology, 34,* 376–384.

Wolpe, J. (1958). *Psychotherapy by reciprocal inhibition.* Stanford, CA: Stanford University Press.

Wood, W. (2000). Attitude change: Persuasion and social influence. *Annual Review of Psychology, 51,* 539–570.

Woods, S. C., Schwartz, M. W., Baskin, D. G., & Seeley, R. J. (2000). Food intake and the regulation of body weight. *Annual Review of Psychology, 51,* 255–277.

Woods, S. W., & Charney, D. S. (1988). Applications of the pharmacologic challenge strategy in panic disorder. *Journal of Anxiety Disorders, 2,* 31–49.

Yogo, M. (1991). Self-regulation of affects: Effects of facial expressive behavior on psychosomatic states. *Doshisha Psychological Review, 38,* 49–59.

Zajonc, R. B. (1968). Attitudinal effects of mere exposure. *Journal of Personality and Social Psychology Monograph Supplement, 9,* 1–25.

Zajonc, R. B. (1980). Feeling and thinking: Preferences need no inferences. *American Psychologist, 35,* 151–175.

Zajonc, R. B. (1985). Emotion and facial efference. *Science, 228,* 15–21.

Zajonc, R. B., Murphy, S. T., & Inglehart, M. (1989). Feeling and facial efference: Implications of the vascular theory of emotion. *Psychological Review, 96,* 395–416.

Zanna, M. P., & Cooper, J. (1974). Dissonance and the pill: An attribution approach to studying the arousal properties of dissonance. *Journal of Personality and Social Psychology, 29,* 703–709.

Zillmann, D. (1983). Transfer of excitation in emotional behavior. In J. T. Cacioppo & R. E. Petty (Eds.), *Social psychophysiology: A sourcebook* (pp. 215–240). New York: Guilford.

Zillmann, D. (1996). Sequential dependencies in emotional experience and behavior. In R. D. Kavanaugh, B. Zimmerbegh, & S. Fein (Eds.), *Emotion: Interdisciplinary perspectives* (pp. 243–272). Hillsdale, NJ: Erlbaum.

Zimbardo, P. B., Weisenberg, M., Firestone, I., & Levy, B. (1965). Communicator effectiveness in producing public conformity and private attitude change. *Journal of Personality, 33,* 233–255.

Zimbardo, P. G., Cohen, A., Weisenberg, M., Dworkin, L., & Firestone, I. (1969). The control of experimental pain. In P. G. Zimbardo (Ed.), *The cognitive control of motivation* (pp. 100–125). Glenview, IL: Scott Foresman.

Zuckerman, M., Klorman, R., Larrance, D. T., & Spiegel, N. H. (1981). Facial, autonomic, and subjective components of emotion: The facial feedback hypothesis versus the externalizer-internalizer distinction. *Journal of Personality and Social Psychology, 41,* 929–944.

Index